THE HISTORY
OF
Pirates

THE HISTORY
OF
Pirates

Angus Konstam

The History of Shipwrecks

Printed in Italy by Rotolito Lombarda

ISBN: 1-55821-969-2

Picture Credits

AKG London: 26, 32, 34, 35 top, 37 top right; AKG London/Paul Almasy: 141 bottom; AKG London/Erich Lessing: 5 top; AKG London/Jean-Louis Nou: 24; Ancient Art & Architecture Collection Ltd.: 39 bottom right; Author's private collection: 9, 19, 23 bottom, 25 top, 49 top right, 65 bottom right, 68, 69 top right, 70, 74, 76, 78, 80, 81, 82, 86, 87, 89, 92, 96, 96, 102, 103 bottom left, 104, 105, 106, 107, 107, 110, 110, 111, 112, 113, 115, 116 top left, 119, 130, 131, 132-133, 133, 137 bottom left, 140, 141 top right, 160, 186 top right, 187 top right; Bibliothéque Nationale, Paris: 91 bottom right; Bridgeman Art Library: 20, 33, 179, 185 top; City Arts Centre/Barry Clifford: 108, 109, 109; Corbis/Richard T. Nowitz: 23 top right; Corbis/Tim Page: 183 bottom right; Delaware Art Museum: 11, 75, 91 top right, 124-125, 127, 129 bottom right, 186-187; E.T. Archive: 25 bottom right, 27 bottom right, 28, 38, 62, 69 bottom, 97; Mary Evans Picture Library: 2-3, 5 right, 14, 21, 21, 29, 37 bottom, 39 top, 188; Oliver Frey: 1, 18, 27 top right, 98-99, 100-101, 103 top right, 184; Hispanic Society of America: 59 top; Image Select International: 61 top right; Kobal Collection: 15 top right, 185 right; Ronald Grant Archive: 15 bottom left; Mariners' Museum, Newport News, Viginia: 6, 7, 8 top left, 12, 13, 43, 59 bottom right, 77, 116-117, 117, 125 top right, 149, 150, 151, 156-157, 157, 162-163, 163, 164, 169 top left, 170; Museum of Arts & Sciences, Florida: 71; National Maritime Museum Picture Library, London: 8 bottom left, 10, 35 bottom right, 42, 44, 46, 47, 47, 48, 49 bottom, 51, 51, 52-53, 53, 56-57, 58, 60, 60-61, 63, 63, 64, 65 center, 67, 67, 79, 84-85, 85, 90, 93, 114, 121, 128, 134, 135, 136, 137 top right, 138-139, 144, 145, 146-147, 147, 155, 161, 168, 169 bottom, 171, 171, 172, 172-173, 173, 175 bottom, 176, 177; N.H.F. Historical Services, USA: 165; E.Pasquier/Sygma: 180, 181, 181, 182, 183 top, 183 bottom left; Peabody Essex Museum, Salem, Massachusetts: 159, 159; Salamander Picture Library: 45, 116 bottom, 129 top, 175 top, 178, 189; Ulster Museum, Belfast: 61 center, 61 bottom left.

previous pages: The infamous pirate Bartholomew Roberts is brought to justice when HMS Swallow, under the command of Captain Challoner Ogle, fires a broadside of grapeshot. Roberts was killed instantly. Interestingly, the artist, Charles Dixon, invented a classic skull and crossbones flag for the pirate ship Royal Fortune, but Roberts always flew one of two very different flags (see page 100).

this page top: Two sailing ships from a Roman sarcophagus of the second–third centuries.

this page right: The stern of a late 18th-century British warship, engraved by Charles Tomkins from a drawing by Van de Velde.

Contents

Foreword

Pirates have long been associated with tropical islands and in particular with the islands of the West Indies, and rightly so. The islands provided hundreds of safe anchorages sheltered by offshore reefs. On the deserted beaches of the Bahamas and the Leeward Islands the pirate ships could be cleaned and repaired. There were numerous fresh water streams, turtles and fish in the lagoons, and wild hogs and cattle roaming the islands inland. Passing among the islands were any number of potential victims: merchant vessels laden with rich goods from Europe; ships from Africa with cargoes of ivory, gold, and slaves; Spanish treasure ships loaded with silver from Central America. And for the less ambitious pirates there were local fishing boats and trading vessels to be plundered of fishing gear and barrels of rum.

Apart from the mosquitoes and occasional hurricane, the Caribbean was a pirate paradise, and in the early years of the 18th century there were reckoned to be more than 2,000 of them operating among the islands. They included the alarming figure of Blackbeard, the barbaric Edward Low—of whom it was said, "a greater monster never infested the seas"—and Calico Jack, whose chief claim to fame was not his piratical exploits but the two female members of his crew, Mary Reade and Anne Bonny.

The pirates did not restrict their operations to the West Indies or the Spanish Main. As Angus Konstam graphically demonstrates in this book, they operated throughout the world. For centuries the shipping in the Mediterranean was at the mercy of the oared galleys of the Barbary corsairs. In Northern Europe, along the banks of the Red Sea, in the Straits of Malacca, and wherever trade routes funneled through straits or islands there would be pirates, lurking to pounce.

Many of them operated from bases where they were protected by the local populace, but the more intrepid pirates made vast ocean voyages in search of plunder. Thomas Tew and the infamous Captain Kidd were among several pirates who sailed from North American ports across the Atlantic to Madagascar and the Indian Ocean. Bartholomew Roberts made several voyages from Newfoundland to the Caribbean, then across to the west coast of Africa. Others traveled around Cape Horn into the Pacific in search of treasure. Their charts were decorative but so inaccurate that they relied on good watch-keeping and men with local knowledge to guide them clear of unmarked reefs and shoals.

Many of the pirates were fine seamen, and they showed an impressive ability to outwit the authorities. There was an admirable tradition of democracy that enabled crews to vote their captains in and out of office and ensured that plunder was shared equally. But it would be a mistake to conclude that pirates in any way resembled the romantic heroes depicted by Errol Flynn and Douglas Fairbanks Snr. in the swashbuckling films of the 1920s and 30s. Philip Ashton, a young sailor taken by pirates in 1722, described his captors as "a vile crew of miscreants, to whom it was a sport to do mischief, where prodigious drinking, monstrous cursing and swearing, hideous blasphemies and open defiance of Heaven and contempt of Hell itself was the constant employment...."

Pirate attacks were violent and frequently accompanied by torture and murder. This has been the pattern throughout history, and it continues today, particularly in the South China Sea, where pirate attacks are as frequent and as brutal as they were in the West Indies during the 17th and 18th centuries.

Introduction

Piracy has fascinated us ever since the newspapers of the early 18th century first chronicled the deeds of men like Blackbeard and Bartholomew Roberts. In reality, these seemingly romantic characters were often ruthless killers, and their lives were nasty, brutish, and short.

Reading the word "pirate" conjures up a powerful image; it has a fascination that reaches into the soul of the purest landlubber. The popularity of piracy is heavily colored by imagery created by books, films, and the stage. Pirate symbolism is used by marketing people to sell products as diverse as hotel accommodation and cars. Pirates are portrayed as almost mythical beings, rather like a cross between the vampires of the horror genre and the knights of chivalry.

Like medieval knights (and unlike vampires), this mythical image is based on reality, but true piracy bears little relation to the myth. For example, there is no evidence that pirates made prisoners walk the plank. Instead, pirate captives could be used for pistol practice, or subjected to sadistic torture.

The pirates of fiction—Captain Hook, Long John Silver, Captain Blood, and many others—are pale imitations of the real thing. The tales of these real pirates involved buried treasure, desert

INTRODUCTION

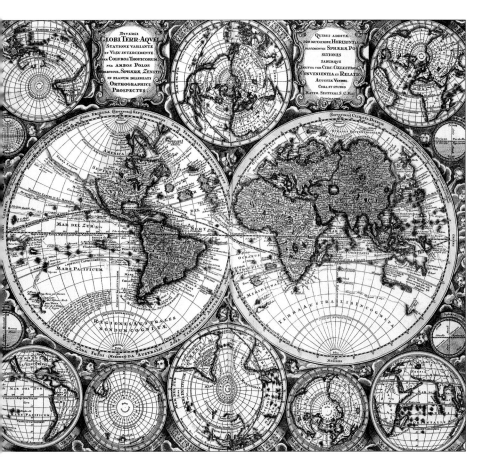

islands, and parrots, but these were minor and infrequent elements. Betrayal, shipwreck, hopelessness, disease, and brutality were recurring themes in the lives of the true pirates. A pirate's life was invariable nasty, brutish, and short.

The popular image of piracy appeals to the smothered desire to rebel against the constraints of society. Pirates may be portrayed as violent, but they are also free-living, lying in a hammock in the sun, and kicking over the traces in a port; things that many people would like to do, but feel that they cannot because of the society in which they live.

There is a certain envy involved in this admiration of the archetypal pirate, fueled by the romantic portrayal of pirates on film and in print. There is no mention of the starving pirate crews who had to prey on ships to survive, or the fact that almost every port was closed to them.

Piracy is not a thing of the past. Piracy may be too romanticized a term for many people to apply to the bandits in fast boats who attack shipping in the waters of the South China Sea. A pirate is a robber who performs his crimes at sea, and this applies as much to a Filipino pirate wielding an AK-47 as it does to Blackbeard with his flintlock pistols. Although tactics and methods have changed, the crimes are the same.

This book examines historical pirates, the times they lived in, the nature of their crimes, and the fate that befell them. From the Ancient Mediterranean to the waters of the Spanish Main, and from the Carolina coast to the Philippines, this wide-ranging study of piracy strips away the romanticism of these characters to show them for what they truly were.

Why become a pirate?

Men have turned to piracy for almost as long as man has sailed on the sea. Whether the pirates operated in ancient galleys, sailing ships, or modern speedboats, many of the reasons behind their choice of occupation are the same.

Pirate crews were often manned by desperate or disillusioned people. Although execution was the expected punishment and life expectancy was short, piracy was an attractive alternative to many of the other options facing seamen. Most 17th century seamen had served on merchant vessels, warships, or privateers before turning to piracy. Most were men in their 20s, with an average age for seaman and pirate alike of 27 years.

One motivating force was freedom. In a restrictive social hierarchy, seamen were at the bottom. The chance to make a profit from piracy then retire was enticing. Piracy provided an opportunity for social advancement through wealth. Unlike working for other ship-owners or serving in the navy, profits went to the pirates themselves.

A seaman's life was grueling, often involving discomfort, danger, and horrific living conditions. Drinking water was often foul, food was frequently rotten, and disease was rife. The life of a seaman did not promise much, but if he was a pirate or privateer there was the chance of huge financial rewards.

The majority of sailors became pirates when their vessels were captured and they chose to join the pirate crew. In law courts, many pirates claimed in their defense that they were pressed by their captors, and joined them unwillingly. In these cases, leniency was sometimes shown by the judge.

Another common route was for privateering crews to turn to piracy. Profit enticed seamen to become privateers, and peace caused massive unemployment among the maritime community, an example being the situation at the end of the War of Spanish Succession in 1714. Despite the great risk of being captured and executed for your deeds, piracy was an attractive alternative to dying of starvation, becoming a beggar or thief on land, or serving in appalling conditions on a ship with no chance of substantial financial reward.

Pirate crews, were composed of men (and a few women) of many nations, classes, and races. Court records show just how varied pirate crews could be. Of the 700 known pirates who were active in the Caribbean between 1715 and 1725, almost all came from the English-speaking Atlantic and Caribbean basin. Englishmen accounted for the majority, at 35 percent; 25 percent were American, 20 percent

came from the West Indies, 10 percent were Scottish, and 8 percent were Welsh. Only 2 percent were from other seafaring countries, such as Sweden, Holland, France, and Spain.

A pirate or privateer crew could also include black men of African descent, while in America free blacks and runaway slaves also joined pirate crews. The crew of Bartholomew Roberts in 1721 contained 187 white men and 75 black men; many of the latter were freed slaves or runaways. Even the misery of a sailing ship was preferable to slavery on a West Indian plantation.

Piracy had many drawbacks. Most condemned pirates displayed a fatalism that hinted at the inevitability with which they saw their capture and execution. For

below: "Gin Lane" by William Hogarth depicts the extreme squalor of the poor in early 18th-century England. Poverty forced many young men to become sailors, and a number of these saw piracy as the only chance to improve their lot.

many desperate, poor, or simply greedy people, piracy provided a slim chance to beat the system.

Privateer, Buccaneer, or Pirate

WHAT'S IN A NAME?

The terms for a pirate have become confused, thanks to their frequent misuse in movies and literature. In their time, the difference between being seen as a buccaneer, privateer, corsair, or pirate could mean the difference between life and death.

One of the problems with any work on piracy is the range of terms used to describe these maritime cutthroats. Not everyone who acted like a pirate was considered a pirate, and some had government authority behind them. A pirate in one country could be considered a patriot in another, like Henry Morgan, Sir Francis Drake, or even John Paul Jones. The various terms that are widely used need to be unraveled.

A pirate in the truest sense attacks any ship, regardless of nationality. It means someone who robs from others at sea, and acts beyond the law. In England and its colonies it fell under the jurisdiction of Admiralty law; a crime committed below the low-tide mark around the shores and rivers, estuaries, and high seas. Convicted pirates were often hanged on the low-tide mark to emphasise the authority of the Lord High Admiral. The same definition was applied in other countries. Many pirates went to great lengths to cover their crimes, trying to hide behind the more forgiving appellations of privateer or buccaneer. Admiralty courts went to equal lengths to uncover such deception and to punish robbery at sea with all the means at their disposal.

A buccaneer was the name given to French backwoodsmen on Hispaniola—modern Haiti and the Dominican Republic—in the early 17th century. The term is derived from the French word *boucan* (barbecue), a description based on the way they smoked their meat. Many early buccaneers were fugitives from the Spanish and maintained a bitter hatred of that nationality.

The original hunters started preying on passing Spanish ships during the mid-17th century, and their numbers were swelled by runaway slaves, seamen, and others. "Buccaneer" later came to refer to the mainly English and French raiders of the Spanish Main, who acted as semi-legalized pirates, based principally in Port Royal and Tortuga.

Privateers, freebooters, and corsairs
A privateer was a man or a ship under contract to a government, allowing them to attack enemy ships during wartime. This contract, called a "Letter of Marque," meant that the government got a share of

below: *In what was largely a man's world, the few female pirates aroused a great deal of popular interest— and the women were just as violent as the men, as depicted in this illustration of Mary Reade.*

the profits in return for issuing it (usually one-fifth of the value of ship and cargo). These contracts were originally called "Letters of Marque and Reprisal" and issued directly by monarchs and governments, but by the late 17th century they were issued by appointed government officials, and later by colonial governors.

In effect, a privateer (or more accurately, a privateersman) was a licensed pirate who didn't attack his own people. Privateering was a useful extension of naval warfare which not only created an income for the government issuing the privateering contract, but also helped to harass enemy shipping in times of war, without the issuing authority having to do anything. The main drawback was that, when hostilities ended, many privateers turned to piracy.

Freebooter and filibuster were names given exclusively to French buccaneers, named after the small, fast *flibotes* (fly boats) they sometimes used. The term fell into disuse, only to be revived during the 19th century, where "filibuster" described a smuggler or blockade runner.

Corsair was the term applied to both privateers and pirates who operated in the Mediterranean Sea, although it was derived from the French *la course* (privateer). The main group of these were the Barbary corsairs of the North African coast. While Europeans regarded them as pirates, these Muslim corsairs saw themselves as privateers, fighting religious enemies under contract from the city states of the Barbary Coast.

Sometimes the names applied to pirates became mixed up. A privateer might turn to piracy (like Captain Kidd), which often happened after a major war. Buccaneers such as Henry Morgan were really privateers, but when he attacked Panama in 1671, England and Spain were at peace—Morgan was acting as a pirate!

Some common terms for pirates were never used historically. Chief among these is "swashbuckler," which was a 16th-century term for a brigand (bandit), but has been applied to pirates by 19th-century novelists and 20th-century scriptwriters.

below: *As with any society, pirate leaders often had to prove themselves in combat. "Which shall be Captain," by Howard Pyle.*

The Pirate in Popular Culture

THE PUBLICITY MILL

As long as man has sailed the seas, there have been pirates, but through a clever marketing ploy, we now mostly think of pirates as swashbuckling heroes of print and screen.

When we think about pirates, much of the popular image that we have dates from one brief historical period, the so-called "Golden Age of Piracy," which at most lasted for 40 years, between 1690 and 1730. The real pirate heyday fitted into just a decade, between

1714 and 1724. Ask anyone to name a pirate and chances are they name someone from that short period, a pinprick of history.

A quick poll conducted outside a dockside tavern in the author's home town showed that the majority of people named Blackbeard as the most readily identifiable pirate. Piracy existed since man first launched a dugout canoe, so why are we so obsessed with a few characters who lived in the early 18th century? The answer is publicity.

In 1684 Alexander Exquemelin published a book in London entitled *Buccaneers of America*. An earlier version had been published the year before in Amsterdam, but the English edition proved to be a best-seller. The author took part in several buccaneer raids and knew characters like Sir Henry Morgan. Although his tale was almost certainly embellished to help sales, it provided the first portrayal of pirates for the general public. Readers reveled in the atrocities and hardships, the heroism and cowardice contained in its pages.

The main era of the Golden Age was not even over when Captain Charles Johnson published *A General History of the Robberies and Murders of the Most Notorious Pirates* in 1724. It also provided its publisher with a runaway success, and while its biographical account of the lives of many pirates may have contained many inaccuracies, it remains one of the most popular pirate books of all time. It says much about the enduring popularity of both of these books that they are still in print today.

Moving toward center stage

At the same time as Johnson's book was released, a play called *The Successful Pyrate* was playing in London's Drury Lane,

left: *"X" marks the spot—one popular image of the pirate, counting his hoard of golden doubloons, hidden in a secret cave.*

a production based on the exploits of the pirate Henry Every. Even while some of these pirates and their victims were still alive, piracy was being romanticized. This process has continued until today, and only in the past decade has the tendency been seriously addressed by historians.

While the work of pirate historians such as David Cordingly, Robert Ritchie, and Jan Rogozinski has tried to strip the fact from the fiction of piracy, they are swimming against the stream of popular culture. Since the early 18th century, the romantic view of piracy, running in tandem with an image of demonic cruelty personified by Johnson's Blackbeard, has proved too deeply ingrained to eradicate. We want our pirates to be swashbucklers who make their victims walk the plank!

In the past three centuries since the Golden Age of Piracy, a number of milestones have marked this enshrinement of the pirate in popular culture. In the early 19th century romantic fiction writers and poets looked to piracy for suitable subject matter. Lord Byron's poem *The Corsair* (1814), Sir Walter Scott's novel *The Pirate* (1821), and Giuseppe Verdi's opera *Il Corsaro* (1848) are all examples of this romantic trend.

Robert Louis Stevenson invents piracy

What really raised piracy above the subject matter of romantic writers and placed it into the realm of popular culture was the work of Scottish writer Robert Louis Stevenson (1850–94). In 1883 he published *Treasure Island*, a work that became the most influential book on public perception of pirates. It has been reprinted

opposite page: *Treasure Island introduced all the elements of the pirate myth.*

13

above: *The evil (and incompetent) Captain Hook takes on his juvenile nemesis, Peter Pan. Illustration by Alice B. Woodward from The Peter Pan Picture Book of 1907.*

nobody could accuse Bartholomew Roberts of lacking professional ability. *Peter Pan* also gave us pirate hats with skull and crossbones symbols on them. Reality and myth were split even further apart.

Pirates were a popular theme in children's books during the late 19th and first half of the 20th centuries. Writers for this "Boy's Own" style of idealized adventure fiction often went back to Exquemelin and Johnson for inspiration, but added a new breed of pirate character: the smart, young (white, Anglo-Saxon, Protestant) hero who battles the evil pirates and beats them at their own game. This provided the basis for the swashbuckling heroes of the silver screen.

In 1920 the silent movie *Treasure Island* was released, followed four years later by *Captain Blood*, then *The Black Pirate* (1926). While the first two made an impact, the latter, starring Douglas Fairbanks Senior, created a genre. Fairbanks was the first pirate figure in history to stick a knife in a sail and slide down to the deck on it. These were the first "swashbucklers," featuring sea fights, pirate gentlemen, and the righting of wrongs. Many more were to follow.

Pirates flood the silver screen

In the 1930s and 40s there was a profusion of talking-picture swashbucklers, of which the remake of *Captain Blood* (1935), *The Sea Hawk* (1940), and *The Black Swan* (1942) are regarded as classics of the genre, making stars of pirate screen heroes such as Errol Flynn and Tyrone Power. While the pirate genre continued into the 1950s and beyond, there was a growing trend for pirate movies to lampoon themselves, *The Crimson Pirate* (1952) being a prime example.

When historical pirate characters were portrayed, they were frequently given the persona of an evil incompetent first seen in Captain Hook. Scriptwriters combed the pages of Charles Johnson's work to find historic pirate characters who could provide a demonic foil for the movie hero. The exceptions were pirates who could be identified as national heroes, and the

countless times and four film versions have been made, the latest in 1990, starring Charlton Heston as the pistol-wielding Long John Silver. Stevenson introduced all the elements that are an indelible part of the pirate myth: treasure maps, buried plunder, parrots, wooden legs, eye patches, and "Fifteen men on a dead man's chest." Most have no place in the reality of piracy.

In 1904 a play written by another Scotsman, J.M. Barrie (1860–1937), was performed in London. *Peter Pan* has enchanted children ever since, with its mix of fairytale and children's adventure story. Its pirates were portrayed as evil incompetents, and that angle has followed in many later pirate portrayals. While Captain Hook was considered incompetent, screen portrayals of pirates such as Sir Francis Drake (*Seven Seas to Calais*, 1963) and Jean Laffitte (*The Buccaneer*, 1950) were more flattering.

Hollywood did not create the pirates of fiction, it only adapted existing pirate characters, often in an incredibly inaccurate way. Many of the early pirate movies were based on the novels of Rafael Sabatini (1875–1950), whose works fell into the category of boy's adventure tales, which in turn influenced the portrayal of pirates by actors such as Errol Flynn. The latest Hollywood "swashbuckling" movie, *Cutthroat Island* (1997), followed the same romantic approach, with the twist that the hero was a woman (played by Geena Davis).

It is now almost impossible to divide myth from reality in the context of popular perception of piracy. The damage done by novelists, playwrights, and film producers has been too extensive, and the best we can probably hope for is to enjoy the popular image of the pirate, while we develop a fresh one, based on historical reality.

above: *The embodiment of pirate as swashbuckling hero—Errol Flynn in The Sea Hawk.*

left: *The pirates in Swiss Family Robinson were altogether a more heartily horrid bunch.*

CHAPTER ONE

Piracy in the Ancient World

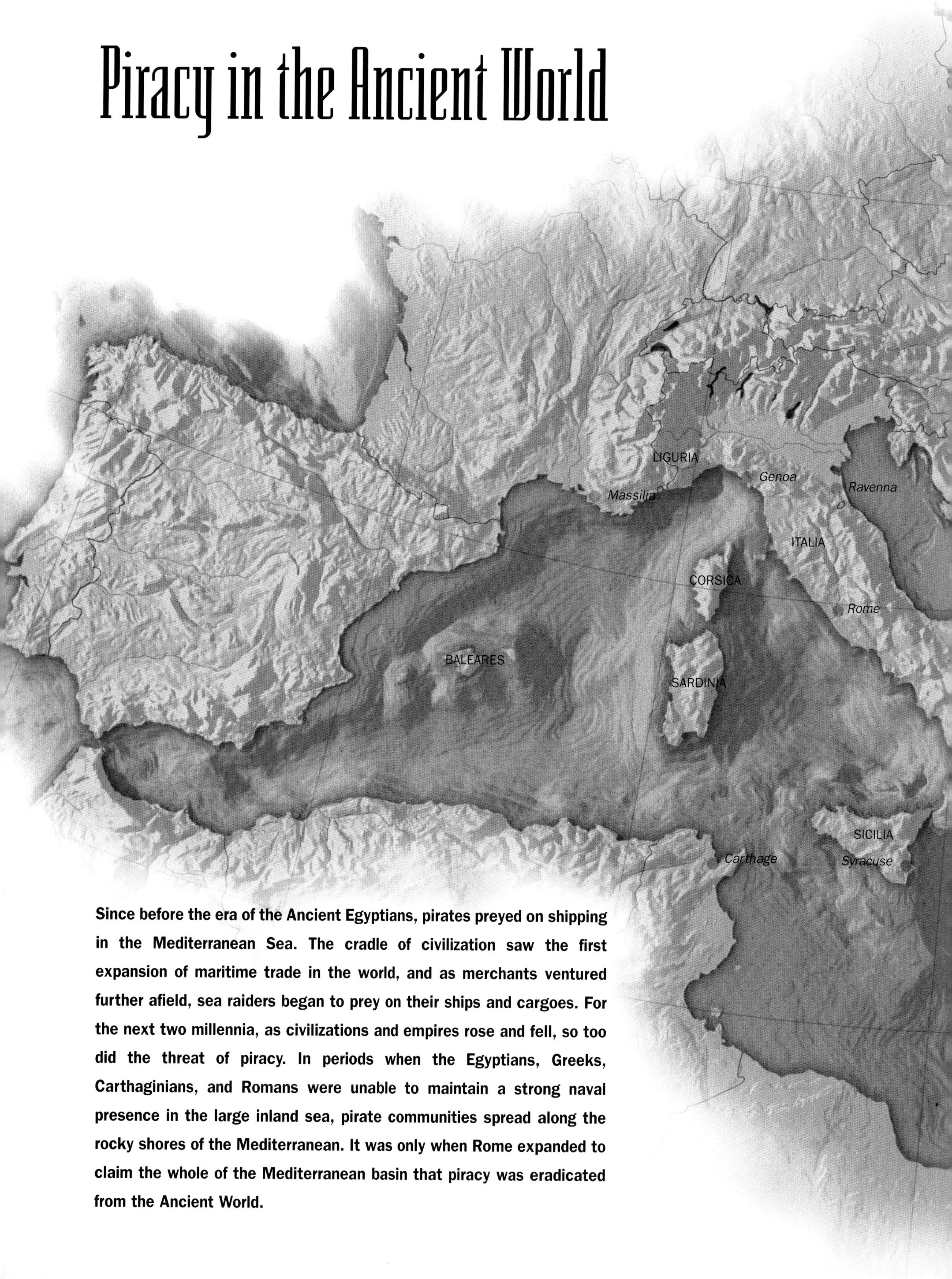

LIGURIA

Genoa

Massilia

Ravenna

ITALIA

CORSICA

Rome

BALEARES

SARDINIA

SICILIA

Carthage

Syracuse

Since before the era of the Ancient Egyptians, pirates preyed on shipping in the Mediterranean Sea. The cradle of civilization saw the first expansion of maritime trade in the world, and as merchants ventured further afield, sea raiders began to prey on their ships and cargoes. For the next two millennia, as civilizations and empires rose and fell, so too did the threat of piracy. In periods when the Egyptians, Greeks, Carthaginians, and Romans were unable to maintain a strong naval presence in the large inland sea, pirate communities spread along the rocky shores of the Mediterranean. It was only when Rome expanded to claim the whole of the Mediterranean basin that piracy was eradicated from the Ancient World.

DALMATIA

THRACE

MACEDONIA

EPIRUS

Tarentum

AETOLIA

Athens

ACHAEA

CILICIA

LYCIA

RHODES

CRETE

CYPRUS

MEDITERRANEAN SEA

PIRACY IN THE ANCIENT WORLD

Some of the earliest pirates to emerge from the pages of history date from before the pyramids were built. Some of the first maritime commerce in history was based in the Mediterranean, and so were some of the first pirates. The Lukka were sea raiders based on the coast of Asia Minor (modern Turkey), and their attacks date from as early as the 14th century BC, although there are clues that piratical activity in the eastern Mediterranean predated even this. During the 14th century, Egyptian records state that Lukkan pirates raided Cyprus, and by the 13th century BC had allied themselves with the Hittite Empire, the enemy of Egypt. Although these first pirates are not mentioned after the 11th century BC, they clearly demonstrate that piracy was not an invention of the past half-millennium.

The decline of the Lukkan raiders in the 12th century and their subsequent disappearance from history has been explained by their assimilation into the group of maritime nomads known as the "Sea Peoples." The appearance of these sea raiders brought the Bronze Age cultures of the eastern Mediterranean basin to their knees, and helped usher in a "Dark Age" of ancient civilization. It seemed inevitable that maritime trade would dwindle during this Dark Age, therefore piracy would decline. While there is historical evidence of this, pirates can be traced in Greece, Crete, and even the western Mediterranean throughout the Dark Age.

During this period pirate activity was also recorded in the Persian Gulf, where in the seventh century BC Assyrian kings sent expeditions to combat pirates operating in the area who prevented the flow of maritime trade between India, China, and the Near East. Phoenician and Greek merchants of the same period reported pirate attacks, and there is even archæological evidence for these early pirates from the wreck of a Greek trading ship, its side pierced by arrows.

Curbed by the Roman Empire

The rise of the Greek and Persian civilizations created the need for powerful navies, and for the first time since the days of the Egyptian New Kingdom piracy could be countered by naval patrols and punitive expeditions. On pages 24–25, a number of accounts show the effectiveness of this naval activity on piracy in the Greek world.

below: A recpnstruction of an Egyptian seagoing vessel that was built for Queen Hatshepsut's expedition to the Land of Punt. No one is sure today where the Egyptians' "Punt" was located, but it is believed to be somewhere down the eastern coast of Africa. A ship like this would have sailed close to the land.

c.2800 BC	c.2000 BC	c.1500 BC	c.1400–1100 BC	14th century BC	13th century BC	1220–1186 BC	10th century BC
Canoe-like vessels used on the Aegean Sea.	Vessels on the Aegean Sea use sails.	Egyptians build sailing vessels with double rudders.	Height of the Mycenaean civilization, dominating Mediterranean sea trade.	The Lukka sea raiders attack shipping from the coast of Asia Minor.	Lukkan sea raiders ally themselves with the Hittites, also from Asia Minor.	The eastern Mediterranean basin is dominated by the "Sea Peoples."	Minoan civilization is overrun by Dorian Greeks, who use Cretan cities as pirate bases.

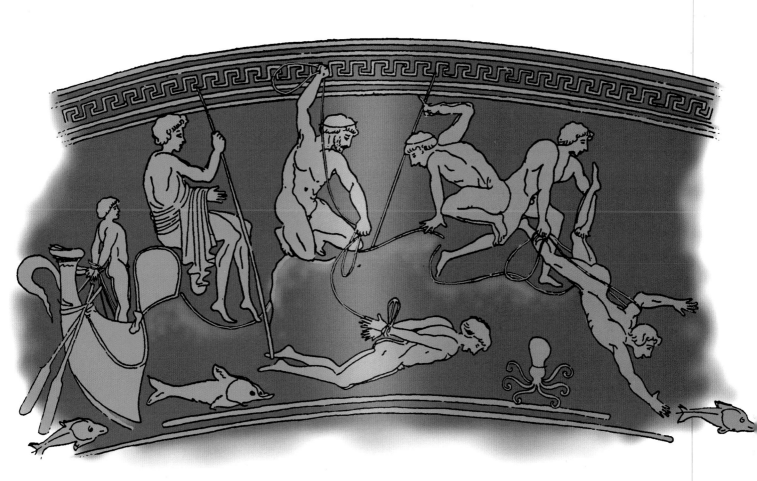

The authors and historians of the classical Greek period, such as Thucydides and Herodotus, frequently mention the exploits of pirates and the attempts of the Greek city states, and then Alexander the Great and his successors, to curb the pirate threat. While this naval activity did much to reduce piracy in its eastern waters, a political void was created throughout the Mediterranean in the second century BC. The war between Rome and Carthage to the west and the decline of the Macedonian successor states to the east allowed whole pirate communities to establish themselves. These communities in Cilicia, Illyria, and some western Mediterranean islands played one power against another and provided mercenary pirate navies for the highest bidder.

As the power of Rome came to dominate the Mediterranean, pirate communities were gradually destroyed and their territory incorporated into the Roman sphere of influence. The anti-pirate campaign of Pompey the Great in 67 BC that destroyed the Cilician sea raiders was followed by subsequent expeditions against Illyrian pirates. By the foundation of the Roman Empire under Emperor Augustus, the Mediterranean was a Roman sea, and shipping was immune from pirate attack for four centuries.

The collapse of the Western Roman Empire in the early fifth century plunged that part of the Mediterranean into anarchy, and piracy spread rapidly. While the eastern portion of the Roman realm developed into the Byzantine Empire, further to the east, Arabic (or Moorish) expansion threatened the stability of the eastern Mediterranean. The Byzantines placed a strong emphasis on the maintenance of a powerful navy, and while the region never reverted to the secure existence it enjoyed during the Roman heyday, both pirates and invaders were held at bay for another half-millennium.

above: *It may be thought that the terrible punishment known as keelhauling is an invention from the Golden Age of Piracy, but this Greek illustration proves otherwise.*

7th century BC	509 BC	c.480 BC	5th century BC	332 BC	2nd century BC	168 BC	67 BC
Phoenician and Greek merchants are attacked by pirates; Assyrians come to their aid.	Founding of the Roman Republic.	A navy is developed at Carthage. A Greek fleet defeats the Persian navy.	The Athenian navy attacks Greek pirate islands, such as Kithnos, Mikonos, and the Sporades.	Alexander the Great conquers Egypt.	War with Carthage loosens Rome's grip on Mediterranean; pirate communities take advantage.	The Romans annex Illyria in order to curb piracy.	An anti-pirate campaign by Roman general Pompey the Great eliminates the Cilician sea raiders.

The Bireme

WORKHORSE OF THE ANCIENT PIRATE

Low, sleek, and capable of avoiding slower, more cumbersome warships, galleys were perfectly suited to the style of attack favored by the pirates of Greece and Asia Minor. Unfortunately for them, the Romans worked out that the best way to catch a bireme was to use a similar vessel.

Some of the first pirate peoples in history used oared pirate craft. The "Sea Peoples" of the late Bronze Age and the later Cretan pirates of the 10th century BC both used a form of galley, as shown in contemporary carved images. These early craft were probably related to the Greek pirate ships mentioned by Homer, small open-decked galleys with between 10 and 25 oars per side. These were the "black ships before Troy" that Odysseus sailed in during his epic return voyage from the Trojan War.

During the "Dark Age" following the collapse of the Mediterranean Bronze Age cultures, several types of vessel appeared in representations of contemporary shipping. While merchant trading ships developed into pure sailing vessels, as well

as oared broad-beamed galleys that could use oar or sail, other illustrations depict narrower, more sleekly designed craft. These were the types of vessel used by pirates—fast enough to evade or overhaul other ships, but unlike warships they retained cargo capacity for captured plunder.

Illustrations of Phoenician ships from the eighth century show fast galleys mounting their oars in two tiers, a form of warship known as the bireme. By the sixth century BC warships were more specialized, and Greek biremes are shown as having more oars to increase speed, a fighting platform for marines, and a ram to help sink enemy ships. The last thing a pirate wanted to do was sink his prey before he could plunder its cargo, so smaller pirate biremes remained less specialized than their naval opponents in the Greek and Phoenician navies.

This naval specialization continued as naval warships developed into triremes by the fifth century BC, where a third bank of oars produced greater speed for short distances, such as when trying to ram another vessel. This specialization also tended to reduce the range of warships. While triremes were excellent warships, they were unsuitable for long ocean voyages, and therefore unable to escort merchant shipping. This gave the smaller and more seaworthy pirate biremes an advantage.

Variations on the bireme
By the era of the Roman Republic and the Macedonian Empire of Alexander the Great, open-decked biremes known as *lembo*s were used by Illyrian pirates in the Adriatic Sea, able to evade less maneuverable naval triremes and quinqueremes (galleys

below: *A fresco from Knossos Palace shows a naval expedition setting sail in 1500 BC.*

with five banks of oars). The Romans later copied the design during the second century BC and used their own version as anti-piracy craft. Another *lembo* variant was the *liburnian*, an adaptation of the pirate bireme that could be used as a warship. When pirates such as the Cilicians were hired as mercenaries by the Mediterranean powers, *liburnian*s formed the backbone of their naval strength.

Yet another pirate adaptation of the classic bireme was the *hemiola*, which first appeared in Greek waters during the fourth century BC. The *hemiola* (from the Greek word for one-and-a-half) was a light, fast bireme that combined oars and a large square sail. Just before a *hemiola* boarded a prize, the crew removed and stowed away half of the top row of oars, and the mast would be stepped (lowered). This created a fighting platform from which the pirates could board the enemy vessel.

For much of the third and second centuries BC the island of Rhodes maintained a fleet of *triemiola* to hunt down and destroy pirate craft. These smaller, faster, open-decked versions of the *hemiola* allowing a number of oars to be removed before coming into contact with another vessel. This increased her ability to swamp the pirate ship with marines.

When Pompey the Great fought his anti-pirate campaign in the first century BC, he relied on hired Rhodean biremes and Roman-built *liburnian*s to catch pirates, and supported these light ships with heavier but slower warships. His campaign broke the back of the pirates in the Mediterranean, and although the Roman Navy maintained a fleet of fast biremes to prevent any resurgence of piratical activity, they were hardly ever used after the foundation of the Roman Empire.

above: *A light fighting ship from classical Greece, with oars assisted by wind power.*

below: *A Roman bireme with only one set of oars showing.*

The Sea Peoples

MIGRATING TRIBES, PIRATE TENDENCIES

Some of the earliest reports of piracy on the high seas can be found at Karnak, hundreds of miles from the sea, on the walls of an Egyptian temple on the banks of the River Nile—an account of how Egypt was attacked by the Sea Peoples.

opposite page below: *In a mighty clash, the Egyptian warships battle with the Sea Peoples off the Nile Delta in 1186 BC.*

The "Sea Peoples" was a collective name given to those who invaded the Egyptian Empire in the late 13th and early 12th centuries BC. The name created by Egyptian chroniclers referred to migrating tribes who originally came from the Aegean and Adriatic basins and the western Mediterranean. Six tribes of Sea Peoples were specifically mentioned by the Egyptians: the Shardana, Denyen, Peleset, Shekelesh, Weshesh, and Tjeker people. This mass migration has been credited with several cataclysmic events in the late Bronze Age Mediterranean world, including the end of the Mycenaean Greek civilization and the destruction of the Hittite Empire in Asia Minor.

The main source of Egyptian information comes from inscriptions in temples at Karnak and Medinet Abu, the tomb of Ramesses the Great. Both mention a link between these northern peoples and the known Egyptian enemies in Libya and Palestine, so it may be possible that these migrating tribes formed an alliance that threatened to destroy Egypt, although swift military action by Ramesses prevented any such catastrophe.

Several historians suggest that the Tursha and Lycian peoples of Asia Minor formed part of this group, but avoided contact with the Egyptians. The Shardana, Shekelesh, and Peleset tribes possibly originated on the northeast Adriatic coast, although the Shardana have also been linked to Sardinia. The Karnak inscription states that the Libyans hired mercenaries from the northern lands of what are now Sardinia, Sicily, Italy, Greece, and Turkey. Whatever their origin, in Egyptian eyes these migrating raiders came from the northern rim of the known world.

Although the Sea Peoples were not strictly pirates in the true sense, but more accurately were formed from aggressive migrating tribes with ships, their actions can be considered as piracy on a grand scale. The Ramesses inscriptions record a tumultuous sea battle, where a confederation of Sea Peoples invaded Egypt from Palestine and were comprehensively defeated. This battle, fought off the Nile Delta in 1186 BC, marks the end of the Sea People's piratical attacks. From around 1220 BC until their defeat in 1186 BC, the Sea Peoples had almost complete control of the eastern Mediterranean basin, and captured ships, then cities, then whole regions.

After the defeat by the Egyptians, there is evidence that most of the Sea Peoples settled in Palestine, where the Peleset

tribe have been credited with being the ancestors of the Philistines. While many of these tribes turned to farming rather than raiding, the Tjeker tribe made a name as a maritime people.

The first pirate confederation

They engaged in maritime trade throughout the region, but also engaged in piracy. These coastal people probably developed into the Phoenicians. Tjeker settlements located around Dor, in modern Israel, form the earliest recorded pirate havens. By the mid-10th century, coastal trade had replaced piracy as the mainstay of the Tjeker economy.

The Medinet Abu carvings provide information about how they fought. A depiction of the 1186 BC sea battle on the tomb is the earliest known depiction of a naval engagement in the world. The Sea Peoples are shown in smaller boats than their Egyptian enemies, and also appear to lack armor and bows, both vital tools in Bronze Age warfare. The depiction supports the notion that these were raiders, intent on easy spoils and the acquisition of territory rather than warfare.

The sea battle was shown as a one-sided fight, but other evidence suggests that the Sea Peoples were not as vulnerable as they were depicted. Sherden (Shardana) warriors hired by both Egypt and the Libyans have been depicted elsewhere wearing armor and helmets and carrying swords and shields. Similarly, accounts of Bronze Age warfare elsewhere in the eastern Mediterranean describes the Sea Peoples as being great warriors and seamen, well armed with long swords and helmets. There is also evidence that they were feared raiders who preyed on shipping and coastal towns, and defeated all the forces sent against them, apart from the Egyptians. If we accept this, the Sea Peoples were the first pirate confederation in recorded history, resembling the Buccaneers of the 17th century, but who also came to settle as well as conquer.

above: Egyptian bas-relief c.1200–1100 BC, showing the Sea Peoples.

Piracy in the Greek World

CRETE, ATHENS, AND THE ADRIATIC

The blue waters of the Aegean and Adriatic seas were infested by pirates for centuries, operating from secluded bases on islands or rocky inlets. The Greek pirates of the Ancient World preyed on passing shipping until the Romans destroyed their lairs with crushing military force.

right: *Fishermen and shipbuilders from a classic Grecian vase. As in most eras, the victims of piracy were mariners trying to make a living. Fishing boats were more commonly plundered than vessels carrying treasure.*

During the period between the end of the Bronze Age and the rise of the Roman Republic, piracy was commonplace throughout the eastern Mediterranean. Certain regions formed pirate havens, which were used as bases from which to attack shipping. Later, a number of Greek States either actively encouraged piracy or created navies to curb the threat of piracy in their home waters.

Crete was an ideally located pirate haven, astride some of the Ancient World's busiest shipping lanes. In the 10th century BC, the Minoan civilization was overrun by Dorian Greeks, who engaged in piratical raids using Cretan cities as bases. In Homer's *Odyssey*, the Cretans were described as pirates.

Crete continued to be a pirate base for almost 800 years, and Cretan cities provided thriving markets for captured slaves and contraband. This reign of lawlessness was brought to an end in the second century BC, when Rhodean anti-pirate patrols cleared the waters of the eastern Mediterranean.

Further to the north, a number of Greek islands provided secluded pirate bases. Pirates from Lemnos even raided Athens itself, and an Athenian naval expedition was sent to crush the pirates and occupy the island in the early sixth century BC. Other pirate islands, including Kithnos, Mikonos, and the Sporades, were attacked by the Athenian navy during the fifth century BC.

In Greece itself, during the fourth century BC, the Aetolian League was formed, and within a century this confederation became the dominant power in central Greece. The league encouraged piracy against rival Greek and Persian states, using it as a means of extending its power. During the third century BC, Aetolian pirates dominated the Aegean and exerted protection payments from coastal settlements. In 192 BC, Rome conquered the Aetolian League and pirates were forced to look elsewhere for a base, the majority relocating to Cilicia.

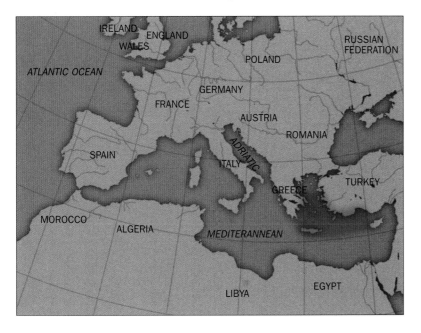

A profusion of pirate bases

In the Adriatic Sea, piracy flourished along its northeastern coast. While the Aetolian League exerted control over Greece itself, further north the inhabitants of the neighboring regions of Dalmatia and Illyria looked to piracy for their major source of income. These pirates raided the coasts of the Adriatic and central Mediterranean, with their activities reaching a peak in the third century BC. The growing amount of Roman trade meant that they were ideally located to prey on shipping, and the pirates even established forward bases on Corfu, Santa Maura, and Cephalonia.

The activities of the Illyrian pirates were curbed when the Roman army fought and defeated the Illyrians, and established a puppet government. Many pirates moved to the regions of Istria and Dalmatia and continued their attacks, and a revival of piracy in Illyria led to the Roman annexation of the area in 168 BC.

Istria, a semi-autonomous area in the northern Adriatic, provided a safe haven until an attack on a Roman grain convoy led to two punitive Roman expeditions destroying the region's bases; the Romans later annexed the region. Dalmatia was another semi-autonomous region of Illyria that seceded in 180 BC. It provided the last pirate refuge on the Adriatic coast after Roman occupation of Illyria and the destruction of pirate bases off the Greek Adriatic coast. The broken coast of Dalmatia made their bases difficult to locate and attack, and a number of pirates continued to operate from them until the region was annexed by Rome in AD 9.

Other Greek peoples settled in the western Mediterranean and engaged in piratical activities until the Romans crushed them. The Etruscans frequently attacked Greek shipping during the sixth and fifth centuries BC, but this was less true piracy than national policy, as the Etruscans sought to exclude Greek merchants from interfering with their trade monopoly. The Greeks called the Etruscans "Tyrrhenians," meaning pirates, but the word was eventually used to refer to any western Mediterranean pirates.

True pirate bases were located in the Lípari Islands off the northern coast of Sicily, in the Balearic Islands, and on the Ligurian coast, but all were conquered first by the Carthaginians then the Romans, ending organized piracy in the western Mediterranean.

above: *Greek naval warfare. Hoplites carried on-board two biremes prepare to clash in a boarding action.*

below: *This Roman mosaic detail of Ulysses and the Sirens shows a late bireme, with the mast raised to provide some relief for the rowers.*

The Cilicians

TAKING ADVANTAGE OF ROMAN TREATIES

The southern coast of modern Turkey once provided a haven to a brotherhood of pirates. The Cilicians plagued the eastern Mediterranean for centuries, and even captured Julius Caesar. Their reign of terror ended when Rome turned its might against them.

right: *As a young man, Julius Caesar was captured by Cilician pirates and held to ransom. Once freed, he returned and destroyed the pirate lair.*

opposite above:

This illustration shows a Roman merchant vessel. These plump trading vessels were easy prey for the Cilician pirates.

Cilicia was the most famous pirate haven of the Ancient World, and the Cilicians formed one of the largest pirate bands in history. The region was located along the southern shore of Asia Minor, in what is now Turkey.

Bordered to the north by the Taurus mountains, Cilicia was a mountainous and inhospitable region. Naturally, the inhabitants looked toward the sea for sustenance, and later for plunder. During the latter second and much of the first century BC, it was a haven for pirates, whose attacks disrupted the shipping around the eastern Mediterranean. It was ideally located for the purpose, astride the main maritime trade route from Syria to Italy and Greece, and close to the sea lanes of Egypt and Palestine. The Cilician

coast was broken by numerous rocky inlets, promontories, and hidden anchorages.

During the early second century BC, the Seleucid kings of Syria and Asia Minor stopped maintaining naval patrols along the Cilician coast. Internal disputes and warfare created a large void in the naval control of the eastern Mediterranean, and the pirates took full advantage.

As a result of the Roman military victory over the Seleucid Empire in 190 BC, the Treaty of Apamea was signed two years later. Under its terms, Western Asia Minor (now Turkey) became a Roman protectorate and the Seleucid navy was withdrawn. No Roman fleet was sent to take its place. Seleucid power in Asia Minor was replaced by that of Pontus, whose king preferred to ally himself with the Cilician pirates than with Rome. As a result, the pirate communities prospered and thousands flocked to join them.

Initially, the Cilicians restricted their attacks to the eastern Mediterranean and its shores. Coastal villages were attacked as readily as ships on the high seas, and captives fueled the slave markets of Crete

and the Aegean. Like all piratical economies, they relied on friendly communities to supply markets for their stolen cargo and slaves. These were the cities of the Roman protectorate: Miletos, Ephesos, and Smyrna. As long as a ready supply of skilled slaves was guaranteed, the Roman provincial governors and citizens were prepared to "turn a blind eye."

Threatening Roman control

By the end of the second century, the pirates began to directly challenge the power of Rome and hinder her trade. Soon, shipping throughout the Aegean was being attacked, then Cilicians ventured into the western Mediterranean, operating off the coast of Italy. Senior Roman citizens were captured and held for ransom, including Julius Caesar! The Senate decided that the pirates had to be curbed, or else the Roman Republic herself would be threatened, through a strangulation of trade.

In 101 BC, the Senate passed its first anti-piracy law, closing the harbors of Rome's Asia province to the pirates. Cilician pirates therefore ventured all over the Mediterranean in search of plunder.

War again changed the dynamics of Mediterranean piracy in 89 BC. King Mithridates of Pontus invaded and captured the Roman protectorate. Allying himself with the Cilicians, he besieged Rhodes and sent troops into northern Greece. In 86 BC, a pirate fleet defeated the only Roman squadron afloat at the time off Brindisi, in southern Italy. By this time the pirates were organized into large naval fleets, capable of crushing any opposition. Due to his alliance with the pirates, Mithridates held undisputed control of the western Mediterranean.

While Mithridates controlled the seas, the Roman army reigned supreme on land. Roman general Cornelius Sulla defeated the Pontic army in 86 BC, and a peace treaty the following year restored the Asian provinces and Greece to Rome. Rome then planned the restoration of her naval control of the Mediterranean, while pirate attacks continued unabated.

By 67 BC the Romans were ready. A

devastating attack on the Cilicians spearheaded by Pompey the Great led to their almost complete destruction. While pirates were still occasionally encountered in Mediterranean waters, they would never again be organized into a major force. At their peak, the Cilicians had threatened the very survival of the Roman Republic, making them one of the world's most influential pirate communities.

below: *Roman warships, from a mosaic at Casa dei Vetti, Pompeii, c.AD 79. These vessels closely resemble the biremes used by Cilician pirates, and by the Romans in their bid to cleanse the Mediterranean of piracy.*

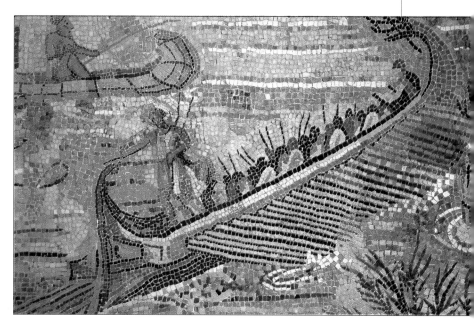

Pompey the Great

MEDITERRANEAN BROOM

The Roman leader Pompey was ordered by the Senate to clear the Mediterranean of pirates. In a short and brilliant naval campaign he swept them from the seas and subdued the pirate lairs of the Cilician coast. His campaign ranks as probably the largest anti-pirate action of all time.

right: *Gnaeus Pompeius Maximus (Pompey the Great) masterminded the Roman campaign to eradicate piracy from the Mediterranean Sea. He continued to dominate Roman military affairs until his death in 48 BC.*

Gnaeus Pompeius Magnus (Pompey the Great) is best known as the ally and triumvirate member of Julius Caesar, then later his bitter rival. His gradual opposition to Caesar's political ambitions ultimately led to the Roman Civil War, where Pompey was defeated in battle by Caesar.

Before Caesar's crossing of the Rubicon and the turmoil of civil war, Pompey served Rome as a politician and a military commander. In 67 BC he was granted an imperium, under the terms of a new anti-piracy law, the *lex Gabinia de piratis persequendis*. This imperium gave Pompey 6,000 talents (units of currency), control of 500 ships, 120,000 Roman troops, and the right to tax and raise militia in cities up to 50 miles (80km) inland. His mission was to completely eradicate piracy in the Mediterranean Sea.

The law was passed despite strong political opposition, as the powers granted to Pompey were immense, amounting to a virtual military dictatorship. That it happened at all was evidence of how serious Rome took the pirate threat. To translate the situation into modern terms, it was as if the US Government gave a general the entire American military machine plus an unlimited budget, with powers to attack anywhere he wanted, in an effort to eradicate drug-trafficking!

Pompey started by dividing the Mediterranean into 13 districts, each under the command of a legate (deputy commander). Simultaneously in each area, the legates sought out pirate bases and blockaded them, while searching the coasts for hidden pirate locations. The army was then sent in to kill or capture the pirates, seize their ships, and destroy their bases. Mobile reserve fleets prevented any pirate fleets that escaped from linking up with other pirate groups.

The main pirate region in the Mediterranean at that time was Cilicia, on the southern coast of what is now Turkey. Pompey led the reserve fleets, sweeping the western Mediterranean and driving all the pirate ships before them, into the waiting cordon commanded by regional legates. In a number of naval skirmishes, these roving pirate fleets were outmatched and outfought by the Romans, and the remainder surrendered or burned their boats and fled inland.

Within 40 days Pompey had cleared most of the Mediterranean from end to end, and only a handful of pirates remained at large. Most of these were bottled up in coastal fortresses, blockaded by sea and soon to be besieged on land. It appears that many pirates gave themselves up, and Pompey usually proved lenient. Most were pardoned in exchange for information and a ransom, although many were executed, particularly those who offered resistance.

Pompey the merciful

As Pompey's grip tightened on the Cilician coast, the pirates coordinated a simultaneous sortie from several strongholds. These broke through the blockade, but were soon met by Pompey's reserve fleets. In a naval battle the pirates were repulsed and forced to retreat to Coracesium, a fortress on a remote Cilician peninsula. Pompey called up Roman troops and engineers, investing Coracesium from the landward side. After a short siege, the pirates surrendered. Pompey was lenient and the majority were relocated inland in Cilicia or Greece. Other pirates paid heed to Pompey's merciful terms, and the remaining strongholds capitulated.

The entire anti-pirate campaign took three months and resulted in the Mediterranean Sea being clear of pirates for the first time in human history. It has been claimed that 10,000 pirates were killed or executed during the campaign, while many more were spared and relocated away from the sea. Over 120 bases and fortresses were destroyed, along with hundreds of pirate vessels. A useful by-product was the capture of pirate booty, which was shared between the participating troops, with Pompey claiming the largest share. Hostages held by the pirates were also released. Pompey's victory over the pirates was complete.

Pompey was granted further commands before becoming embroiled in the politics surrounding the final years of the Roman Republic, and he was killed in 48 BC. Despite his later military failures against Caesar, Pompey remains one of the most successful pirate hunters of all time.

below: *A reconstruction of a Roman flagship leaving port. Most of Pompey's galleys were far smaller craft, mainly biremes, but each carried a complement of well-trained Roman legionaries or marines.*

CHAPTER TWO

Medieval Pirates

While Viking raiders were causing havoc in the waters of Dark-Age Europe, the Byzantine Empire was seen as the defender of civilization, protecting the eastern Mediterranean against the forces of Islam. As Byzantine fortunes waned, they invited pirates to help them defend their borders, much as the rulers of feudal Europe used piracy as an economic weapon. Both policies led to maritime anarchy. While the Hanseatic League helped fight piracy in northern Europe, it was only the collapse of the Byzantine Empire that brought an end to the piracy that plagued the Mediterranean. Piracy would still continue, but increasingly it was harnessed to help fight the religious and national struggles that engulfed the continent.

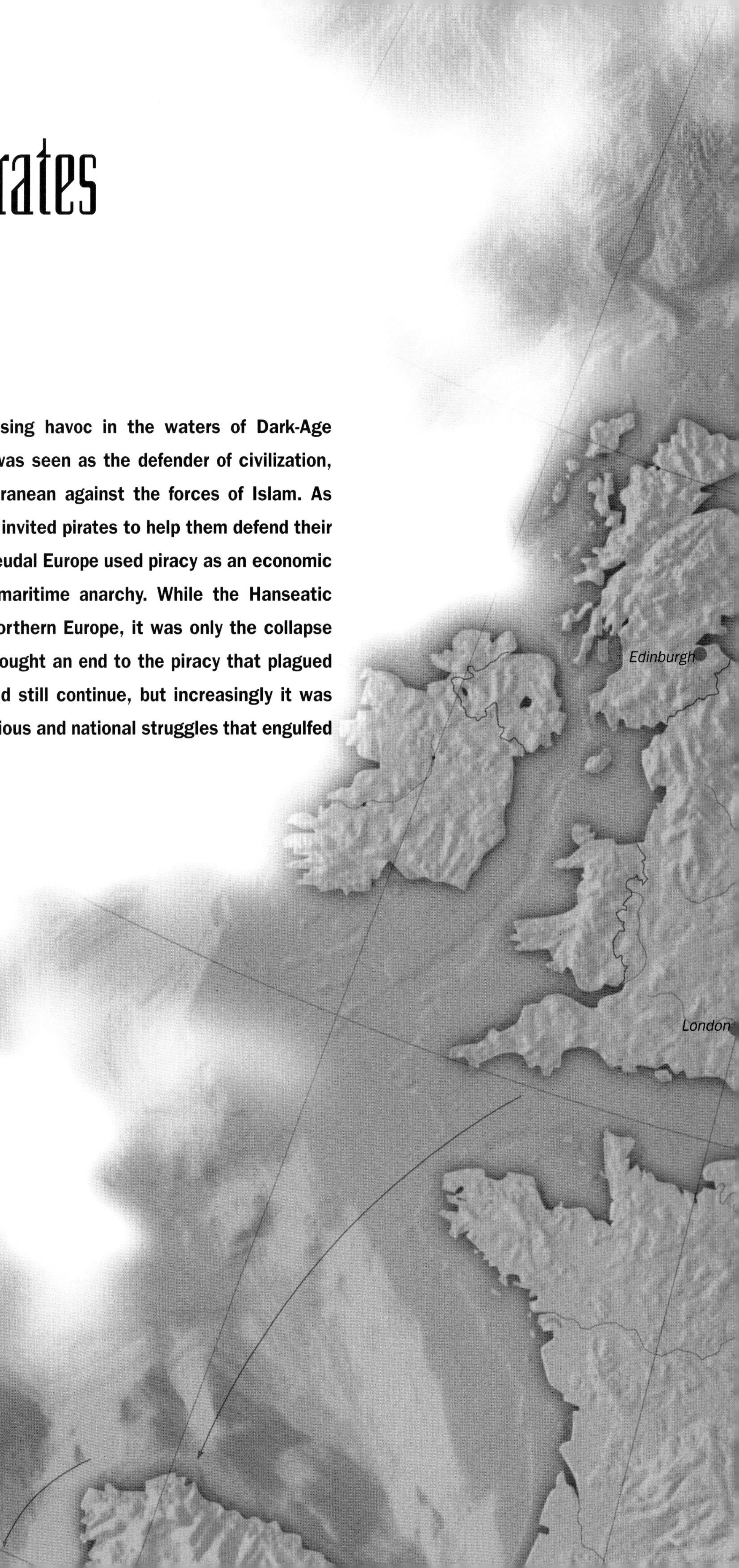

Edinburgh

London

Arrows indicate main trade routes established by the Hanseatic League that were open to pirate attacks

Bergen

Cristiana

Stockholm

Reval

Visby

Riga

Copenhagen

Danzig

Lubeck

Bremen

Amsterdam

Bruges

Genoa
Venice
Pisa
Madrid
Barcelona
CORSICA
Rome
BALEARICS
Naples
Istanbul
Acre
Beirut
Tripoli
Latakia
Cadiz
SARDINIA
Malaga
Algiers
Palermo
Athens
Tunis SICILY
MALTA
CYPRUS
CRETE
MEDITERRANEAN
Tripoli
Alexandria
Cairo

Arrows indicate major medieval trade routes in the Mediterranean c.1200–1400

MEDIEVAL PIRATES

below: *This depiction of a 13th-century vessel shows how the basic craft was turned into a warship by the addition of fighting "castles."*

While the collapse of the Western Roman Empire plunged Europe and the western Mediterranean into the period known as the Dark Ages, the Eastern Empire based in Constantinople weathered the barbarian storm. For the next thousand years the Byzantine Empire would exert its influence over the eastern Mediterranean. While for most of this period this influence would be a benevolent one, as the borders of the Empire contracted and its military power diminished, Byzantine policy invited pirates to help protect its waters.

Following the sack of Constantinople during the Fourth Crusade of AD 1204, the Aegean Sea became a haven for pirates. While Islamic corsairs along the coast of Syria and Egypt protected their own shipping and attacked vessels of their religious enemies, the Byzantines were not even able to protect their own capital. The rest of the eastern Mediterranean became controlled by the Ottoman Turks, who established the stability of maritime trade, but constant deals between the Byzantine court and the Aegean pirates led to anarchy in Greek waters. Many of these pirates were Italians, and the Byzantines used them as a tool to prevent the spread of Venetian and Genoese maritime power into its sphere of influence, creating an anarchical buffer zone.

The rise of the Ottoman Empire meant that the influence of these pirate communities would be curtailed by the 13th century, and the Byzantines were in no position to protect their own shores, still less to turn back the Islamic tide. Italian and Greek pirates owing allegiance to the Byzantine Empire were replaced by

below: *This depiction of a 13th-century vessel shows how the basic craft was turned into a warship by the addition of fighting "castles."*

330	655	c.800	896	c.1000	1066	13th century	1203
Constantine moves to Byzantium (Constantinople) and founds the Byzantine Empire.	A Byzantine fleet off Egypt is defeated by Arabs.	Western Europe's first castles are constructed.	King Alfred of Wessex, England, repels a Danish invasion.	Greenland colonized by Vikings.	Norman conquest of England.	"Reprisal" contracts awarded to wronged European mariners creates principle of privateering.	Venetians fail to clear pirate bases from Ionian Islands in the southern Adriatic.

corsairs serving the Ottoman Empire. The Ottoman Turks saw piracy as a useful extension of religious and territorial expansion, with corsairs harrying the maritime trade and coastlines of the enemies of Islam while protecting Ottoman territory and trade. Following the collapse of the Byzantine Empire and damage to maritime trade, and from the early 13th century the policy of issuing "Reprisal" contracts to wronged mariners led European monarchs to develop the basic principles of privateering. This piracy in the name of a feudal overlord was accompanied by freelance piracy,

above: *A battle between two cogs depicted in an early 14th-century miniature. At this stage, archery still dominated sea battles, softening up an enemy before the battle was joined at close quarters.*

the sack of Constantinople in 1453, the stage was set for a religious conflict that would engulf the whole Mediterranean and see the rise of the Barbary pirates.

The birth of privateering

In northern Europe and the western Mediterranean, centuries of maritime raiding by a succession of migratory Barbarian peoples eventually led to an era of stability, the Middle Ages. While the feudal system imposed a degree of peace on the continent, it established the system that resulted in the dynastic wars which plagued Europe until the 19th century. The spread of peace encouraged business, and as towns grew, maritime trade flourished between these fledgling ports of northern Europe, Spain, and Italy.

United under the banner of Christianity, the realms of medieval Europe combined religious warfare against the Moors, Turks, and Pagans surrounding their periphery with constant internal struggle over land and titles. This warfare inevitably caused

particularly in the waters of the Baltic Sea and the English Channel. The 13th century saw such an upsurge of piratical attacks that European trading ports were forced to band together into protective bodies. In Germany the Hanseatic League developed into a major maritime power, leading the way in the combat of piracy in the waters of northern Europe.

During the late 14th and early 15th centuries, almost continual warfare between England and France led to an increase in national piracy. Using the technology offered by improved ship types and the introduction of shipborne artillery, pirates and privateers roamed the waters of the English Channel and the Bay of Biscay, sailing further from their home ports than ever before. These maritime plunderers would develop into the Sea Rovers of the 16th century, combining warfare in the name of religion and the national interest with a ruthless quest for plunder.

1217	1241	c.1254	c.1300	1348	1392	15th century	1453
Eustace the Monk at large, using a Viking-influenced, clinker-built knorr as a pirate ship.	Hanseatic League formed by Baltic German cities to supervise sea trade and suppress piracy.	Birth of the explorer Marco Polo.	League of the Cinque Ports formed, develops British trade, protects Channel from pirates.	A third of Europe's population die with the bubonic plague.	Hanseatic League is rocked when the port of Bergen is attacked by the German pirates.	Carvel-built ships replace the clinker-built craft that cannot be fitted with artillery.	The Byzantine Empire ends as Ottoman Turks invade Constantinople.

The Ships of Medieval Europe

FROM COASTAL TRADER TO THE PERFECT PRIVATEER

At the start of the Middle Ages, European ships were only capable of making short trading voyages. By the late 15th century, a string of technological breakthroughs produced ships that were capable of carrying European trade to the edges of the known world and beyond.

below: *Embarking troops for the Third Crusade (1189–92) and a sea battle in which the English fleet destroys a Sarazene ship.*

During the Early Middle Ages the standard trading ship in northern Europe was the knorr, a vessel developed from the Viking ships that had dominated European waters since the eighth century. The knorr was pointed at both ends, open-decked, and clinker built—overlapped planks formed the hull. A single mast and square sail provided propulsion, while a steering oar acted as a rudder.

As maritime trade grew in 13th-century northern Europe, these ships were modified to improve their efficiency. An improved sail plan and bowsprit gave the vessel more speed, while raised platforms at the bow and stern provided shelter. They also acted as a fighting platform if the ship was attacked—and as maritime trade grew, so did piracy. The depiction of a battle against the pirate called Eustace the Monk in 1217 shows vessels of this type. As European sailors ventured into the Mediterranean, they encountered vessels based on Arabic lines; carvel-built designs using planking joined edge to edge. These Mediterranean ships used a triangular lateen sail that allowed them to sail close to the wind.

By the mid-13th century northern ship designers produced a development of the knorr called the cog, which rapidly became the dominant ship in northern European waters. It used a stern rudder, so the stern was no longer pointed, and its deck was enclosed, protecting its cargo.

In the mid-1300s the cog had increased in size, and superstructure (or "castles") at the bow and stern developed into true forecastles and sterncastles, providing good fighting platforms. These were the seaworthy trading vessels used by the Hanseatic League, and provided the basis for all warships and pirate vessels of their day. The only difference between a trader and a warship was the size of her crew, and possibly the increased size of her fighting platforms.

Roundship, galiot, caravel, and carrack

These Italian shipbuilders had copied the increased hull size of the cog and adapted it for use in carvel-built ships. The cog

left: Loading supplies onto a 14th-century French Crusading fleet. Note the fighting platforms added to the hulls of the vessels.

below: The cog was replaced by the carrack as the standard late-medieval trading ship in Northern Europe. "A Carrack before the wind, c.1540." Oil painting in the style of Peter Brueghel the Elder.

developed throughout the Middle Ages, and both height of superstructure and hull size steadily increased. The two styles were amalgamated in Italian ports, where northern size was married to a southern sail plan and a carvel hull to produce the roundship. Unlike northern European vessels, these were not used as warships or pirate craft. In Mediterranean waters from the 14th century onward, galleys were used for warfare, and pirates used a smaller variant, called the galiot for attacks.

During the 15th century, a fast sailing ship developed in the Mediterranean combining a stern rudder and lateen sails. The caravel was a lightly built, fast, and responsive vessel that used the similar-sounding carvel frame construction and was easily handled by a small crew. A northern development of the cog emerged around the same time.

Permanent fighting platforms made ships more seaworthy, and the introduction of artillery during the 15th century made them formidable warships. This development produced the carrack, which became the backbone of Europe's merchant fleets and navies. The Spanish and Portuguese referred to the vessel as the nao.

There was also a gradual shift from clinker-built to carvel-built hulls, a trend spurred on by the development of naval artillery. The integrity of clinker-built hulls was compromised by cutting holes in them to make gunports, and the increasingly heavy guns of the period had to be mounted low inside a ship. This meant that warships had to be carvel-built. These large ships combined a strong frame with a streamlined hull, and their cargo capacity was much greater than that of Mediterranean craft of the same period.

While the pirates of the Mediterranean preferred small galleys, those of northern waters used small caravels to attack enemy shipping, or else relied on the firepower of the carrack to overpower opposition. Private ships were constantly being hired for national defense and as privateers. These were the ships that would be used by the explorers of the New World, and by the pirates who preyed on the wealth these explorers revealed.

Byzantine Pirates

PLUNDER IN A RUINED EMPIRE

The Byzantine Empire maintained the sea lanes of the eastern Mediterranean for almost a millennium. As the empire declined, its seas became the hunting ground for ruthless pirates, who terrorized the Mediterranean for over 200 years.

The Byzantine Empire was founded in AD 330 when Emperor Constantine moved to Byzantium, renaming the city Constantinople. After the fall of the Western Roman Empire, the Eastern or Byzantine Empire remained a bastion of order in the Mediterranean for a millennium, despite the rise of Islam and Europe's descent into the Dark Ages. Byzantine warships patrolled the eastern Mediterranean defending the empire's maritime trade, while her armies tried unsuccessfully to prevent the spread of Islam.

By the late 12th century the Byzantine Empire had shrunk—her power only extended as far as Greece and most of modern Turkey. Although fabulously wealthy, constant political turmoil

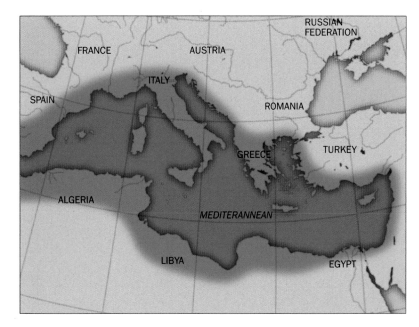

undermined the power of Byzantine military forces, and a disastrous brush with European Crusaders led to the capture and sack of Constantinople in 1204.

One reason for the disaster was the collapse of the Byzantine navy. For years it had recruited Italian seamen. In the late 12th century, conflict with Venice and other Italian states led to the arrest of these seamen, who for the next decade became the scapegoats for Byzantine Imperial decay. Many took to piracy, and although the Byzantines regained control of their capital, their naval power never recovered and piracy became endemic in the Aegean Sea.

These pirates used remote bases, well away from the last bastions of Byzantine authority in the region. Crete and many of the smaller Aegean islands were favored, as were remote mainland harbors such as Anaia (now Kusadasi in southwest Turkey) or Menemvasía in southern Greece. The Ionian Islands of the southern Adriatic were also considered pirate havens, ruled by the Italian knight Margaritone of Brindisi. The Venetians attacked the pirate bases on their way to attack Constantinople in 1203. The pirates soon returned, and these Italian and Greek renegades used the islands of Corfu, Zante, Ithaca, and Cephalonia as bases until they were annexed by Venice in the late 14th century.

From piracy to Rhodes' overlord

The real pirate heyday in the waters surrounding the crumbling Byzantine Empire came in the late 13th century. A Byzantine revolution led to the ascension of a provincial governor as the new emperor in 1259. During the early 1260s Emperor Michael III recaptured Constantinople and large tracts of Greece that had been occupied by feudal Italian overlords. While these petty nobles welcomed pirates to their waters, and saw them as an extra source of income, the Byzantine emperor used them as a political tool. He hired pirate captains to form a reconstituted Byzantine navy, and these corsairs were encouraged to attack Italian shipping in the Aegean. Most were Italian, and according to Italian historian Torsello writing in the early 14th century, most Aegean pirates were originally from Genoa and Venice.

The typically Byzantine expedient of turning Italian against Italian resulted in the naming of many of these pirates in a Venetian claim for compensation in 1278. A document bears out Torsello's claim. The names of Michael Balbo, Manuel de Marino, and Bartolomeo Foscolo betray their north Italian origins. One pirate in the service of the emperor, Giovanni de lo Cavo, rose to prominence as a naval commander and became overlord of Rhodes in 1278. Not all of these Aegean pirates were Italian; local Greek or Balkan pirates operated in the region, like Bulgarino d'Anaia, George de Malvasia, and George Makrycheris.

The growing naval power of Rhodes and the Ottoman Empire curbed lawlessness in the region during the 14th century. While

the Byzantine navy found it difficult to maintain control of the waters surrounding Constantinople, Turkish warships dominated the Aegean and the eastern Mediterranean, bringing the era of medieval Italian pirates to an end. One exception was a group known as the Catalan pirates, Spanish mercenaries who established their own community based around Athens. They eventually amalgamated with the Islamic corsairs. While Turkish pirates attacked the shipping of Byzantium and the Italian city states, they fought for the Ottoman Empire as much as they did for plunder, an amalgam of roles that would be repeated by the later Barbary pirates.

above: *The Crusaders played an active role in undermining Byzantine control in the Mediterranean. Here Louis IX departs on the Sixth Crusade in 1248.*

left: *At the request of the Genoese, whose trade had been adversely affected by African corsairs, a French and English expedition set out in 1390 to do battle with the pirates.*

The Pirates of Northern Europe

EARLY EUROPEAN PIRATES

During the Middle Ages, merchants and trading ports flourished along the shores of the Baltic and North seas. An increase in maritime trade also created an increase in piratical attacks, forcing the merchants to form defensive leagues.

right: *Execution of the German pirate Henzlein on September 10, 1573, along with his 32 crew. He was one of the later pirates operating on the Baltic, preying on local shipping after the decline of the Hanseatic League.*

Following the Barbarian Invasions, Europe was plunged into the period known as the Dark Ages. Raiders brought maritime commerce to a virtual standstill, and any resurgence was ended by the Viking attacks of the late eighth century. For the next 300 years Scandinavian raiders dominated the waters of northern Europe, and in their wake came Norse settlers. While the 10th and 11th centuries saw the adoption of the feudal system, Scandinavian traders established fortified posts that gradually developed into ports by the 12th century. An increase of maritime trade also brought piracy.

During the early medieval period, piracy formed part of everyday life, as Norse raiding parties reached as far afield as Russia and the Mediterranean. By the 1200s, national and city identities led to more selective attacks, and the feudal rulers of Europe tried to harness piracy for their own ends.

The Plantagenet kings of England and parts of France did their best to suppress piracy. In 1228 William de Briggeho became the first recorded pirate executed for his crimes in England, evidence of a tougher stance against piracy. The growing

importance of towns and the revenues they produced for their feudal protector meant that piracy impeded political and national growth.

One of these pirates was a renegade cleric known as Eustace the Monk. This Flemish pirate operated in the English Channel and enjoyed the protection of the English crown, as long as he confined his attacks to French ships. His assaults on English shipping forced him to flee to France, where the French king engaged him as a mercenary sea captain. Eustace led a French raiding force against the English coast in 1217, but was intercepted off Dover. In the ensuing battle, the English used lime as a form of early chemical weapon, then captured the French raiders.

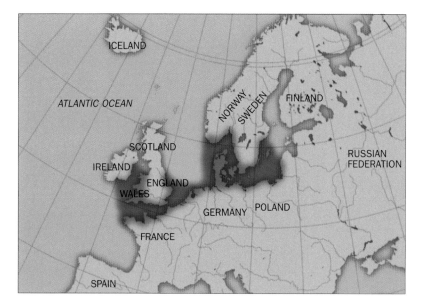

The monk was summarily executed.

In 1241 the Baltic German cities of Lübeck and Hamburg combined to form the Hanseatic League, a merchant guild that supervised maritime trade and the suppression of piracy. Other free (i.e. non-feudal) cities joined, until by 1300 this trading fellowship incorporated 19 ports. The Hanse had become a major force, and took the lead in combating piracy in northern European waters. Similar organizations were to follow, although on a smaller scale.

Channel and Baltic under threat

In England, the League of the Cinque Ports was established in the early 14th century to protect the English Channel from pirates and to encourage trade from its ports, which included Dover and Hastings. While the Hanseatic League remained true to its ideals, the English equivalent degenerated into a semi-legal piratical organization, where it protected its own shipping but attacked that of everybody else.

Almost continuous warfare in Europe in the late 14th and early 15th centuries encouraged a rise in piratical activity. In the Baltic several German pirates formed a band known as the Victual Brothers and waged war against the Hanse. They attacked the Norwegian Hanse port of Bergen in 1392, threatening the survival of the Hanseatic League. The pirates were caught in 1402 by a fleet of Hanse ships from Hamburg, and pirate leader Stertebeker and his followers were executed in Hamburg.

In the waters of the English Channel, the prevalence of piracy was influenced by the almost constant state of warfare between England and France. English seamen such as John Hawley of Dartmouth in Devon and Henry Pay from Poole in Dorset frequently attacked French and Spanish shipping, inviting reprisal attacks from foreign pirates such as Pero Niño of Castille and Frenchman Charles de Savoisy. The right of "Reprisal," issued by a monarch to ship owners who had suffered losses, encouraged this form of national raiding, and the system developed into the "Letter of Marque" licenses that allowed private vessels to plunder enemy ships. Peace with France and the reestablishment of order brought an end to widespread piracy by the late 15th century, although random piratical attacks continued in northern European waters in the following century.

CHAPTER THREE

The Barbary Pirates

FRANCE

Holy Roman Empire

Venic

Genoa

Marseilles

SPAIN

Barcelona

CORSICA

Italian
States

Seville

BALEARIC ISLANDS

SARDINIA

Naples

Cadiz

Tangier

Algiers

Salé

SICILY

Tunis

MALTA

Tripoli

For more than 150 years, from the late 15th century onward, a pirate community plagued the waters of the Mediterranean. This highly organized community of corsairs were known as the Barbary pirates, named after the string of North African ports they used as their bases. They combined piracy with naval service on behalf of the Ottoman Empire, and for much of the 16th century they were at the forefront of the bitter religious war fought for the domination of the Mediterranean basin. The Barbary pirates used small, fast galleys to attack European shipping and raid coastal settlements, and their bases became bustling markets for the sale of slaves and plunder.

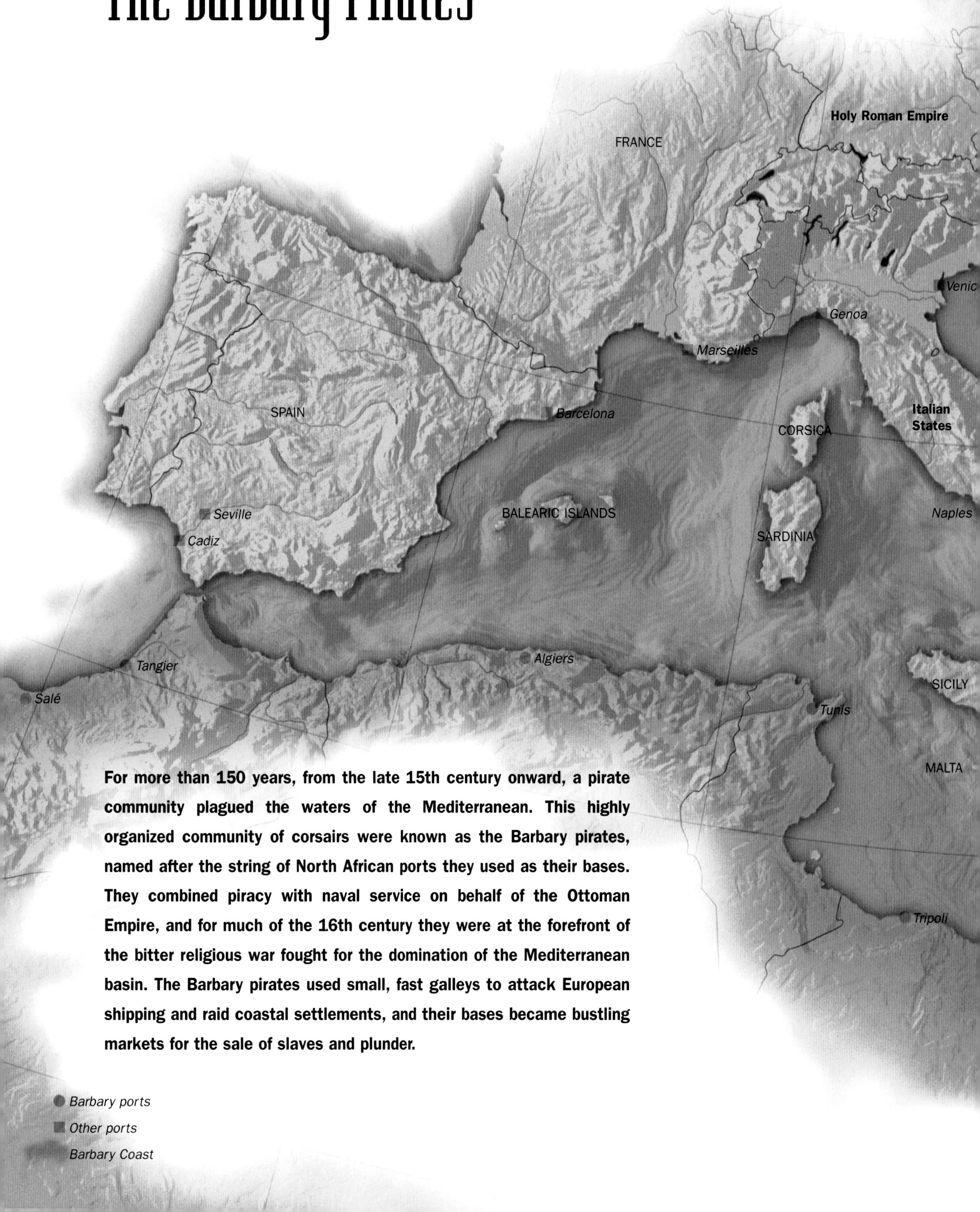

● *Barbary ports*

■ *Other ports*

Barbary Coast

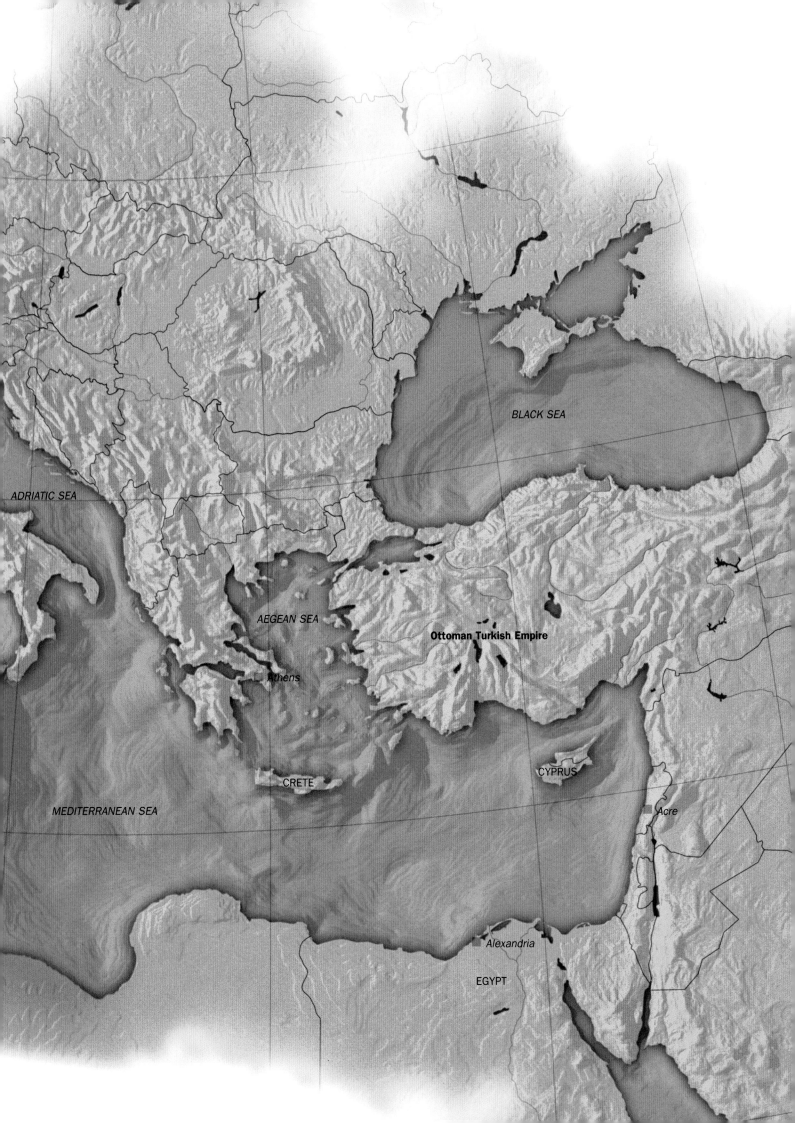

BLACK SEA

ADRIATIC SEA

AEGEAN SEA

Athens

Ottoman Turkish Empire

CYPRUS

CRETE

MEDITERRANEAN SEA

Acre

Alexandria

EGYPT

THE BARBARY PIRATES

From the 15th century, a string of city states that skirted the Mediterranean shore of North Africa played host to a group of corsairs known as the Barbary pirates. For centuries their long, sleek galleys would attack shipping and coastal settlements from the entrance to the Atlantic to the Holy Land, and their reputation for ferocity was legendary. These men were not simple pirates, but served the Ottoman Empire, combining acts of piracy with warfare on behalf of their Muslim overlord.

The cities of Algiers, Tunis, and Tripoli, plus a score of smaller coastal towns, were strung out along the southern Mediterranean shore, ideally located to act as bases from which to harass passing shipping. They were ruled by local potentates—Beys or Beylerbeys—who owed their position to the Ottoman Turkish sultan (in effect, an emperor).

These coastal towns sat on the edge of the Sahara Desert, and their sparsely populated hinterland of small African settlements produced the barest essentials required to support the cities. Any wealth had to come from the sea, so during the late 15th and early 16th centuries local rulers encouraged corsairs to use their ports as pirate havens. In return, they expected a percentage of the profits, and treated piracy as a lucrative business. During the 16th century these local rulers were often appointed from the ranks of the pirates themselves, making piratical activities an integral part of policy and economics along the Barbary Coast.

The Barbary corsairs were well organized. A ruling captain's council, the Taife Raisi, supervised the running of the pirate havens and acted as a link between the corsairs, local potentates, and the Ottoman Empire. The policy of the Barbary states was to confine attacks to non-Muslim shipping, and piratical attacks were further restricted by treaties between certain Christian states and the Ottoman Empire. As an example, the city state of Venice was at peace with the Ottoman Turks for much of the 16th century, therefore attacks on Venetian ships were discouraged.

Lucrative trading opportunities

The city states of the Barbary Coast were considered part of the Ottoman Empire, and Turkish troops assisted the local potentates in defending the ports. The corsairs often combined

below: A Royal Navy crew board an Algerian corsair in the early 19th century. Corsairs were still active in the Mediterranean until after the Napoleonic Wars, when European powers and the United States combined forces to pacify the Barbary Coast.

15th century	1405	1415	c.1440	1453	c.1470	1492	1493
The Barbary pirates, based on the North African shore, are rife in the Mediterranean.	The Chinese voyage around the Indian Ocean.	The English win the Battle of Agincourt.	Malacca, southeast Asia, is established as a major commercial port.	The Byzantine Empire ends as Ottoman Turks take over Constantinople.	The Greek Barbarossa brothers are born; their pirate careers involve raids on mostly Spanish ship and towns.	Christopher Columbus reaches America.	Founding of Hispaniola, the first Spanish settlement in the Americas.

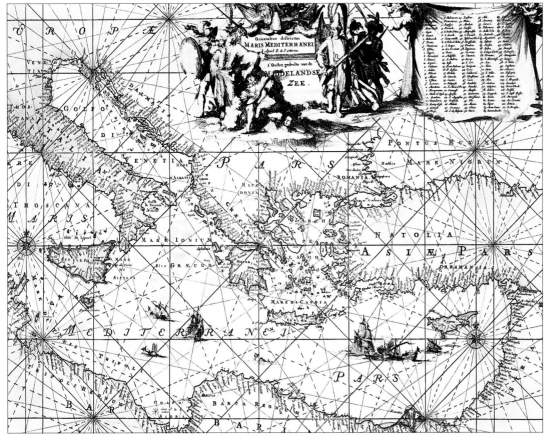

piratical attacks with service in the Ottoman navy. Corsair commanders and their fleets of galleys and galiots fought in the major naval battles of the 16th century. They also helped to defend the Barbary Coast from attack by Christian forces, and a bitter struggle for control was fought with Spain for much of the century.

By the end of the 16th century a form of stalemate had been reached in the Mediterranean Sea, and although conflict continued between Christians and Muslims in the Balkans, the Barbary Coast was considered an integral part of the Ottoman Empire and its security was no longer threatened. The ports of the Barbary Coast continued to play host to corsairs, but the heyday of these pirates was over by the mid-17th century. Although Barbary pirates still attacked passing ships as late as the early 19th century, they never again rivaled the Christian powers for control of the Mediterranean.

Barbary pirates were often portrayed as fanatical Muslims, waging an undeclared war against their religious enemies. In fact, many corsairs were born as Christians, and adopted the Islamic faith in order to pursue a piratical career. Renegade Christians formed a substantial portion of corsair numbers.

While they nominally served the Ottoman Empire and both the local potentate and the Taife Raise, each captain (or Rais) owned his own ship and had almost complete freedom. He was assisted by the aga, who commanded the boarding party, and a scribe appointed by the Taife Raise ensured that booty was shared between the Rais and the local potentate at the end of the cruise. Typically, the local Bey claimed 10 percent, plus a fee for usage of his port. As the Barbary ports were excellent markets for contraband and captured slaves, the system suited the corsairs and the local authorities.

1498	16th century	1500	1520	1530	1534	c.1650	c.1800
Vasco da Gama becomes the first person to make a return voyage from Europe to India.	A larger, taller galley is developed; pirates use galiots, smaller, faster variants.	Pedro Cabral discovers Brazil.	Italian Uluj Ali is born as Giovanni Dionigi, a pirate who led an Ottoman fleet.	Christian corsairs the Knights of Malta are granted control of Malta by Hapsburg Emperor Charles V.	Albanian Murat Rais is born, a pirate who was made "Captain of the Sea" by the Sultan of Algiers.	The heyday of the Barbary pirates comes to a close.	A few bands of Barbary pirates still operate.

The Galley

RUNNING RINGS AROUND ITS VICTIMS

The Barbary pirates adopted oared galleys as their main striking force. Sailing from their bases along the North African coast, they allied themselves with the galley fleet of Ottoman Turkey, and tried to drive their Christian rivals from the Mediterranean.

During the 16th century, a naval phenomenon swept through the Mediterranean. It seemed as if the navies of the region were trying to recapture the days of antiquity by building fleets of war galleys. The galleys of the Renaissance were developed along the lines of earlier galleys but retained a number of differences. They carried a party of corsairs or marines who were ready to swarm aboard an enemy ship, but also employed artillery. A specially constructed forecastle carried from one to five main guns in a forward-facing battery, and swivel guns were used for point-blank fire. Unlike the larger sailing ships of the era, which carried their armament in large broadside batteries, these galleys had to point their bow at an enemy, in the process presenting a narrow target to the enemy.

The galleys carried one or more masts fitted with lateen sails, allowing them to take advantage of wind to supplement oar propulsion. A typical galley carried 20–30 oars or sweeps, each manned by three, four, or even six rowers, usually slaves or prisoners, seated on wooden benches. This human engine room was able to go from dead in the water to full speed in a matter of seconds.

In the light airs of the Mediterranean, this gave the galley a natural advantage over the sailing ship. While the latter was capable of carrying a heavier armament and her higher structure served as a bulwark against attack, the sailing ship was slower and more cumbersome. A nimble galley could dance around a sailing vessel, keeping out of the angle of fire of the enemy's broadsides while bombarding her.

For Barbary corsairs and other pirates, artillery fire was to be avoided at all costs—the ideal prize was one that was captured without a fight. Artillery could seriously damage a potential prize, particularly if it was a galley.

below: *A Barbary galley, from a 17th-century engraving. Artillery is carried in the bow, and can only be fired directly forward.*

above: *This cutaway reconstruction shows a corsair galley of about 1770. It had 24 oars on either side, each manned by between four and six slaves—the inevitable fate of prisoners taken alive by Barbary pirates. In addition to powerful armament, the galley could carry a large force of fighting men.*

Variants from the Mediterranean

The galleys of the Barbary pirates carried a large crew of well-armed corsairs, who would swing aboard an enemy as soon as they came alongside. A preferred tactic was to maneuver behind an enemy ship, swarm aboard over the forecastle, then overpower the enemy vessel in a hand-to-hand fight. Unlike the galleys of antiquity, ramming was never an attractive option.

Mediterranean regions developed their own variants of the basic galley design. The Venetians placed an emphasis on speed, favoring long, narrow galleys with almost racing lines. They were also less stable than their contemporaries. Most of the other Christian states and the Ottoman Turks of the eastern Mediterranean preferred a broader and taller galley, which provided a better gun platform.

Full galleys were expensive to maintain, and only a small number were retained by the navies of the Mediterranean, including the principal Barbary ports. The rest of the galley fleets of the 16th century comprised a smaller version of the galley known as the galiot. These were faster than the larger war galleys, and ideally suited to Mediterranean pirates.

A typical galiot was flush-decked and fitted with a single mast carrying a lateen sail. Between six and 12 oars per side were each manned by an average of two oarsmen, and on true corsair galleys these were free pirates rather than slaves, as the smaller size of the vessel precluded carrying anyone who was not able to board an enemy prize. These long, sleek craft were the mainstay of the corsair fleets of the Barbary Coast and the Ottoman Empire, although corsair commanders often used their own galleys as command craft. Larger galleys did go on pirate raids, and provided the basic transport for coastal raiding parties or amphibious assaults. The tartan was a variant of the galiot that placed greater emphasis on the use of sail, having two masts.

Although use of the galley declined throughout the 17th century, oared corsair craft of various types remained in use along the Barbary Coast until the early ninth century.

The Barbarossa Brothers

THE SCOURGE OF THE SPANISH

Two Greek brothers rose to eminence among the Barbary corsairs of the 16th century. Within a few short years they gained control of much of the Barbary Coast, and waged a holy war against the Spaniards, who were equally set on driving the Moors from the Mediterranean.

above right:

The infamous Barbary corsairs, the brothers Aruj (left) and Hizir Barbarossa.

The two Barbarossa brothers—Aruj and his younger sibling Hizir—were born in Greece during the 1470s. Traditionally their father was a retired Ottoman soldier who married a local girl on the Aegean island of Lesbos. During the 15th century Lesbos was a haven for pirates, both Greek and Moslem, and a bustling, cosmopolitan port where the cultures and religions of the Mediterranean mixed freely. Officially, the island fell under the control of the Ottoman Empire.

During the last few years of the 15th century, Aruj Barbarossa serving on a corsair galley based at Lesbos, attacking shipping in the Aegean. His ship was captured by the Knights of Rhodes, a religious order who combined piracy with religious fervor. He served as a galley slave until an Egyptian emir (ruler) secured his release.

Brought to Alexandria, Aruj sent for his brother, and together they fitted out corsair galleys, funded by the emir. The brothers proved themselves to be skilled captains. By around 1505, the Barbarossa brothers had moved their galleys to the western Mediterranean. The Sultan of Tunis allowed them to use the island port of Djerba, 200 miles (322km) south of his own capital at Tunis.

Soon the Barbarossas' galleys ranged as far north as the Ligurian Sea. Aruj captured two Papal galleys off the island of Elba, so clearly the corsairs were powerful enough to attack warships as well as merchant vessels. A becalmed Spanish sailing warship was captured off the Lipari Islands north of Sicily, showing the advantages of corsair galleys over sailing ships in light winds. The base in Djerba swelled with prizes, and other corsairs flocked to serve under the brothers. A disagreement with the Sultan of Tunis in 1511 meant that the brothers moved their base to Djidjelli near Algiers, where the Sultan of Algiers sought their help defending his territory from the Spanish. This was to prove a costly mistake.

Trapped in Tlemcen

Occasionally, the Barbarossa brothers overestimated their abilities. In 1512 an attack led by Aruj on a Spanish-held fort

on the North African coast was repulsed; the elder brother lost his arm in the engagement. Seeking revenge, he attacked again two years later, but failed a second time.

This represented a change in the brothers' activities. Increasingly, the Spanish were singled out as their enemy, and pirate attacks were frequently combined with amphibious operations against Spanish coastal settlements and shipping. The sultan's lack of response to the Spanish threat led to a popular rising against him, and Aruj Barbarossa took full advantage of the situation. In 1516 he led a corsair force into Algiers, murdered the sultan and claimed the Sultanate for himself.

The Spanish retained a toehold in Algiers bay, and it was used as a springboard for a Spanish attack in 1518. The corsairs repulsed the assault, assisted by a severe storm. Another Spanish toehold was at Oran, 200 miles (322km) west of Algiers. Aruj went on the offensive, but while securing the hinterland around Oran he was surprised and forced to take refuge in the town of Tlemcen. After a six-month siege, Aruj led a night-time attempt to break out of the town, but was defeated and killed.

Hizir Barbarossa

was now in charge. By this time he was called Khair-ed-Din ("the gift of God") and continued to resist Spanish attacks around Algiers. He allied himself with the Ottoman emperor and as a reward was officially named Sultan of Algiers, and sent Ottoman troops and galleys to defend his territory.

Now an Ottoman commander, Khair-ed-Din launched repeated raids on Spanish possessions in the Mediterranean. Although the Spanish captured Tunis in 1535, he sacked Majorca and Nice and helped to defend Ottoman interests in the eastern Mediterranean by defeating a Christian galley fleet.

By the time of his death in 1547, the younger Barbarossa brother had helped to establish Ottoman control throughout the Mediterranean, and although increasingly based in the court of Constantinople, he maintained a tight grip on his extensive North African territory.

above: *Christian slaves in the streets of a Barbary town. The capture of slaves was one of the most profitable business enterprises on the Barbary Coast.*

below: *The Barbarossa Brothers waged a near-constant war against the Spanish in the western Mediterranean. "Spanish Men of War engaging Barbary Corsairs." Oil painting by Cornelis Vroom.*

Murat Rais

THE AUDACIOUS CORSAIR

A young Albanian fisherman who was captured by Barbary corsairs was accepted into their ranks. He became one of the most notorious of the pirates, and even led his ships in devastating attacks on Spanish possessions in the Atlantic Ocean.

below: *In the 17th century, the French blockaded Algiers. In reprisal, French residents of the city were blown from the mouths of cannons.*

Murat Rais was probably born on the Albanian coast in 1534, at a time when the region was a no-man's land between Christian Europe and the Muslim Ottoman Empire. As a teenager in 1546 he was captured by Kari Ali Rais, the Barbary pirate ("Rais" being a local term for "captain"). His initial name is not recorded, but he adopted the Muslim "Murat" and joined the corsairs.

After Kari Ali's death in 1565, Murat Rais launched his pirate career with his first independent cruise—and was ignominiously shipwrecked, probably off the southern Italian coast, but his small band captured a passing Christian sailing vessel and continued their cruise. The small Albanian took three Spanish trading vessels, which he sold in one of the North African Barbary ports. Basing himself on the North African coast, he specialized in attacks on Spanish and Italian shipping, and coastal raids around the Christian shores of the Mediterranean.

Murat steadily gained a reputation as an audacious corsair. As profits from his activities mounted, others joined his group, and by the 1570s he was regarded as one of the most successful corsairs. Reputedly, one of his tricks was to lower the masts of his smaller galiots, tow them hidden behind his other galleys, and encourage the enemy to underestimate his strength.

He occasionally cruised in consort with other Barbary pirates, and in 1570 his enthusiasm caused a rift with a corsair ally. During an attack on a war galley manned by the Knights of Malta, he attempted to board ahead of his consort, the powerful Barbary ruler Uluj Ali. It appears that Murat Rais frequently turned his back on the codes of Barbary society's conduct, which may explain why his later appointment as an officially sanctioned naval commander was not approved for 20 years.

Murat Rais, Captain of the Sea

In 1578 Murat Rais captured the Spanish viceroy of Sicily, returning home to Spain in two powerful galleys. The attack sent shockwaves throughout the Mediterranean and incurred the wrath of Spanish King Philip II. Three years later Murat attacked and captured three French sailing ships carrying a fortune in silver and gold to Toulon; other equally audacious attacks secured his reputation.

He was appointed the "Captain of the Sea" by the Sultan of Algiers in 1574, and as such was held responsible for the defense of the sultanate's shores, but the

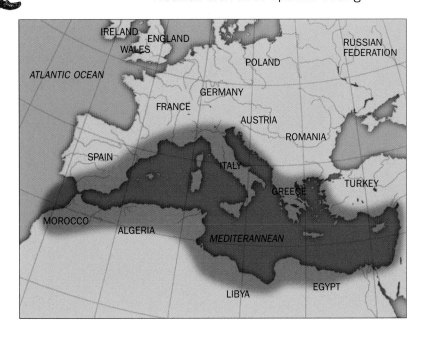

post was already held by the more cautious Muslim naval commander, Memmi "Arnaut" Rais. The position wasn't officially approved by the Ottoman Emperor until 1594, when the older captain left Algiers to serve as a commander in the Ottoman navy. As the Ottoman representative in the western Mediterranean, Murat Rais was in a position to use his forces to attain political and strategic objectives, combining piracy with policy.

In 1586 he sailed into the Atlantic Ocean and attacked the Spanish town of Lanzarote, in the Canary Islands. He held the town for several weeks and ransomed his captives. Three years later he captured a large galley of the Knights of Malta, by which time his attacks on Christian settlements and warships had made him the most notorious corsair in the Mediterranean. Following his official adoption as Captain of the Sea, Murat Rais led the Algerian contingent in a large-scale Ottoman attack on southern Italy, and in 1595 operations off the coast of Sicily produced his most spectacular string of prizes, when he captured three Spanish Sicilian warships and repulsed a Maltese galley attack that outnumbered his smaller squadron.

By the early 17th century Murat was frequently found in the eastern Mediterranean, where he commanded increasingly large detachments of the Ottoman navy and served as a land commander. From 1607 until his death in 1638 Murat Rais and his galleys dominated the waters of the eastern Mediterranean, crushing piracy in the Aegean and raiding Christian ports and settlements in the Adriatic. He was killed during the Ottoman siege of the Albanian town of Vlorë, and his loss was considered a tragedy for the Ottoman Empire.

above: *A Spanish expedition launches an attack on one of the fortified towns of the Barbary Coast during the mid-16th century.*

below: *The Barbary Coast port of Algiers in the 17th century. This was Murat Rais' main base for much of his piratical career.*

Uluj Ali

THE CORSAIR WHO SAVED AN EMPIRE

A daring corsair, this Italian-born pirate embraced the Muslim faith, and went on to become the commander of the Ottoman Turkish fleet. A skilled pirate and a natural leader, his achievements mark him as one of the great naval commanders of the 16th century.

opposite page below: *Christian slaves being brought ashore in the Barbary Coast port of Algiers around 1700. Although the port's fortifications are shown to be crumbling, the city was still a formidable stronghold.*

Giovanni Dionigi was born in southern Italy in 1520. The son of a fisherman, he followed his father's trade until captured by Barbary pirate Giafer Rais in 1536. Giafer Rais was an Algerine pirate who raided the Italian coast under the command of Khair-ed-Din Barbarossa. The young Italian was made a galley slave, but when given the opportunity to convert to Islam and join the corsairs, Dionigi accepted, changing his name to Uluj Ali.

By the late 1560s he served under the Barbary leader Turgut Rais, who was based in Tripoli, and commanded his own small galiot. In 1560 Ali acted as a scout for the Ottoman fleet that fought and beat the Spanish off Djerba, and his actions were commended by the Ottoman admiral. Five years later he served in the Ottoman attack on Malta, and again he distinguished himself. Following the fall from grace of Turgut Rais, Uluj Ali was made Governor of Tripoli, and coordinated Barbary raids from the port. His corsairs attacked shipping and coastal settlements in Sicily and southern Italy, and within three years he was given the even more prestigious title of Beylerbey (Supreme Governor) of Algiers.

For the next decade he acted as a thorn in the side of the Spanish, capturing Tunis and supporting Moorish revolts in southern Spain. He also attacked the shipping of the Knights of Malta, capturing a powerful Maltese squadron in 1570. Although Uluj Ali held important Ottoman appointments, he continued to see himself as a corsair, and when not performing official duties he cruised in search of plunder.

Esteemed commander

In 1571 Ali was recalled to the east, where he commanded a wing of the Ottoman fleet at the Battle of Lepanto, fought on October 7, 1571. The allied Christian powers defeated the Ottoman Turks, but Uluj Ali's tactics almost saved the day, and his performance was widely praised. As the defeated Ottoman navy was reorganized, Ali was named its supreme commander, and over the next year his skilled campaigning prevented the collapse of Ottoman power in the central Mediterranean.

A resurgent Spain recaptured Tunis in 1573, and Uluj Ali was recalled to the western Mediterranean. He brought a powerful Ottoman force with him, and a combined naval blockade, amphibious attack, and land assault brought about the

surrender of the city in June 1574. Ali went on to consolidate Ottoman power along the North African coast from Oran to Tripoli, and he greatly improved the Barbary ports' defenses.

Spain was increasingly embroiled in a struggle against the Protestant powers of Northern Europe, and consequently needed to focus her resources. As a result, the Holy Roman emperor and the Ottoman emperor signed a truce, ending the near-permanent warfare that had existed between Spain and the Barbary Coast for the past 50 years. While the Italian states and Hapsburg Austria were not included in the truce, it guaranteed the continued Ottoman control of the Barbary Coast.

Uluj Ali retained his position as commander of the Ottoman navy, but following the treaty his services were needed back in the east. He led several raids in the waters of the Adriatic and the Black Sea, securing Ottoman supremacy of her Greek and Turkish waters. Returning to Algiers, he planned one last campaign in Morocco, to drive the pro-Spanish autonomous government out and capture

the port of Salee. The project was abandoned following disagreements between various Ottoman commanders.

Regardless of this failure, by the time of his death in 1587, Uluj Ali had secured the Barbary Coast for the Ottoman Empire and had contained the power of the only Christian coalition that ever threatened the Ottoman territories.

above: *Ottoman Turks attacking a Greek corsair in a print dating from around 1800. Corsair activity remained a problem in the Aegean until the late 19th century.*

The Knights of Malta

PIRATES IN THE NAME OF CHRIST

The Knights of Malta were a Christian brotherhood who fought their Muslim enemies throughout the Mediterranean. Although it started as a holy war, they made their religious order rich through plunder, and their attacks were little more than pirate raids.

above right: *The Barbary Coast corsair Dragut Rais portrayed in a 19th-century print. The corsair served under Aruj Barbarossa, and was killed during the siege of Malta in 1565.*

Not all the corsairs in the Mediterranean Sea were Muslims based on the Barbary Coast. The religious order of the Knights of Malta acted as Christian corsairs, harassing Muslim shipping from their island fortress. When the Ottomans captured the island of Rhodes in 1522, the old crusading order of the Knights Hospitalers was forced to flee to the west.

In 1530 the knights were granted control of Malta by Hapsburg Emperor Charles V, where he hoped they would provide a bulwark protecting the western Mediterranean from Ottoman expansion. In return the knights gave the monarch the annual tribute of a Maltese falcon. The newly formed Knights of Malta also controlled Tripoli on the North African coast,

until the port was captured for the Ottomans in 1551.

The Knights maintained a small fleet of war galleys and participated in naval campaigns against the Ottoman Empire during the mid-16th century, part of a large allied fleet of Christian maritime powers. When the Maltese war galleys were not engaged in larger campaigns they cruised off the Barbary coast, raiding settlements and harassing and capturing Muslim shipping. Jewish and on occasion Christian ships were also attacked. As the Venetians were at peace with the Ottomans for much of the 16th century (until 1571), the ships from this prosperous Christian port were also singled out for attack, against the wishes of both the Pope and the Holy Roman Emperor.

Maltese raids ranged as far east as Egypt and the Aegean Sea, and the Knights of Malta were regarded as fearsome opponents. These attacks were little more than pirate raids, with any strategic importance overshadowed by the desire to collect plunder. All booty was taken back to Malta to replenish the coffers of the knightly order.

Corsairs parading crosses

In 1544 the Italian-born galley captain Brother Gattinaro captured a rich Ottoman prize off the North African coast, as well as one of the most notorious Barbary

pirates, Kara Mufsa Rais. On his return, Gattinaro and his fellow captains tried to swindle the knights, but were discovered. The galley commander and his captains were imprisoned. This harsh treatment acted as an incentive for future captains to turn over all of their booty; successful galley captains were always well rewarded by the order to further encourage propriety.

During the 1550s attacks by the Knights of Malta seriously disrupted the maritime commerce of the Ottoman Empire. Consequently, Ottoman Turks seized the order's secondary port of Tripoli in 1551, attacked Malta itself without success, and plundered the nearby Maltese island of Gozo. Christian support for the Knights of Malta had dwindled following their raids on Venetian shipping, and money was needed to improve the island's defenses. Consequently, the Grand Master and his council refused to obey the Pope's decree to stop attacking Venetian ships, and the knights appeared to cross the line between privateering and piracy. A Venetian official in 1588 called the Knights of Malta "corsairs parading crosses," an indication of the low esteem in which they were viewed by their non-Muslim victims.

In the decade preceding 1565, Maltese raids into the eastern Mediterranean increased, often spearheaded by one of the order's most successful commanders, Brother Romegas. The Knights of Malta sanctioned independent cruises that allowed the Maltese commanders greater freedom of action and potentially more profit. The capture of an Ottoman galleon in the Adriatic by Romegas in 1564 enraged the Ottoman emperor, who ordered a full-scale assault on Malta to wipe out the knightly corsairs for good. A massive Ottoman force besieged Malta in 1565, but a resolute defense led by Grand Master La Valette held the island, and the Ottomans withdrew after four months.

The order continued to act as semi-legal corsairs throughout the 17th century, but their power was waning. By the 1650s the Maltese had become an anachronistic relic, and although the Knights retained Malta until 1798, the island ceased to be regarded as a dangerous haven of Christian corsairs.

below: The galleys and galiots of the Barbary corsairs were ideally suited for attacking sailing ships in light winds. "Spanish Engagement with Barbary Corsairs." Oil painting by Andries van Eertfeldt.

CHAPTER FOUR

The Spanish Main and the Sea Rovers

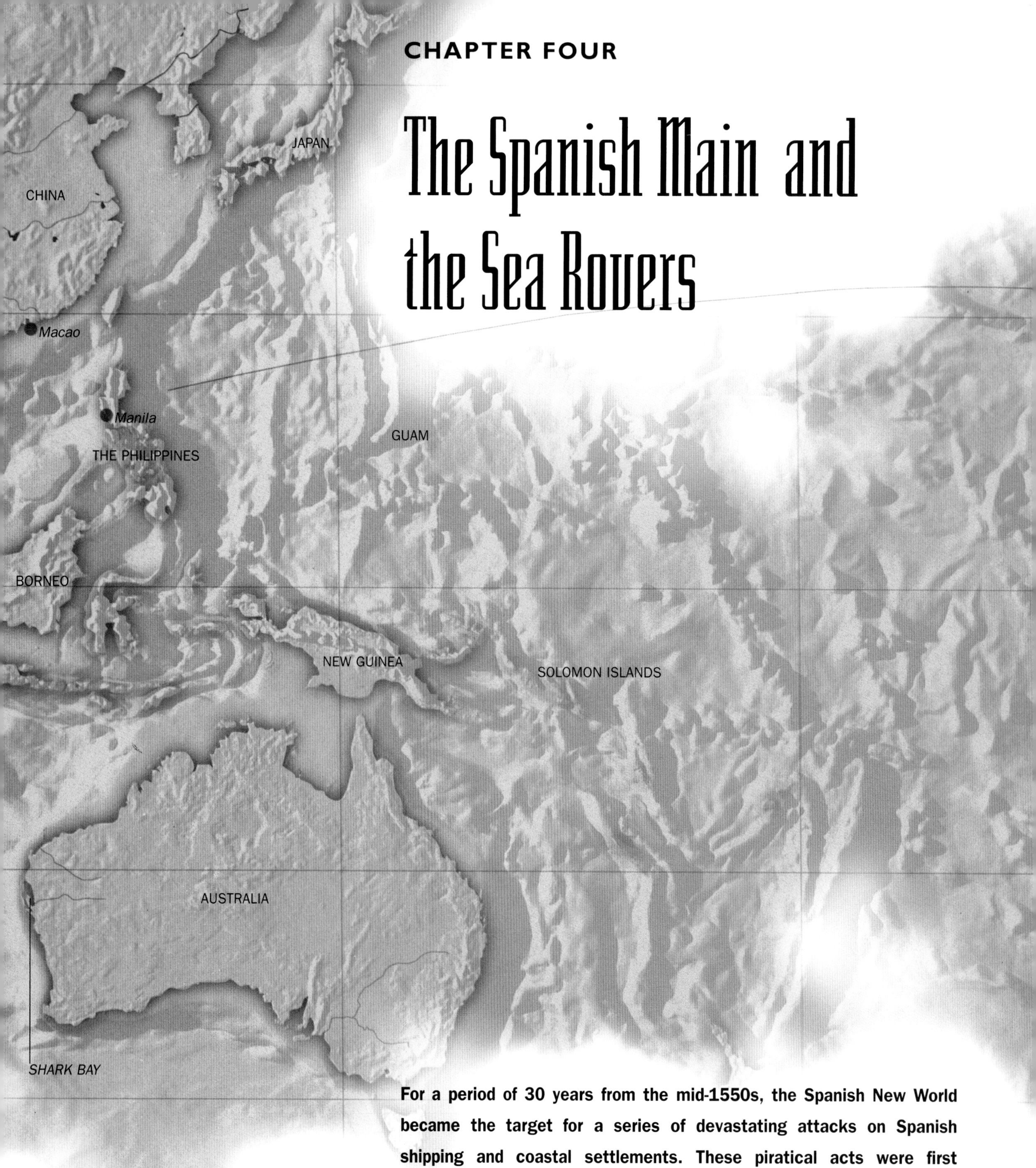

CHINA

JAPAN

Macao

Manila

THE PHILIPPINES

GUAM

BORNEO

NEW GUINEA

SOLOMON ISLANDS

AUSTRALIA

SHARK BAY

For a period of 30 years from the mid-1550s, the Spanish New World became the target for a series of devastating attacks on Spanish shipping and coastal settlements. These piratical acts were first conducted by French, then later by English raiders, the attackers combining religious and national rivalry with greed. The wealth of the Spanish Main was fabulous, and the region was increasingly harried by Elizabethan Sea Rovers (or Sea Dogs) seeking to plunder the Caribbean in the name of the English queen. These English sea captains included men like Sir Francis Drake and Sir John Hawkins, national heroes in their own country. To the Spanish, they were nothing other than pirates.

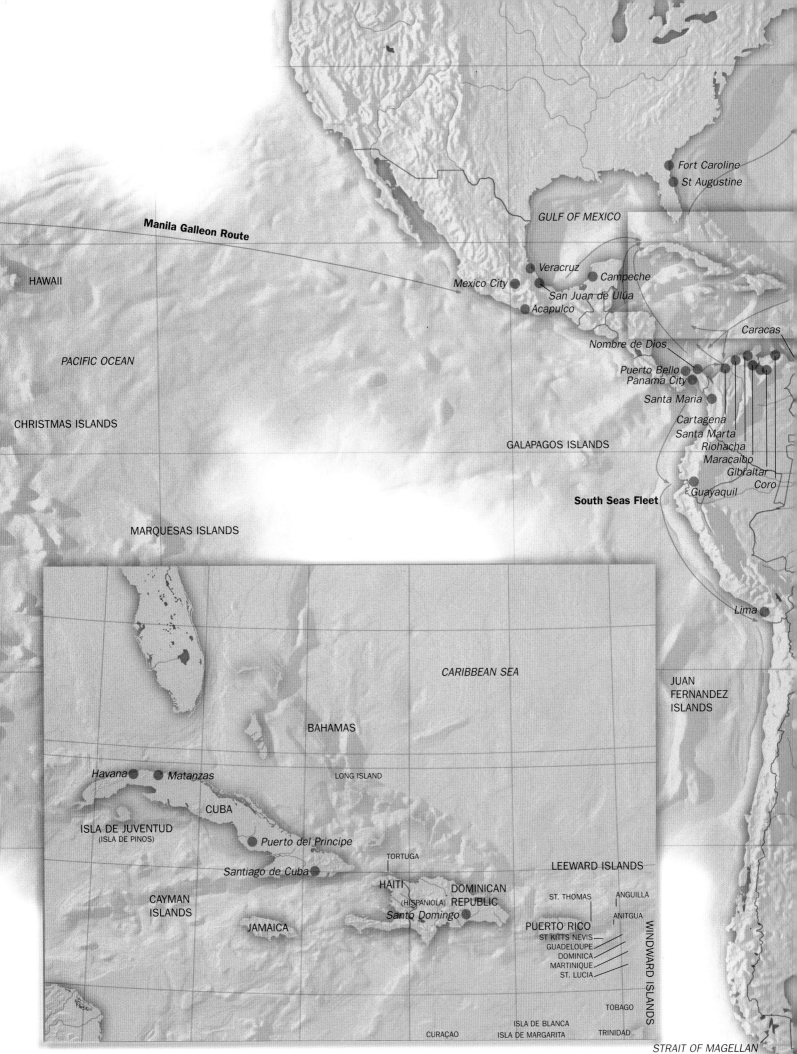

Fort Caroline
St Augustine

GULF OF MEXICO

Manila Galleon Route

Veracruz
Campeche
Mexico City
San Juan de Ulúa
Acapulco

HAWAII

PACIFIC OCEAN

Caracas

Nombre de Dios

Puerto Bello
Panama City

CHRISTMAS ISLANDS

Santa Maria

Cartagena
Santa Marta
GALAPAGOS ISLANDS
Riohacha
Maracaibo
Gibraltar
Coro
Guayaquil

South Seas Fleet

MARQUESAS ISLANDS

Lima

JUAN
FERNANDEZ
ISLANDS

CARIBBEAN SEA

BAHAMAS

LONG ISLAND

Havana
Matanzas

CUBA

ISLA DE JUVENTUD
(ISLA DE PINOS)

Puerto del Principe

TORTUGA

LEEWARD ISLANDS

Santiago de Cuba

HAITI
DOMINICAN
REPUBLIC
(HISPANIOLA)

ST. THOMAS
ANGUILLA

CAYMAN
ISLANDS

Santo Domingo

ANITGUA

PUERTO RICO

JAMAICA

ST KITTS NEVIS
GUADELOUPE
DOMINICA
MARTINIQUE
ST. LUCIA

WINDWARD ISLANDS

TOBAGO

ISLA DE BLANCA
CURAÇAO   ISLA DE MARGARITA   TRINIDAD

STRAIT OF MAGELLAN

CAPE HORN

THE SPANISH MAIN

When Christopher Columbus discovered the islands of the Bahamas in 1492, he launched Spain on a course of colonial expansion that would lead to her control of almost the entire continent of South America, plus the Caribbean basin. The New World was an overseas empire first scouted by the Spanish ships of discovery, then carved out by small, brutal armies of conquistadors. After decimating and enslaving the native population, the Spanish were free to exploit the wealth of their new-found lands, and to ship that wealth back to Spain.

Under the terms of the Treaty of Tordesillas of June 1494, the Pope, together with Spanish and Portuguese diplomats, divided the undiscovered territories of the New World in two. A line was drawn through the middle of the Atlantic. While the Spanish were allowed to settle to the west of the line, Portugal retained control of the east side, ensuring her monopoly of trade into the Indian Ocean.

By the late 16th century the Caribbean basin had developed into a sprawling lagoon known as the Spanish Main, where Spain's business of exploiting the region was allowed to continue almost unimpeded. The Tordesillas line also included the entire continent of North America, but the Spanish were unable to prevent French, Dutch, and English settlement along the Atlantic seaboard. However, any attempt at encroachment into the Spanish Main was quashed.

The waters of the Caribbean were exclusively controlled by the Spanish until the early 17th century, when other European powers secured a number of toeholds among the islands of the West Indies. These embryonic European settlements were regularly attacked by the Spanish, who still upheld the terms of the Tordesillas treaty. The line drawn by the Spanish territory and the phrase "no peace beyond the line" represented Spanish official policy toward interlopers.

By the mid-17th century French and

below: *A great fleet of Spanish treasure ships sets sail from the Spanish Main, heavily laden with New World wealth bound for the coffers of the Spanish Treasury.*

English colonies in the Caribbean were strong enough to resist attack, and these territories played host to a fleet of pirates who specialized in preying on Spanish shipping. Their establishment also brought an end to the Spanish monopoly of the region, and the treaty of 1494 was consigned to the history books.

Formation of the Spanish Main

The term "the Spanish Main" was originally applied only to part of the Caribbean basin, the northern coast of South America. It stretched from the isthmus of Panama to the mouth of the Orinoco river, incorporating a number of offshore islands such as Trinidad, Tobago, and Margarita. The Spanish divided their overseas empire into a number of regions: New Spain, which was centered on Mexico, Tierra Firme (or "mainland") incorporating the territories of Venezuela, Colombia, and Panama, then the Viceroy of Peru, which controlled the Pacific coast of South America, including Ecuador. The term "Spanish Main" was therefore first applied to the Spanish Mainland by English and French interlopers.

By the late 16th century the phrase came to represent all of the Spanish territories and islands in the Caribbean region, and even the Gulf of Mexico. It has also been widely used in pirate fiction and today it has connotations with Spanish treasure fleets, Caribbean islands, and the raids of Elizabethan Sea Dogs and 17th century buccaneers.

The territory was based around a number of fortified harbors, many of which served as secure anchorages for the Spanish treasure fleets. They were also seen to contain the wealth of the Spanish Empire, and were subject to attack by European interlopers and buccaneers. The chief Spanish ports of the region were Havana in Cuba, Cartagena in modern Colombia, Vera Cruz in Mexico, and Panama on the Pacific coast. Secondary ports such as Porto Bello, Santo Domingo, Caracas, and Campeche served as local administrative and trading centers. These were all subject to raids by 16th- and 17th-century pirates, including Sir Francis Drake and Sir Henry Morgan.

above: *The capture of San Domingo. Along with Caracas and Campeche, San Domingo served as a local administrative and trading center. All three ports were subject to raids during the 16th and 17th centuries by pirates, including Sir Francis Drake and Sir Henry Morgan.*

Unable to maintain a monopoly of trade, the Spanish New World went into a decline during the 17th and 18th centuries, and two centuries after the death of Sir Francis Drake it began to break apart as a wave of regional nationalism swept through the Spanish overseas empire.

The ultimate pirate prize

For over two centuries, Spanish galleons sailed the Atlantic Ocean, taking European goods and settlers from Spain to the Spanish Main, and returned laden with the treasures of the New World. These Spanish treasure ships were seen as a major target for 16th century pirates; the ultimate prize.

The Spanish galleons rarely sailed alone, but formed part of a sizeable treasure fleet. Attacking a large fleet was a hazardous undertaking, but pirates such as Sir Francis Drake constantly sought fleets laden with treasure. A less vulnerable target was the Manila galleon, a single heavily armed ship that sailed annually from the Philippines to Mexico, carrying a

crop of wealth from the Orient on its journey to Spain. Drake's capture of the Manila galleon *Cacafuego* was one of the most stirring pirate conquests of all time.

The whole treasure fleet (or Flota) was run by a complex administrative system that ensured that these fleets sailed annually, bringing the Spanish crown the wealth it needed. In the 16th century Spain's empire covered large parts of Europe and the New World. The king needed silver from the New World to run this empire, and without the treasure fleets Spain would become bankrupt. Administrators in Seville supervised every aspect of the operation in what was one of the largest bureaucratic organizations of its time. They maintained a complete monopoly of transatlantic travel within the Spanish Empire, ensuring vast profit for the Spanish crown.

The annual Flota operation

Almost every year from 1530 to 1735 a fleet sailed from Seville, bound for the Spanish Main. Once there the fleet split

left: *The richest silver mine in the world was the mountain of Potosi in Peru. The Spanish engineers (in the foreground) used Incan slaves to mine the raw silver ore from the mines sunk into the mountain.*

into three groups. The Tierra Firme fleet sailed to Porto Bello to collect silver from the rich mines of Peru, which had been shipped over the isthmus of Panama and was ready in the port's warehouses. The galleons then sailed to Cartagena to collect gold from Ecuador, emeralds from Colombia, and pearls from Venezuela. The New Spain fleet went to Vera Cruz in Mexico to collect the silver from Mexican mines and the goods shipped across the Pacific in the Manila galleon, mainly silks, porcelain, and spices from the Orient. A small Honduras fleet called at Trujillo in modern Honduras to load indigo dye and spices from Central America.

All three fleets met in Havana in Cuba and prepared to sail home in a vast convoy. Additional fleets transported the goods of the empire to meet the Flota galleons. The South Seas fleet shipped Peruvian silver to Panama, while the Manila galleon sailed from the Philippines to Acapulco in Mexico. Once these ports were reached, the treasure was loaded onto the backs of mules and transported overland to the ports of the Spanish Main, Porto Bello, and Vera Cruz.

The twin aims of interlopers into the Spanish main were to disrupt the Spanish Empire and to make a profit, and the best way to achieve this was to intercept and capture part of the treasure fleet. Certain sections of the system were more vulnerable than others. Catching small sections of the fleet as they lay at anchor in port was one such opportunity, and this reasoning lay behind Drake's raid on Cartagena. Similarly, Drake tried to ambush the overland mule convoy from Panama to Porto Bello, but without success.

By the early 17th century the system was in decline. The Spanish had swamped Europe with silver and the value of the metal fell, causing widespread inflation. The fleets steadily declined in size, until by the end of the century they numbered less than a dozen ships. By 1740 the treasure fleet system was all but abandoned, and individual warships carried the valuable cargoes back to Spain, ending a commercial organization that had once been the envy of the world and the ultimate target for daring pirates.

below: *A Dutch map of 1708 showing the Spanish Main toward the end of the great era of Spanish treasure fleets.*

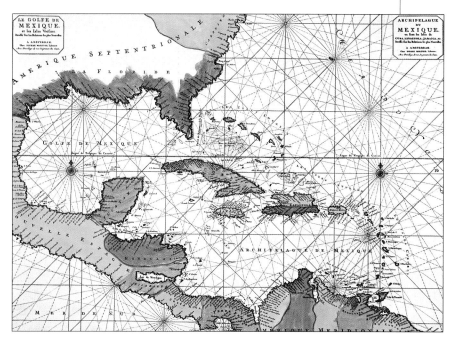

THE SEA ROVERS

right: *The defeat of the Spanish Armada was only the most dramatic incident in a long-running war between Spain and England. Most of the action was fought in the Caribbean by England's Sea Dogs. "The Armada in the Strait of Dover, 1588."*

below: *Drake's attack on the Spanish Main port of Cartagena, 1586. Various stages of the action are depicted, with the English fleet entering the inner bay, then landing troops and storming the city.*

Following the discovery of the Americas, the Spanish carved out an empire in the New World that provided her with fabulous wealth. In the wake of Spanish explorers and conquistadors came priests and settlers, and the local population who were spared decimation through war and disease were often enslaved by their new Spanish masters. The conquistadors had revealed just how wealthy the region was, and by the 1530s Spanish mines extracted vast treasures of gold and silver from Mexico, Venezuela, and, above all, Peru. By 1550 output from the mine in Potosi alone exceeded the rest of the world's combined silver production.

The Spanish transported this wealth from their ports in the Caribbean (or Spanish Main) using a convoy system of treasure fleets, which almost always ensured the safe arrival of the precious metals in Spain. Well-armed galleons guarded the treasure when it was at sea, while the treasure ports of the Spanish Main were protected by substantial fortifications.

Spain jealously guarded her New World possessions and the wealth they produced, and resented the presence of interlopers such as the English and the French. The wealth of the Spanish overseas empire also encouraged these same outsiders to look for ways to muscle in on the Caribbean region, and try to benefit from the opportunities it provided. The French started by establishing settlements on the fringe of the Spanish Main that would act as springboards for attacks on Spanish ships and coastal settlements. Later, following the destruction of these colonies, the French conducted piratical raids on the Spanish Empire.

Although French and later Dutch pirates preyed on the Spanish Main, it was the English who undertook this at a strategic level. Initial English trading voyages in Caribbean waters were driven off by Spain's naval power. English sea captains such as Drake returned to the Spanish Main seeking revenge.

English monarch condones piracy

In the 1570s and intermittently over the next two decades, English expeditions ventured into the Caribbean in ever-increasing numbers. Intent on piracy and plunder, they attacked Spanish shipping, plundered her towns, and attempted to disrupt the flow of treasure from the New World. These attacks were spearheaded by

1494	c.1510	1519	1520	1521	1530	1532	1534
Treaty of Tordesillas divides undiscovered areas of New World between Spanish and Portuguese.	African slaves are first transported to America.	Sikh religion is founded by Guru Nanak.	Ferdinand Magellan crosses the Pacific Ocean.	Beginning of the Protestant Reformation.	The Spanish treasure fleets begin their annual trading voyages.	John Hawkins is born, a pirate and slave trader who later reorganized the English navy.	Baghdad, Mesopotamia, and Tunis are captured by Ottoman Turks.

Francis Drake, a man who combined piracy with national aggrandizement. Officially, most of his raids were conducted without the knowledge and approval of the English monarch. In reality, Queen Elizabeth I probably secretly condoned his activities, and from 1577 onward she provided secret financial support for the piratical ventures conducted in her name.

The legal status of these Elizabethan Sea Rovers or Sea Dogs varied, although the Spanish consistently saw them as pirates, and if caught they could expect to be treated accordingly. For much of his career, Sir Francis Drake was a privateer, fighting his nation's enemies under the protection of a Letter of Marque issued by the queen. When he captured the Spanish treasure ship *Cacafuego* in 1579, he told her captain that he was "to rob by command of the Queen of England." Earlier attacks against the Spanish were less clearly the act of a privateer, as both England and Spain were at peace, and no Letter of Marque lent validity to his piratical actions.

In England the activities of Drake, Frobisher, and Hawkins were seen as being conducted in the national interest, and the performance of these Sea Rovers during the Spanish Armada campaign of 1588 raised them to the status of national heroes. Certainly, the line between piracy and privateering was constantly being blurred, and indiscretions were frequently overlooked by the English authorities, who secretly condoned these piratical activities. Queen Elizabeth even referred to Drake as her "pirate."

These Elizabethan Sea Dogs, supported on occasion by other European privateers, played havoc in the waters of the Spanish Main for over 20 years, and disrupted the flow of precious metals from the mines of the Americas into the coffers of the Spanish king. The pirates fought for reasons of religious and national rivalry, but their actions were constantly influenced by the desire to pluck whatever plunder they could from the heart of the Spanish New World.

above: *In her long-running battle with King Philip II of Spain, Queen Elizabeth I of England used any weapon, including the secret sanction of piracy.*

left: *The Spanish mined gold and silver in Mexico, Bolivia, and Peru. Gold was minted into doubloons,* **below,** *and silver into pieces of eight,* **above**. *As the most valuable coin, large quantities of doubloons were shipped to the Spanish treasury.*

1540	1541	c.1550	1555	c.1570–1590	1577	1579	1588
Francis Drake is born, a privateer who was knighted in 1581 for his attack on the galleon *Cacafuego*.	Hernando de Soto discovers the Mississippi river.	The riches of the Spanish New World become a prime target for pirates.	French Protestant Huguenot pirates, led by Jacques de Sores, capture Havana.	The English travel to the Caribbean to attack Spanish shipping and colonies.	Queen Elizabeth I first provides financial support for piratical raids in the New World.	Sir Francis Drake uses the *Golden Hind* to capture the *Cacafuego* treasure galleon.	The Spanish Armada is defeated as it attempts to invade England. John Hawkins is knighted.

Privateers of the Elizabethan Era

SPANISH GALLEONS AND ENGLISH PRIVATEERS

During the late 16th century English shipwrights began constructing low, sleek ships, ideally suited as pirate or privateering craft. In the hands of captains such as Sir Francis Drake they were formidable naval weapons.

On March 1, 1579, Sir Francis Drake in his small English race-built galleon *Golden Hind* fought a small Spanish galleon nicknamed *Cacafuego* ("Shitfire"). The galleon was captured, yielding one of the richest ever hauls of pirate booty. The struggle also served to show the differences between the two ship types: the Spanish galleon and her English race-built derivative. These English privateers served as the basic design followed by later Dutch shipbuilders, and paved the way for the pirate ships used by buccaneers of the 17th century.

The galleon was a variant of the carrack, designed by Spanish shipwrights to protect the annual treasure fleets sailing between Spain and the New World. The typical galleon was a vessel of between 300 and 500 tons (272–454 tonnes), although they could displace as much as 1,200 tons (1,089 tonnes). Some, like the *Cacafuego*, were even smaller—less than 200 tons (181 tonnes)—although these were not considered true galleons.

The largest galleons were used as fleet flagships, rather than as escorts for the annual treasure fleets. These were the ships that formed the backbone of the Spanish Armada, but they were never used against English privateers in the Spanish Main. There the English Sea Rovers would expect to meet small galleons and well-armed *naos* (carracks).

Spanish galleons adopted certain distinctive features. One was a high forecastle and massive sterncastle, making them unwieldy. They had a large cargo capacity, due to their role as treasure ships. As the most prestigious ships sailing between Spain and the New World, they also carried passengers, which proved a hindrance in action. They carried a powerful armament of artillery and Spanish soldiers, but their value was limited by a flawed tactical doctrine. The Spanish used gunfire as a prelude to fighting a boarding action. Better English and Dutch gun carriages using four small wheels instead of two large ones meant that they

below: *The Golden Hind, an English race-built galleon, with sleeker lines than its Spanish prey, took Sir Francis Drake into battle in the Spanish Main.*

could fire far faster than the Spanish. The best soldiers in the world were useless in a long-range gunnery duel. Despite these drawbacks, a combination of the convoy system and the imposing appearance of these Spanish galleons usually deterred potential attackers, including the most persistent of the English Sea Rovers.

Streamlined and efficiently armed

The ships used by the English privateers of the period were designed along completely different principles. Sir John Hawkins used the royal warship *Jesus of Lubeck* in his expedition of 1567, an old carrack of Henry VIII's navy that was similar to many of the armed warships used by the Spanish. She had been modified by removing much of her superstructure, creating a lighter and more seaworthy warship.

Most English privateers used vessels designed from the keel upward to be fast, well-armed, and maneuverable. A new breed of English shipwrights, such as Matthew Baker, produced plans for a new type of race-built galleon, and these became the leading warships of a new Royal Navy. England relied on privateers to supplement her navy in times of war, and many of these armed private ships imitated the designs of the royal shipwrights. English race-built galleons combined a far sleeker hull shape than the galleon, with a low superstructure rising gradually toward the quarter-deck, but avoiding the towering superstructures of their Spanish counterparts.

Privateers and royal warships carried powerful armament mounted on efficient four-wheeled carriages, and their crews were trained to use their weapon, avoid close contact with the enemy, and rely on gunnery to win the battle for them.

Sir Francis Drake's *Golden Hind* is typical of these ships, being about 75 feet long, 20 feet wide (23 by 6m), and displacing a mere 120 tons (109 tonnes). She carried 18 guns of various sizes, combining fast, racy lines with high maneuverability and a powerful striking ability. These were the ships used by English privateers and pirates to raid the Spanish Main and prey on Spanish shipping, from the Pacific to the coast of Spain.

below: *The beginning of modern map-making—Hack's waggoner (atlas of sea charts) took its detail from stolen Spanish manuscripts.*

below: *A model of the classic Spanish galeón that made up the treasure fleets. These slow-moving galleons became the preferred prize of English privateers.*

Sir Francis Drake

PIRATE OR NATIONAL HERO?

Sir Francis Drake is probably the best-known English seaman of the Elizabethan era. He became the scourge of the Spanish Main and, with the capture of the galleon *Cacafuego*, brought back the greatest ever treasure stolen from the Spanish.

right above: *The damage Drake did to the Spanish treasury can be appreciated in his haul from the Cacafuego—over £100,000, millions by today's standards.*

Francis Drake was born in Plymouth, England, in 1540, and sailed in the ships of John Hawkins in 1566 and 1567. In the latter expedition, Drake was given command of a captured prize, but his ship was trapped with the rest of Hawkins' force in the Spanish port of San Juan de Ulúa. The English were forced to fight their way out, and only Drake's and Hawkins' ships escaped. Although a disaster, the Hawkins expedition showed Drake the potential of the Spanish Main. The 29-year-old seaman was soon to launch a one-man war against the Spanish that would earn him the nickname "El Dragón" (The Dragon).

Drake led his own expedition against the Spanish Main in 1570, then repeated the raid twice more in succeeding years. Unlike Hawkins, he refused to engage in trade, but concentrated on raiding Spanish ports and capturing their ships, a semi-legal privateering war fought in the name of Queen Elizabeth I.

In his expedition of 1572 he captured Nombre de Dios, but was wounded and forced to withdraw. He hid further up the coast and tried to ambush the annual mule convoy carrying silver across the isthmus. The Spanish were forewarned and the ambush failed. Drake sailed off to lick his wounds and formed an alliance with a French pirate. Together they attacked and captured the next annual convoy. Drake returned to England with his loot. England and Spain were technically at peace at the time, so his attacks were acts of piracy. The queen refused to condone Drake's activities and he went into hiding for two years.

In 1577 he was back in favor and the queen secretly backed a new expedition. He set out again, this time leading an expedition of five ships, including his flagship *Golden Hind*. The expedition was to sail down the African coast, before crossing to South America. Drake's squadron sailed down the South American coast, but a storm off Cape Horn sank some ships and forced others to return home. On her own, the *Golden Hind* sailed up the Pacific coast of South America, sacking Valparaiso in Chile.

Massive destruction for little reward

In March 1579 Drake caught up with the Spanish treasure ship *Cacafuego*. After he fired a broadside the galleon surrendered, yielding one of the richest prizes of all time, her holds containing silver and gold. Drake chose to sail home, heading north to the Californian coast, then west in July. After a mammoth voyage of circum-navigation, he arrived back in Plymouth in September 1580. The voyage brought him fame, wealth, and the queen's admiration; he was knighted in 1581.

attack on Puerto Rico was thwarted, and after several assaults on the port were repelled, he was forced to withdraw. Drake cruised off the coast of Venezuela, capturing a number of small towns without finding much booty. He captured Nombre de Dios, but an attack on Panama was thwarted, and the English again withdrew.

Drake caught a fever and died at sea in February 1596. Drake died a national hero, and is remembered as one of England's greatest sea captains. To the Spanish, he remained El Dragón.

below left: *The complicated instrument believed to belong to Drake was made by Humphrey Cole in 1569. Cole—a leading Elizabethan scientific instrument-maker—provided lunar and solar dials, as well as the latitudes of many cities.*

below: *This engraving shows Drake's Golden Hind attacking the Spanish galleon Cacafuego in 1579.*

Five years later Drake led a fleet of over 25 ships to the Spanish Main, this time in an officially sanctioned expedition. Once in the Caribbean he caused mayhem, capturing Santo Domingo in Hispaniola, Cartagena in Venezuela, and St Augustine in Florida. However, the voyage was not a great financial success, and the threat of a Spanish invasion of England prevented another expedition for a decade. Raids on the Spanish coast in 1587 failed to prevent the sailing of the Spanish Armada in 1588, but the massive Spanish force was comprehensively defeated by the English fleet. Drake took a leading part and received national renown for his actions.

Sir Francis Drake returned to the Spanish Main in 1595, leading a fleet of 27 ships. The expedition's aim was to capture Panama, but Drake was distracted by the opportunity of plunder elsewhere and attacked Las Palmas in the Canary Islands, but was repulsed. A surprise

Caca Fogo.

Caca Plata.

Sir John Hawkins

ELIZABETHAN TRADER, PIRATE, AND HERO

Hawkins was knighted for his efforts in reorganizing the English navy that would later destroy the Spanish Armada, but his exploits against Spain in earlier years were openly piratical and an inspiration to his younger cousin, Francis Drake.

Hawkins was a fascinating figure, combining commerce, warfare, and piracy with national defense. At various times he was a slave trader, pirate, naval administrator, and national hero. He was one of the first Elizabethan Sea Dogs to try and break the monopoly of the Spanish Main, and his piratical attacks set the tone for later English raids against Spain's overseas empire.

John Hawkins was born in 1532 in the port of Plymouth in Devon, a region of southwest England renowned for maritime activity. His father was a local merchant who made repeated voyages to Africa and Brazil. Although trade with Spain was not technically forbidden, any dealings had to be approved by the Spanish government, which strove to maintain a monopoly of trade to the New World. When the young Hawkins

commanded his own ships in the early 1560s he realized that official channels could be bypassed, and the profits produced by illicit trade with the Spanish New World could greatly outweigh the risk.

In 1562 he took a cargo of slaves from West Africa to the Spanish Main, selling them illegally in small towns on Hispaniola, well away from the main settlement of Santo Domingo. The enterprise produced a huge profit and Hawkins was encouraged to repeat the venture. He also saw that piracy could increase his profit margin, as he had taken the slaves from two Portuguese ships that he attacked off West Africa!

The following year relations between England and Spain deteriorated, and the Spanish crown forbade any trade with English merchants. Undeterred, Hawkins planned a second slaving voyage to the Caribbean. Queen Elizabeth I was one of his backers, and lent him the warship *Jesus of Lubeck*.

A series of upsets

John Hawkins left Plymouth in October 1564, with four ships bound for Africa. Through a combination of slave raiding and piracy he collected 400 slaves, then sailed for the Caribbean. He arrived in the Spanish Main off the coast of Venezuela and sold the slaves in the small port of Rio de la Hacha, despite the hindrance of local Spanish officials. He reaped a healthy profit from the slaves, and the expedition returned safely to Plymouth in September 1565.

The Spanish were furious and pressured Queen Elizabeth to forbid further interloping voyages. She agreed but secretly continued to back Hawkins, who planned a new voyage in 1566. He was

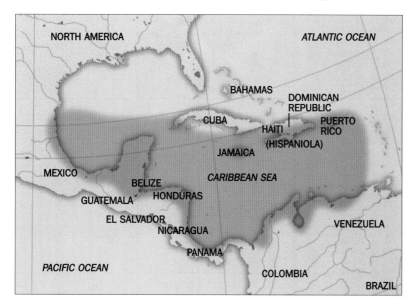

ships escaped, commanded by Hawkins and another young captain from Devon, his cousin Francis Drake. He left behind the queen's flagship, most of his crew, and all of his profits. This disaster signaled the end of Hawkins's trading expeditions; Drake would take up where Hawkins left off.

Hawkins became treasurer of the navy in 1577 and began reorganization that reaped rewards during the battle against the Spanish Armada a decade later. In 1588 he was knighted and appointed chief administrator of the navy, leading a squadron against the Armada in the same year.

In 1590 Hawkins tried to attack the returning Spanish treasure fleet off the Azores but failed. It appeared he was losing his touch, and in his last expedition in 1595, the 63-year-old commander fell out with Drake during a joint raid on the Spanish Main. He died onboard his flagship while the English ships lay off San Juan in Puerto Rico.

left: *He may have been knighted, but Sir John Hawkins was a notorious slaver and pirate.*

below: *In the same year that Hawkins was knighted, 1588, the "Mariner's Mirrour" was published. It was the first English sea atlas, although its information was all based on Dutch charts.*

unable to take part and it was a failure.

Hawkins led the next trading voyage, sailing in October 1567 with five ships, including the *Jesus of Lubeck*. As usual he attacked Portuguese slaving ships and stole their human cargo, then crossed the Atlantic. Back in Rio de la Hacha, the governor refused to deal with the Englishman—until Hawkins burned part of the town and captured hostages.

A storm forced Hawkins into San Juan de Ulúa—the later site of Vera Cruz—in September 1568. He was followed into the harbor by the annual treasure fleet and, despite a truce, the Spanish attacked the English interlopers a week later. Only two

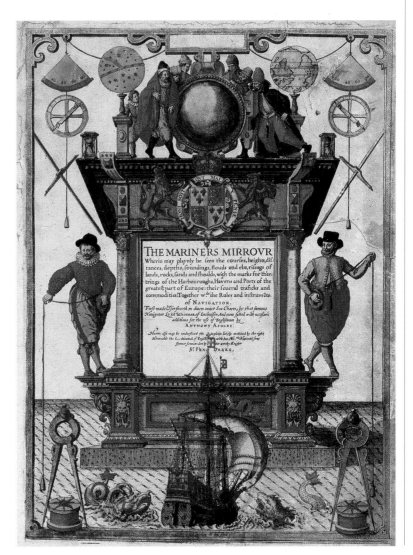

THE MARINERS MIRROVR

Huguenot Pirates

RELIGIOUS PIRACY ON THE SPANISH MAIN

Bitter enemies of the Spanish, the French were first to challenge Spain's monopoly of the New World. In the mid-16th century, French Protestant Huguenot pirates fought a religious war against the Roman Catholic Spaniards in the Americas, combining national policy with personal profit.

right above:

Huguenots raiding a Cuban port in the mid-16th century. The plunder is carried out to the waiting French ships as the town is burned in the background.

n 1523 Spain and France were at war, and French privateering captain Jean Florin (also written as "Fleury") encountered three Spanish ships off the Spanish coast, returning home from the New World. He captured them and discovered that their holds were full of treasure. The gold, emeralds, pearls, Aztec souvenirs, and exotic wildlife were in transit to the Spanish king by Hernando Cortez, the Spanish conqueror of Mexico. Clearly the Spanish colonies were producing more wealth than could possibly be imagined by her European rivals.

Refusing to recognize Spanish domination of the New World as established by the Treaty of Tordesillas in 1494, the French crown sanctioned attacks on Spanish ships and settlements in the New World. Privateering Letters of Marque were issued, ensuring that the French government would secure a share of any profits these raiders produced. These privateers began to attack Spanish shipping in European waters and in the New World itself.

Treasure ships were the ultimate prize for these early privateers, laden with the spoils of the Spanish Empire. Single treasure ships were vulnerable to attack, so the Spanish quickly instituted a system of convoys that became the Spanish treasure fleet, an organization unrivaled in maritime history. Jean Florin participated in these renewed attacks, but was captured and hanged as a pirate in 1527.

French privateers retaliated by raiding ports on the Spanish Main. Lack of fortifications made the treasure houses vulnerable, and French privateers began causing mayhem in the Caribbean. Puerto Rico was attacked, as were the pearl beds off the island of Margarita, near the Venezuelan coast.

These were mere pinpricks compared with the more ambitious raids launched by French pirate fleets in the 1540s and 1550s. Havana port was caught napping and raided. A French piratical attack on Cartagena in 1544 used information supplied by a Spanish deserter to find a rear path into the city. It was plundered and razed to the ground, while the French raiders made off with a fortune in booty. A peace treaty between France and Spain in 1544 failed to end these raids, and the two countries declared war on each other again in 1552.

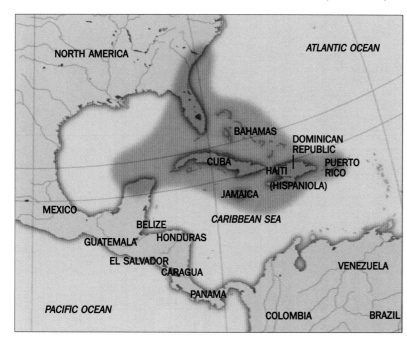

Adventurous gentlemen, reckless soldiers, discontented tradesmen

François le Clerk was a French pirate known as "Jambe de Bois" (Pegleg) and caused mayhem in the Canary Islands, Spain's launching pad for voyages to the New World. In 1553 raids along the coast of Hispaniola were followed by a devastating attack on the Cuban city of Santiago the following year. In 1555 it was the turn of Havana again, as Huguenot (16th-century French Protestant) pirates captured the city for the second time and held it to ransom. The assault was led by one of Le Clerk's deputies, Jacques de Sores, who demonstrated a startling ruthlessness. Havana and the surrounding countryside was devastated by the French. By the late 1550s French privateers appeared able to rampage through the Caribbean with impunity. The Spanish monarch was forced to strengthen the ports of the Spanish Main.

Further French raids were delayed by the spread of a religious civil war in France, but by the 1560s the Huguenots continued their attacks on the Spanish Main. French Admiral Gaspard de Coligny financed an expedition to found a settlement in the Americas, and Protestant exiles established a settlement at Fort Caroline in Florida in 1564, near present-day St. Augustine. These people were no colonists, and de

Coligny said of them, "There were no tillers of the soil, only adventurous gentlemen, reckless soldiers, discontented tradesmen, all keen for novelty and heated by dreams of wealth." The colony was clearly designed to provide a base for Huguenot attacks on Spanish ports and shipping.

The Spanish crown sent Pedro de Menéndez to destroy the French, and in 1565 his small force captured Fort Caroline and executed all the Protestant Frenchmen they took prisoner. Organized French resistance to Spain in the New World was broken, and it was left to the English Sea Rovers to disrupt the commerce of the Spanish Main.

above: *A clash between Huguenot raiders and a lightly armed Spanish convoy off Havana, in the mid-16th century. French raids caused havoc in the Spanish Main until the Spanish launched a concerted campaign to eradicate the Huguenot threat.*

left: *The French Hugenots established a base at Fort Caroline on the eastern seaboard of Florida, but came as raiders, not colonists.*

Pedro de Menéndez de Avilles

When Spain's New World Empire was threatened by French pirates, their ablest commander was called on to destroy the interlopers. De Menéndez launched a crushing campaign that removed the Huguenot threat and ended with a brutal massacre.

below: *Pedro de Menéndez de Avilles, an able pirate hunter, decimated the French settlement in Florida and secured the safety of the Spanish treasure fleets.*

The Spanish king Philip II was increasingly concerned about the protection of his New World Empire. As French interlopers continued their raids, Philip sought a commander to restore order to his territories. The Spanish nobleman Pedro de Menéndez de Avilles was the perfect choice. In April 1562 de Menéndez sailed from Spain to the Caribbean as captain general (admiral) of the combined annual treasure fleet. His orders carried a warning: "In the Indies sailing routes go some French, English, and Scotch corsair ships, seeking to steal what comes." It recommended ruthless treatment of any pirates he caught.

De Menéndez was no stranger to the New World or transatlantic shipping, and he owned several vessels engaged in trade between the old world and the new, a business venture he ran with his brother, Bartolomé. He had already been asked to conduct a study of the defenses of the Spanish Main for Philip II, and his findings revealed serious security problems at many treasure ports. Havana and Cartagena both required improvements to their fortifications. De Menéndez also recommended maintaining squadrons of galleons to patrol likely avenues of attack, and the establishment of a fortified settlement in Florida to protect homeward-bound fleets.

De Menéndez sailed with the joint treasure fleet when it returned to Spain, but it included a number of his own ships whose cargo manifests were questioned. Charges of smuggling were leveled against him when he arrived back in June 1563. The king was concerned and a letter was sent to Seville ordering that the matter be resolved in the admiral's favor. This interference was resented and his prosecutors continued to press charges. De Menéndez confessed and was arrested, tried, and in January 1564 he was found guilty. De Menéndez was fined and released.

While he was in Seville, news reached him that his son had been lost in a shipwreck off Hispaniola, along with several of his own ships. Apart from the personal loss, his finances had been damaged, and the king threw him another lifeline.

Stalking and routing the French

Before Pedro de Menéndez left Havana for Seville, he received a request from Philip II to help him defeat the French. His co-planner was to be Diego de Mazariegos, Governor of Havana, and the two were ordered to investigate reports of a French settlement in Florida. Before plans could be finalized, de Menéndez sailed for Seville. It was only when the trial was over that he could resume his pirate-hunting duties.

Initially, de Menéndez was to fund the project himself, but King Philip contributed ships, troops, and money. The expedition's aim was to establish a fortified settlement in Florida and use it as a base from which to attack the French. By June 1565 a force of 30 ships and 2,000 soldiers and marines, plus 600 settlers, was ready in Cadiz, and de Menéndez sailed for Florida. A storm scattered the fleet, but de Menéndez continued with five ships and 600 men.

In September he arrived off the French settlement at Fort Caroline, but found it too powerful to attack. He sailed south to a place with "a good harbor" and founded a colony he named St. Augustine. De Menéndez sent his ships south, only to see the French interlopers sail past him in pursuit.

The admiral was left at St. Augustine with 500 men and decided to march north to attack the now poorly defended French

fort. The French were slaughtered. Leaving most of his men at Fort Caroline, he hurried back to St. Augustine. There he heard that the French pirate fleet had been shipwrecked to the south, where he found and captured 200 shipwrecked survivors of the fleet. The prisoners were executed *en masse*.

Two weeks later de Menéndez caught one remaining group of Frenchmen and executed them, too, including the French leader, Jean de Ribault. He marked their grave with a sign: "I do this not to Frenchmen but to heretics." De Menéndez was rewarded for his actions by an appointment as Governor of Havana and further royal positions. His brutal campaign had almost single-handedly protected the Spanish Main from attack.

above:
De Menéndez led a small group of Spanish troops in an attack on the Huguenot fortified settlement of Fort Caroline in 1565. The garrison was slaughtered without mercy.

CHAPTER FIVE

The Buccaneers

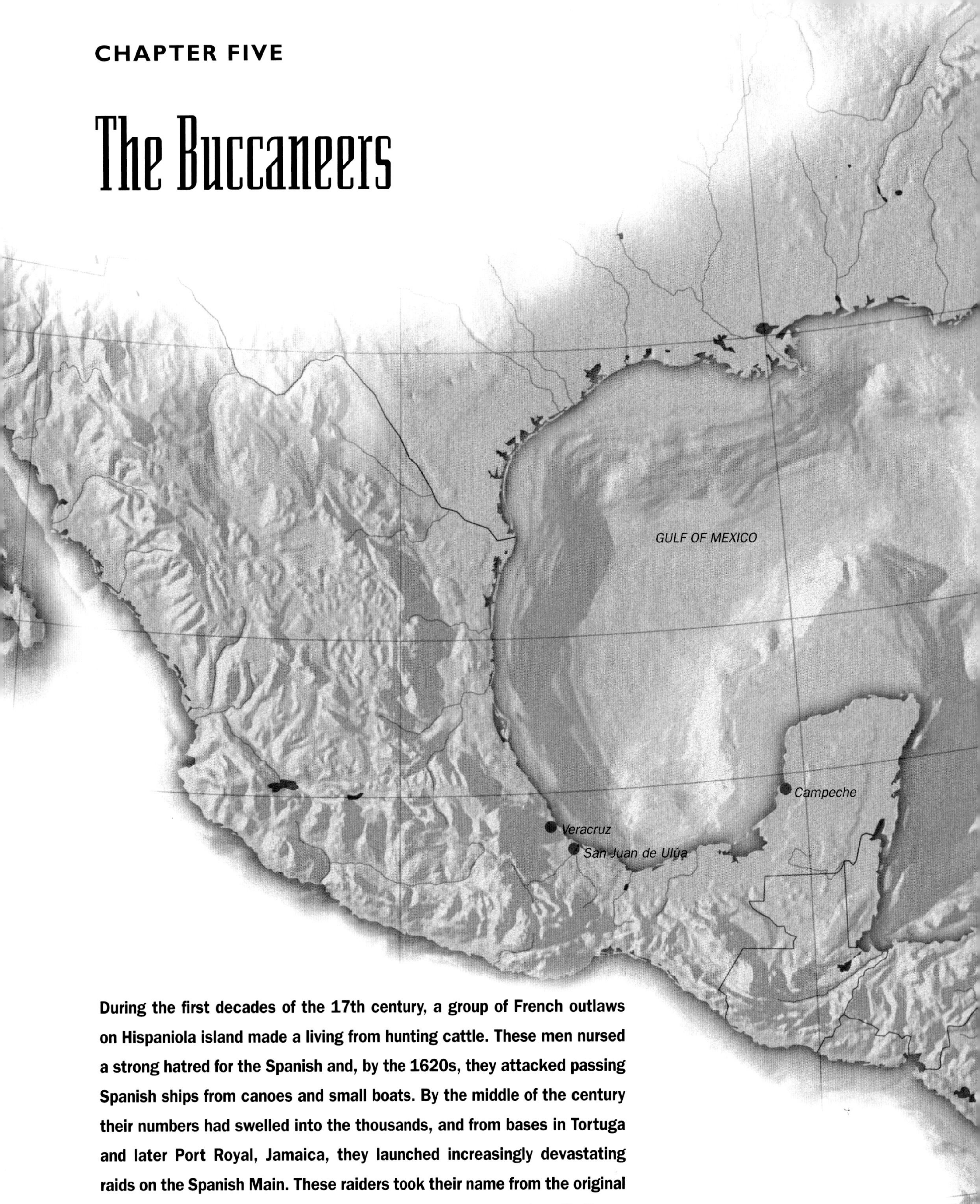

GULF OF MEXICO

Campeche

Veracruz

San Juan de Ulúa

During the first decades of the 17th century, a group of French outlaws on Hispaniola island made a living from hunting cattle. These men nursed a strong hatred for the Spanish and, by the 1620s, they attacked passing Spanish ships from canoes and small boats. By the middle of the century their numbers had swelled into the thousands, and from bases in Tortuga and later Port Royal, Jamaica, they launched increasingly devastating raids on the Spanish Main. These raiders took their name from the original French hunters: buccaneers. Their number included men like Sir Henry Morgan, who combined profitable attacks on the Spanish with national aggrandizement. The buccaneers terrorized the Spanish Main for half a century, creating a legacy that survives to this day.

St. Augustine

BAHAMAS

LONG ISLAND

Havana Matanzas
CUBA

ISLA DE JUVENTUD
(ISLA DE PINOS)

CAYMAN
ISLANDS

Puerto del Principe

Santiago de Cuba

TORTUGA

HAITI

(HISPANIOLA)

Petit-Goave

DOMINICAN
REPUBLIC

Santo Domingo

PUERTO RICO

LEEWARD ISLANDS

ANGUILLA
ANITGUA

ST. THOMAS
ST. KITTS NEVIS

GUADELOUPE

DOMINICA

MARTINIQUE

ST. LUCIA

JAMAICA
Port Royal

WINDWARD ISLANDS

TOBAGO

ISLA DE BLANCA

TRINIDAD

ISLA DE MARGARITA

CARIBBEAN SEA

CURAÇAO

Coro Caracas

Riohacha

Santa Marta Maracaibo

Cartagena

Gibraltar

Puerto Bello

Panama City

Guayaquil

73

THE BUCCANEERS

above: *An early 17th-century buccaneer (or "boucannier") on Hispaniola. The three lower scenes depict the way in which he hunted and cooked game for a living.*

opposite: *The early buccaneers used small boats to attack Spanish shipping off the island of Hispaniola. "Buccaneer attack on a Spanish Galleon." Oil painting by Howard Pyle.*

During the 1620s, men with a hatred of the Spanish began to menace Spain's coastal shipping between Hispaniola and Cuba. These men were French settlers driven from their homes by the Spanish. On Hispaniola (modern Haiti), these "buccaneers" roamed the island, hunting wild animals. The name buccaneer comes from the Arawak word *buccan*, a fire used to smoke meat.

The early buccaneers were tough frontiersmen living beyond the law. Dressed in rough rawhide and skin clothing, they each carried a hunting musket, knives, and sometimes a sword. The Spanish tried to rid Hispaniola of buccaneers in the 1630s, and many turned from hunting to piracy. A buccaneer haven was established on the fortified island of Tortuga, off the northwestern corner of

Hispaniola. Tortuga acted as a haven for fugitives of any nation, and numbers grew steadily.

By the 1640s buccaneers were seamen rather than hunters and dressed appropriately, in coarse shirts, woolen breeches, and hats. The tactics of these early buccaneers were simple. They used small sailing or rowing boats (flyboats or pinnaces) to creep up astern of larger Spanish ships, preferably under cover of darkness, and boarded them before the alarm was raised. While marksmen shot the helmsmen and officers, other buccaneers wedged the ship's rudder to prevent escape, then swarmed up the side of the Spanish vessel. They acquired a fierce reputation for cruelty and torture when opposed, and this was often enough to encourage the Spanish to surrender without firing a shot, hoping their lives would be spared.

In 1655, when the English drove the Spaniards from Jamaica, many buccaneers moved to Port Royal. The Jamaican buccaneers, known as "The Brethren of the Coast," were mainly English, and their attacks on the Spanish were encouraged by successive governors of Jamaica.

By the 1660s the buccaneers began to raid Spanish towns; Christopher Myngs led a number of attacks, including a raid on the city of Santiago in Cuba. The high point of buccaneering came that decade, when thousands preyed on Spanish ships and towns.

Skilled and terrifying soldiers

Buccaneer numbers were sufficient to allow attacks on coastal towns since the late 1650s. In these raids they favored fast, hard-hitting commando-style tactics, making surprise attacks from the landward side after going ashore further down the coast. Henry Morgan perfected this style of raid in the 1660s and 1670s, and his assault on Porto Bello in 1668 is a classic

c.1620	1623–1638	1625	c.1630	1646	1652	c.1653	1654
French outlaws on Hispaniola become buccaneers as they begin attacking Spanish shipping.	Approximately 500 Spanish and Portuguese vessels are captured by the Dutch off the Americas.	Christopher Myngs is born, an important English navy officer who also raided Spanish vessels and colonies.	The Spanish fail to drive French buccaneers from Tortuga island, off Hispaniola.	The Bahamas are colonized by the English.	Cape Town, South Africa, founded by the Dutch.	Frenchman Jean "L'Olonnais" Nau attacks Spanish ships at the start of a brutal piratical career.	Dutch privateer Rock Braziliano arrives at Port Royal, Jamaica; the Spanish capture him, but he escapes.

example of a buccaneer attack.

Buccaneers were originally hunters and backwoodsmen, so they were skilled with musket and knife. In stand-up land battles such as the battle outside Panama in 1671, they outfought the local Spanish soldiers, including cavalry, and some leaders even trained their men to fire in volleys, like regular soldiers.

Although characterized as a lawless group, buccaneers developed codes of conduct. From their earliest days, buccaneers operated in pairs, living and fighting together. It is reported that this partnership continued in Port Royal, where wives were shared. Buccaneer partnerships were especially useful in battle.

The number of early buccaneers was increased by a stream of runaway slaves, seamen, servants, and adventurers. They were capable of acts of extreme cruelty, even by the standards of the time. Terror was a weapon, and a record of cruelty discouraged resistance.

The French buccaneer L'Ollonais is described interrogating Spanish prisoners: "L'Ollonais grew outrageously passionate; insomuch that he drew his cutlass, and with it cut open the breast of one of those poor Spaniards, and pulling out his heart with his sacrilegious hands, began to bite and gnaw it with his teeth like a ravenous dog."

Following the Treaty of Madrid in 1670, where Spain and England made peace, the English demanded that buccaneers stop their raiding. Henry Morgan's attack on Panama was the last great buccaneering venture, and even he faced charges of piracy on his return. While some buccaneers turned to farming, many turned to full-scale piracy, using bases in the Bahamas.

c.1655	c.1655	1664	1670	1674	1683	1689	1700s
Port Royal, Jamaica, becomes a haven for buccaneers.	Portuguese seaman Bartolomeo arrives in Port Royal, at the beginning of an unlucky pirate career.	The Dutch lose New Amsterdam to the English, who rename it New York.	Spain and England make peace under the Treaty of Madrid and buccaneer raids come to an end.	Henry Morgan, a buccaneer acting under a privateer commission, is knighted.	Michel de Grammont finds a new ally, Dutch buccaneer Laurens de Graff—attacks Vera Cruz.	Jean Du Casse and Baron Jean de Pointis capture the Spanish port of Cartagena.	Schooners, variations on the sloop, are commonplace in American and Caribbean waters.

The Sloop

Although a number of pirates and buccaneers such as Blackbeard and Bartholomew Roberts hunted in large, well-armed ships, most pirates used smaller craft. The typical pirate vessel was the sloop, ideally suited for the hit-and-run tactics of the pirate trade.

During both the buccaneering era (1640–90) and the subsequent Golden Age of Piracy (1690–1725), pirates in American and Caribbean waters adapted regular cargo vessels for their particular needs. When ships were captured they were sold, destroyed, or turned into pirate vessels. Certain types of ships were favored over others. The ideal ship had to be fast enough to catch—or run from—more powerful enemies, so

vessels, so space onboard was limited. The ideal ship also had to carry powerful armament.

This is theory, as there is little contemporary evidence to show what a pirate ship looked like. Evidence clearly indicates that pirates and buccaneers used sloops and, to a lesser extent, brigantines, while schooners became steadily more popular during the 18th century. Their specifications show how ideally they were suited to the needs of piracy.

Sloops

Sloops were the main small workhorse vessel of the 17th and 18th centuries. The name was used to describe a wide range of vessels, and sloops formed the largest single type of vessel found in American and Caribbean waters.

They were small, single-masted craft, carrying a vast spread of sail, in proportion to their size. This made them fast, maneuverable vessels. Their shallow draught and fast lines added to this suitability. Their sail plan was normally a fore-and-aft rig, with a mainsail and a single foresail. A typical sloop of around 1700 was capable of carrying up to 75 men and 14 small guns.

In the 18th century the term "sloop" also referred to similar small vessels with one, two, or three masts. Jamaican shipbuilders produced an especially highly regarded sloop variant with a reputation for seaworthiness and speed, and this was a favorite of buccaneers. Traditionally constructed of red cedar, they were strongly enough built to carry an extra armament of guns. By the 18th century,

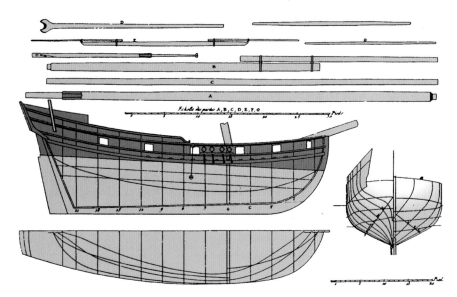

above: *The hull lines of a Bermudan sloop, c.1700. Along with sloops built in Jamaica, these Bermudan vessels were highly sought after as sound sloop designs.*

smaller, lighter craft were preferred, such as sloops, brigantines, and schooners. Occasionally, some pirates favored larger, better-armed ships.

Ideally, they were commodious enough to carry plunder and stores. The crew had to be fed and kept in readiness. It was also the storeroom for plunder. Pirate crews were larger than those on other

Bermudan shipwrights had also acquired a high reputation for building sloops and schooners.

A variant of the sloop was the cutter, a small single-masted vessel with a fore-and-aft mainsail, foresail, and jib.

Schooners

An American variation of the sloop was the schooner, which became increasingly common in American and Caribbean waters as the 18th century progressed. Their narrow hulls and large spread of sail made them fast and sleek, capable of sailing at almost 12 knots (22km/h) in the right winds. Typically, they also had a shallow draught, allowing pirate schooners to hide amid the shallow waters and shoals of the Bahamas and the Carolina coast.

Their principal disadvantage was the lack of hold space that limited both cruising range and storage for plunder. Typically, schooners displaced up to 100 tons (91 tonnes) and could carry around 75 men and eight small guns.

Brigantines

Brigantines were in common use for coastal trading in American waters, and their two masts allowed these vessels to take advantage of different wind conditions. The foremasts carried square-rigged sails, while their mainmasts used a fore-and-aft-rigged mainsail and a square-rigged topsail. They measured up to 80 feet (24.4m) long, weighed up to 150 tons (136 tonnes), and could carry a hundred men and 12 small guns. A variation of the classic brigantine was the snow, which had a gaff-rigged sail at the back of the mainmast set on its own spar, or trysail.

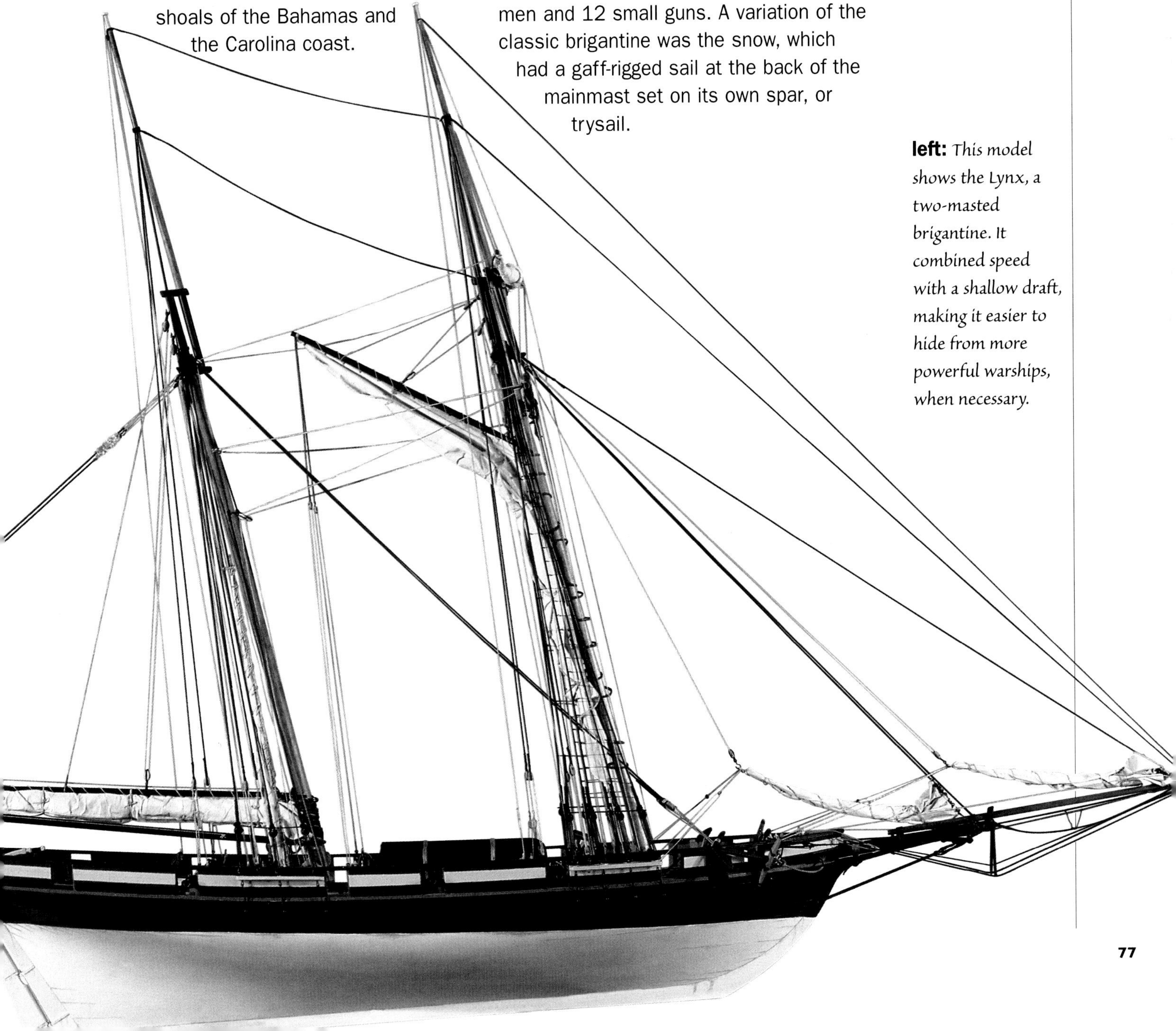

left: This model shows the Lynx, a two-masted brigantine. It combined speed with a shallow draft, making it easier to hide from more powerful warships, when necessary.

Sir Henry Morgan

THE MOST SUCCESSFUL BUCCANEER

While Morgan's buccaneering career only lasted a decade, he came to be seen as the most successful of all the buccaneers. He terrorized the Spanish Main, captured several town and cities and held the inhabitants hostage. Unlike many, he also survived to live off his ill-gotten gains.

above right:

Sir Henry Morgan, as depicted in Exquemelin's "The Buccaneers in the Indies." In reality, he was not as portly as this when he was at the height of his notoriety.

Morgan is perhaps the best-known buccaneer, thanks to the author Alexander Exquemelin, who vividly described his raids. Exquemelin disliked Morgan, although he respected his accomplishments. Henry Morgan assembled and maintained the largest expeditions ever undertaken by a buccaneer and was an inspiring leader, as well as a master politician. Morgan occupied Panama, which Sir Francis Drake had failed to take in 1596, and his fame stemmed more for attacks on cities than on ships.

Born into a Welsh farming family, Morgan never spoke of his early life. It is rumored that he went to Barbados as an indentured servant, then moved to Jamaica when it was conquered by the English in 1655. His appointment as a militia officer in 1662 suggests some military experience, and he received a privateering commission in the same year.

In early 1664 Morgan sailed for central America with a small buccaneering squadron. During an epic two-year voyage, the buccaneers plundered three cities. On his return, Morgan remained in Jamaica, invested in the first of several plantations, married the daughter of his uncle, Sir Edward Morgan, and cultivated a friendship with Thomas Modyford, the governor.

Despite a non-aggression pact between Spain and England in 1667, Modyford claimed that the Spaniards planned to invade, and in January 1668 he ordered Morgan "to draw together the English privateers and take prisoners of the Spanish nation, whereby you may gain information of that enemy."

Morgan's commission permitted the capture of Spanish ships but not the use of his ships to take Spanish cities— explaining Morgan's preference for taking to the land to attack: under English rules, if he took booty at sea, half went to the English government. Since Morgan's commission didn't mention land actions, he and his men could split the entire haul. Attacks on cities were illegal piracy,

but extremely profitable.

Morgan assembled 10 ships and 500 men and sailed to the southern coast of Cuba, where he was joined by French buccaneers from Tortuga. The group decided their force was too small to attack Havana, so instead they marched on Puerto Principe, a prosperous town 30 miles (48km) inland. The Spaniards learned of the raid and laid various ambushes, but the buccaneers overcame Spanish resistance.

Holding Porto Bello to ransom

At Puerto Principe, according to Exquemelin, the raiders locked the inhabitants in a church. To make them reveal their treasures, the wretched prisoners "were pained and plagued by unspeakable tortures." Morgan agreed not to burn the town in return for a ransom in cattle. Nothing bulky could be carried down mountain trails, and Puerto Principe yielded only 50,000 pesos. Disappointed with this poor booty, the French contingent sailed off. However, another English ship joined Morgan, leaving his force close to 500.

Morgan proposed an assault on Porto Bello, the port from which treasure ships left for Spain. Three massive forts guarded the port, but Morgan learned that their garrisons were undermanned and badly equipped. Some argued against the venture, but Morgan ignored his critics.

Anchoring a few miles from the city, he transported his men in canoes to the outskirts of Porto Bello, then attacked. Sentries warned the defenders, but the garrison was poorly prepared. In a series of savage assaults, the buccaneers took Porto Bello and its forts on July 11 and 12, 1668. To capture San Geronimo castle, they apparently forced women, nuns, and old men to carry ladders up to the walls, as a human shield.

After the town was captured, the pirates celebrated for days, and again tortured prisoners to reveal the hiding places of their personal possessions. The governor of Panama sent militia to recapture Porto Bello after Morgan demanded 350,000 pesos in ransom. After negotiations and a small skirmish, 100,000 pesos were handed over in return for the city. The pirate returned to Jamaica in mid-August with 250,000 pesos in booty.

The Porto Bello raid exceeded the terms of Morgan's commission and violated the treaty with Spain, but many agreed with the expedition, and Morgan and Modyford avoided censure. In March 1669 the Admiralty court decreed that the Porto Bello booty was a legal prize. At Port Royal, the pirates ran through their money in a drunken spree, while Morgan bought more land.

below: *The Battle of Panama, 1670, is probably one of the largest battles fought in the Americas before the start of the 18th century. Morgan and his buccaneer army defeated the Spanish garrison in front of the city, aided by the stampeding cattle shown in the engraving.*

The scourge of the Spanish Main

In October 1668, Morgan arranged a rendezvous off Hispaniola with French buccaneers for a joint attack on Cartagena. Modyford lent him an English warship, *HMS Oxford*, but it was destroyed in a magazine explosion that killed 200 crew and Morgan's chances of taking the Spanish city. A Frenchman suggested they repeat L'Olonnais's 1667 raid on Maracaibo and Gibraltar, located on Lake Maracaibo in Venezuela.

At both cities, Morgan's pirates chased the residents, who had fled into the jungle. Anyone they caught was tortured. As Morgan sailed out of the lake in late April 1669, he met three Spanish warships sent to intercept him. Twelve of Morgan's men

below: *Morgan and his men interrogate and torture Spanish prisoners at Panama in an effort to find out where they have hidden their personal treasure. Much of the wealth of the city was removed by sea before the buccaneers arrived.*

ran a fireship into the Spanish flagship and blew up both vessels. The pirates captured another warship and the third was scuttled. A sum of over 20,000 pesos in silver was captured from the Spanish squadron, plus 10,000 from the land raid.

The raiders reached Port Royal in May 1669, where, yet again, most wasted their money in taverns. Morgan put his money into a plantation.

While Morgan was raiding Venezuela, England had adopted a friendly policy with Spain. On June 14, 1669, Governor Modyford unhappily announced peace with Spain, but small Spanish reprisal raids soon gave Modyford an excuse. He gave Morgan ambiguous orders in August 1670, allowing him "to doe and performe all matter of Explo_{y}ts which may tend to the Preservation and Quiett of Jamayca." He was allowed to commission captains, and the raiders could split the spoils "according to their usual rules." To Modyford's credit, he also suggested that Morgan stop torturing prisoners. Morgan called for volunteers, and nearly every buccaneer in the Caribbean responded.

In December 1670, Morgan and 2,000 English and French buccaneers in 33 ships sailed for Panama, the richest prize in the Caribbean. Leading an advanced party, Joseph Bradley captured the fortress of San Lorenzo at the mouth of the Chagres river with 500 men, opening the way to Panama. In mid-January, the buccaneers paddled up the Chagres River by canoe, then cut across the jungle toward the city. They attacked and routed Panama's defenders: 1,200 militia infantry and 400 cavalry. When the buccaneer musket fire cut down Spanish cavalry and infantry assaults, the defenders gave up and retreated toward the city. The pirates pursued and killed around 500 Spanish troops.

Morgan escapes punishment

As Morgan's men entered the city, the defending militiamen started fires that destroyed most of the buildings, then fled into the jungle. The buccaneers spent four weeks picking through Panama's smoking ruins, but much of the city's wealth had been taken to the safety of Ecuador. Frustrated by their poor haul, the buccaneers destroyed everything and tortured and raped their prisoners while seeking hidden treasure caches.

Leaving Panama in February 1671, the buccaneers returned to San Lorenzo and divided the small pile of booty. Accused of cheating his compatriots, Morgan sailed off alone to raid the Central American coast, where many ships were wrecked in a storm. The Spaniards abandoned the ruined city, rebuilding Panama (now Panama City) at a better and more defensible harbor six miles (9.7km) away.

By the Treaty of Madrid (July 1670), Spain recognized English holdings in the Caribbean, and both nations agreed to prohibit piracy against the other.

Governor Modyford had exceeded his authority by launching Morgan's raid and appointing him as admiral. A new governor, Sir Thomas Lynch, arrested Modyford in August 1671, and returned him to England where he spent two years in the Tower of London. To further appease Spanish outrage, Morgan was arrested and taken to England in April 1672, but was never imprisoned and soon gained influential political friends.

Lynch was ousted in 1674, while Morgan was knighted and made lieutenant governor. Modyford returned to Jamaica as chief justice. By 1675, Morgan was 40, immensely rich, and the owner of several Jamaican plantations. In another political reversal, Lynch returned as governor in 1682 and removed Morgan from office. Morgan died six years later. His historical legacy is as the most successful buccaneer of the late 17th century, and his actions did much to ensure the survival of English interests in the Caribbean.

above: *Morgan's squadron attacks and defeats a blockading Spanish squadron at the mouth of Lake Maracaibo in April 1669. The buccaneers used fireships to disrupt the Spaniards.*

Jean "L'Olonnais"

THE FLAIL OF THE SPANIARDS

This French buccaneer was regarded as the cruelest man of his time. A torturer, he was driven by a bloodlust that caused havoc in the Spanish Main. He was also one of the first buccaneers to capture entire Spanish towns and plunder whatever he found.

below:

Jean L'Olonnais, as depicted in Exquemelin's "The Buccaneers of America."

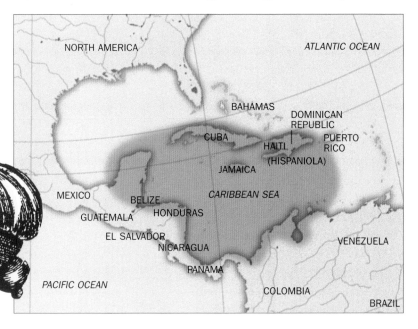

Born Jean David Nau in western France at Les Sables d'Olonne (hence his nickname, "The Man from Olonne"), he was also called Fléau des Espagnols—the Flail of the Spaniards—because of his inhuman cruelty. L'Olonnais went to the Caribbean in 1650. After three years as an indentured servant, he joined the cattle hunters at Hispaniola, then turned to piracy. L'Olonnais moved to Tortuga Island and received a ship from the French governor, an adventurer and buccaneer in his own right.

L'Olonnais's first attacks on Spanish shipping were profitable, although his psychopathic mistreatment of prisoners made it harder to take Spanish prizes. Instead of surrendering, Exquemelin wrote that merchant ships "fought until they could fight no more, for he granted Spaniards little mercy."

During one voyage, L'Olonnais' ship was wrecked on the Campeche coast, where the Mexicans killed most of his men. L'Olonnais escaped by smearing himself with blood and hiding under the corpses. He stole a canoe and eventually reached Tortuga. Next, L'Olonnais attacked a small port in Northern Cuba. His band took a warship in the harbor and L'Olonnais executed the entire crew except one, who was given a letter addressed to the governor of Havana. It stated that L'Olonnais would kill every Spaniard he captured.

L'Olonnais committed these acts during peacetime, but a brief war between France and Spain (1667–68) gave him a legitimate excuse. He planned a larger expedition against Spanish towns in Venezuela, and so in July 1667 he set sail from Tortuga with eight small ships and

660 men. Off eastern Hispaniola, the rovers took a prize carrying a rich cargo, then a Spanish warship.

The buccaneers headed for Lake Maracaibo in Venezuela. They easily occupied the prosperous town of Maracaibo, but its inhabitants fled to the woods with their possessions. The raiders caught some 20 Spaniards, in possession of 20,000 pesos, and tortured them. L'Olonnais hacked one to death with his cutlass. After two weeks, L'Olonnais moved on to Gibraltar, a small town across the lake, and captured it in a bloody fight. L'Olonnais stayed for a month, then returned to Maracaibo to extort a 20,000-peso ransom.

A catalog of bloodlust

Altogether, the buccaneers divided up coins and jewels worth 260,000 pesos. Back in Tortuga, their spoils soon vanished, for as Exquemelin put it: "the tavern keepers got part of their money and the whores the rest."

Taking some six ships and 700 men, L'Olonnais sailed for Lake Nicaragua, but his fleet was becalmed and drifted into the Gulf of Honduras. Pillaging the Indian villages along the way, the pirates reached the impoverished port of Puerto Caballos. The buccaneers plundered the town, but most of the inhabitants had escaped and they found little to steal. As usual, prisoners were tortured to obtain information. Exquemelin wrote: "When L'Olonnais had a victim on the rack, if the wretch did not instantly answer his questions he would hack the man to pieces with his cutlass and lick the blood from the blade with his tongue, wishing it might have been the last Spaniard in the world he had thus killed."

Two prisoners agreed to lead the buccaneers to the nearby town of San Pedro, but *en route* they were ambushed by Spanish troops. After defeating the Spaniards, L'Olonnais turned to his prisoners and "ripped open one of the prisoners with his cutlass, tore the living heart out of his body, gnawed at it, and then hurled it in the face of one of the others." The remaining prisoner quickly suggested a route that would not be protected by troops.

The buccaneers captured and burned San Pedro, but found little booty. Disappointed with their spoils, his captains deserted with the smaller boats while L'Olonnais sailed to Nicaragua in a captured Spanish vessel. It ran aground, and many of the now-demoralized buccaneers sailed home in the ship's boat.

L'Olonnais decided to march to the Gulf of Darien, but on the way he and his small band were attacked by cannibalistic Indians. L'Olonnais was killed and probably eaten; an appropriate end for such a vicious man.

above: *L' Olonnais forces a prisoner to eat the heart he has cut from the victim on the right in one of his legendary instances of cruelty. Any Spaniard unlucky enough to fall into his clutches was assured of a painful death.*

Sir Christopher Myngs

CROMWELL'S PIRATE

Sent by Cromwell to ensure Jamaica's security, Myngs used buccaneers to defend the island. An officer first and foremost, his use of buccaneers as an "offensive" defense was brilliant strategy, safeguarding the English foothold in the Spanish Main.

An English naval officer, Myngs combined his orders to protect the English colony of Jamaica with the opportunity to harass the Spanish. He used buccaneers to raid Spanish settlements, and blurred the line between piracy and actions performed on behalf of the State. Henry Morgan was probably his protégé, who adopted and refined Myngs's tactics.

Born in Norfolk in eastern England in 1625, Christopher Myngs joined the Royal Navy as a young boy shortly before the English Civil War. He sided with Parliament and rapidly rose through the ranks. In January 1656, as a captain in Oliver Cromwell's Commonwealth Navy, he arrived in Port Royal in command of the 44-gun frigate *Marston Moor*.

above right:

During the 17th century, the great maritime nations fought a series of wars to gain control over trade. Buccaneer attacks were a useful extension of this struggle for naval supremacy. Oil painting by Hendrik van Minderhout.

Jamaica had been occupied by English troops since mid-1655, and Myngs saw that the best defense was to take the offensive against the Spanish. In May he took part in a raid on Santa Marta, Venezuela that demonstrated that buccaneers could help in his strategic plans. By January 1657 he was given command of the Jamaican squadron of naval ships and buccaneer vessels, of which the *Marston Moor* became the flagship.

In October 1658, Myngs' squadron hid along the central American coast and narrowly missed taking ships from a treasure fleet. When the Spaniards arrived, most of the English ships had left to obtain fresh water. The *Marston Moor* and another vessel passed through the 29 Spanish ships, hung on their rear, and tried without success to scatter them. The English fleet later burned Tolú (today in Colombia), captured two large ships in the harbor, and devastated Santa Marta.

Profits were limited, as the forewarned inhabitants had fled inland with their possessions, so Myngs decided to split up his fleet, hoping to achieve surprise with a smaller force. The *Marston Moor* and two other ships attacked Cumana, Puerto Caballos, and Coro on the Venezuelan coast, and achieved total surprise. They had also learned to pursue the locals

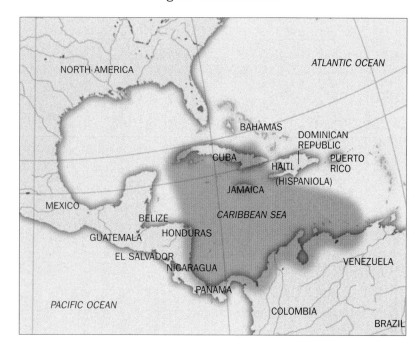

pirates in a dozen ships, Myngs captured San Francisco, in the Bay of Campeche, after a bitter fight. The town produced 150,000 pesos in booty, and Myngs captured 14 Spanish ships at anchor in the harbor.

The Spanish government strongly protested against the raids on Santiago and San Francisco to the English crown and Charles II forbade further attacks. Myngs returned to England in 1665, where he was promoted to the rank of vice-admiral. He took part in the Second Dutch War (1665–67), when he was knighted following his performance in the Four Days' Battle (June 11–14, 1666). In a second battle fought on August 4–5, Myngs was killed by a Dutch cannonball.

Myngs died a distinguished naval officer and hero, but during his time in Jamaica he demonstrated that he was also a skilled buccaneer and, by helping to defend Jamaica, he made Port Royal a haven for pirates. Above all, he encouraged Henry Morgan, who continued Myngs' policy of defending Jamaica by devastating the Spanish Main.

below: *By the time Myngs returned to England to serve as an admiral, he was already an experienced commander, but led buccaneers rather than naval squadrons. Oil painting by Sir Peter Lely.*

inland, and at Coro they captured a large silver shipment belonging to the Spanish crown. The entire haul from the raid was valued at over a quarter of a million English pounds, exceeding all expectations. Myngs split the haul with his men, rather than keep a share for the governor and the English treasury, as ordered.

Saved by confusion, decorated at war

On his return to Port Royal, Myngs was arrested and sent back to England to be tried by the Admiralty on charges of embezzlement. In the confusion surrounding King Charles II's return to power, the case against Myngs was abandoned, and by 1662 he had returned to Jamaica as a captain in the new Royal Navy, commanding *HMS Centurion*. Although by then Spain and England were at peace, the Jamaican authorities continued to harass Spanish possessions.

In October 1662 Myngs and his joint naval-buccaneer command stormed Santiago, Cuba's second largest city. The buccaneers captured several ships and treasure, then destroyed the port's defenses on leaving. Since they had avoided English censure, Myngs made a further raid on the coast of Mexico in February 1663. Leading a force of 1,500 buccaneers, including French and Dutch

Bartolomeo el Portugues and Rock Braziliano

THE UNLUCKY AND THE CRUEL BUCCANEERS

Portuguese seaman Bartolomeo el Portugues and Dutchman Rock Braziliano had two things in common—they operated in the same waters and at the same time. While Rock was moderately successful and cruel, Bartolomeo's career was remarkable only in that it appeared to be a catalog of disasters.

Bartolomeo el Portugues as depicted in Exquemelin's "The Buccaneers in the Indies." A small-time buccaneer, his efforts continually seemed to come to nothing.

Bartolomeo, a Portuguese seaman, arrived in Port Royal soon after Jamaica was captured by the English in 1655. His subsequent buccaneering career is notable less for his achievements than by the bad luck that dogged him.

Bartolomeo served on expeditions raiding the Mexican coast, but he started his independent career by cruising between Jamaica and the southern coast of Cuba in a small vessel with 30 men and four guns. He attacked a larger Spanish ship but was repelled, although he captured it in a second attempt, losing half his crew in the fighting. The prize contained coin chests and sacks of cocoa beans. He abandoned the smaller vessel, but contrary winds prevented him from sailing back to Jamaica, so he headed west along the southern Cuban coast.

Off Cuba's western tip he was chased and captured by three Spanish ships bound for Havana. The ship carrying Bartolomeo and other prisoners was caught in a tropical storm and returned to Campeche, in Mexico. The buccaneers were held onboard while gallows were erected, but they escaped and swam ashore. The fugitives cut across the Yucatán peninsula, heading for the eastern coast, and found a buccaneering ship that took them back to Port Royal.

Bartolomeo was bent on revenge, and so he returned to Campeche with 20 men and a seagoing canoe. He "cut out" the ship that had captured him, still laden with goods. He escaped, only for his bad luck to plague him again. He ran aground on the Isle of Pines, off southern Cuba, and was forced to abandon ship and cargo, escaping to Jamaica by small boat.

Apparently, he continued his attacks on the Spanish, as Exquemelin reported he made "many violent attacks on the Spaniards without gaining much profit from marauding, for I saw him dying in the greatest wretchedness in the world."

Roasting prisoners like pigs

Braziliano was a Dutch privateer who came to the region when the Dutch held Bahia, in Brazil. When the Portuguese drove off the Dutch in 1654, Rock moved to Port Royal in Jamaica and served as a seaman. He and others quarreled with the captain, made off in the ship's boat, and started a new buccaneering life. They succeeded in capturing a Spanish ship carrying gold and silver, and brought it to Port Royal in triumph.

It is unclear how many cruises he sailed on as captain, but at some stage Rock Braziliano was captured by the Spanish and imprisoned in Campeche, in Mexico. Rock wrote a letter to the Spanish governor that supposedly came from his friends outside. It warned the governor that if Rock was killed, fellow buccaneers would sack the town and kill every Spaniard they found. Rock was shipped to Spain as a prisoner, but, once there, he escaped and eventually returned to Port Royal.

He returned to Campeche in 1669, but his ship ran aground. The small crew abandoned their vessel and cut across land to a known buccaneer rendezvous on the Yucatán peninsula. They were caught by Spanish cavalry, but the riders were held at bay by musket fire, allowing the buccaneers to escape in canoes. They captured a small local craft and used it to take a Spanish merchant ship that was carrying a valuable cargo. Braziliano took his prizes on to Port Royal.

Exquemelin described Rock as particularly brutal, and reported that "he would roam the town like a madman. The first person he came across, he would chop off his arm or leg, and anyone daring to intervene, for he was like a maniac. He perpetrated the greatest atrocities possible

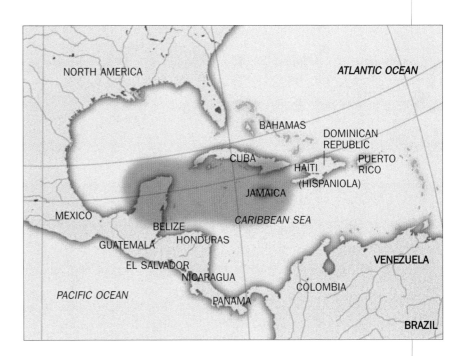

against the Spaniards. Some of them he tied or spitted on wooden stakes and roasted them alive between two fires, like killing a pig." His ultimate fate is unrecorded, but he probably died in Port Royal.

The brutal madman of Port Royal, Rock (or Roche) Braziliano, as depicted in Exquemelin's "The Buccaneers in the Indies." He combined a flair for naval and military action with a brutality that bordered on the psychotic.

Michel de Grammont

A brilliant buccaneer commander, de Grammont excelled in tactics on land and sea. In repeated raids on the Spanish Main, his French buccaneers devastated Spanish settlements. In 1686, while at the height of his power, de Grammont was lost at sea, and the Spanish were saved from further humiliation.

During the 1670s a Frenchmen rose to prominence among the buccaneer communities of Tortuga and Saint Dominique (now Haiti). Michel de Grammont's origins are obscure, but reputedly he was born in Paris and served in the French navy.

By the mid-1670s he had reached the Caribbean, where he commanded a French privateering vessel. When he illegally captured a Dutch vessel, he fell foul of the authorities. Unable to return to France, he chose to remain in Saint Dominique.

In 1678 France and Holland declared war, and de Grammont and other buccaneers decided to raid the Dutch island of Curaçao. A buccaneer flotilla sailed from Petit Goave in May 1678 accompanied by a French naval squadron,

giving a combined raiding force of over 1,200 men.

The fleet was caught in a storm and swept onto the reefs of the Aves islands, west of the Lesser Antilles. Several ships were wrecked and, once the storm passed, the naval squadron returned to Saint Dominique, leaving the buccaneers to salvage what they could from the wreckage. This was a lucrative opportunity and the salvors "were never without two or three hogsheads of wine and brandy in their tents, and barrels of beef and pork."

During this time, de Grammont became the commander of the buccaneers, acquiring the title of "Chevalier." After salvaging what they could, de Grammont decided that his force was too weak to attack Curaçao, so in June 1678 he sailed for the Venezuelan coast. He then commanded around six ships and 700 men.

The French buccaneers entered Lake Maracaibo, an area already plundered by L'Olonnais and Henry Morgan in the 1660s. Clearly the towns in the region had not recovered in the intervening decade, as little booty was recovered. Using captured horses, de Grammont led his men inland to assault Trujillo in September 1678, where he captured a large haul of booty. In late December the buccaneers sailed back to Saint Dominique.

Triumphant return with de Graff

In May 1680 de Grammont led another raid against the Venezuelan coast to attack La Guaira, the harbor that served Caracas, the region's capital. The buccaneers captured the town in a night attack, spearheaded by a small assault force that captured the two forts guarding

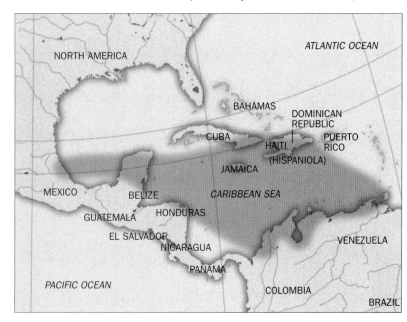

the harbor and then threw open the town gates. By the following day 2,000 Spanish troops from Caracas reached the port and the buccaneers found themselves besieged.

Repeated Spanish assaults were repulsed in bitter fighting, during which de Grammont was wounded in the throat. The buccaneers escaped to sea, taking prominent Spanish prisoners with them as hostages. These were ransomed, but otherwise the raiders withdrew empty-handed, lacking the time to load more than a minimum of booty into their ships. They returned to Saint Dominique.

Three years later, in May 1683, de Grammont joined forces with the Dutch buccaneer Laurens de Graff to attack Vera Cruz in Mexico. De Grammont led the French buccaneering contingent and, following the sack of the city, the raiders took 4,000 prisoners to a nearby island, where they held them until they were ransomed. Although France was at peace with Spain at the time, the governor of Saint Dominique chose not to prosecute de Grammont for his actions.

Two years later de Grammont and de Graff joined forces again for an attack on Campeche, in Mexico. The city and its surrounding countryside were held for three months during that summer, and Spanish attempts to drive off the buccaneers were thwarted. Attempts at ransoming the town to the Spanish Viceroy of Mexico came to nothing, and the city was burned when the buccaneers departed in September 1685.

In the following year de Grammont planned another raid on Mexico, despite promises of respectability and a French colonial position if he gave up his illegal attacks on the Spanish. By April 1686 he was operating off the Yucatán peninsula, but was forced to withdraw to the northeast because of storms. He planned an attack on Spanish Florida but became separated from the rest of his fleet. De Grammont and his ship were never seen again.

The Sack of Cartagena

France took advantage of a war with Spain to strike at the heart of the Spanish Main. A French force combined with an army of French buccaneers to attack Cartagena in 1689. When the French fleet sailed away after the city was plundered, the troubles of Cartagena's inhabitants were only just beginning.

below: *The Siege of Cartagena, 1689. The French combined a powerful military force with French buccaneers to ensure the capture of the Spanish city.*

During the War of the League of Augsberg (1688–97), France fought England, the Netherlands, and Spain. French Caribbean colonists helped by raiding enemy colonies, and Jean Du Casse, the French governor of Saint Dominique, issued numerous Letters of Marque from his office in Petit Goave.

As the war drew to a close, French strategists looked for the opportunity to launch a last lucrative raid on some Spanish city. Cartagena—reputedly the richest city in the Spanish Main—was chosen as an attractive target. It had last been attacked a century earlier by Sir Francis Drake, and since then its formidable defenses had scared off most buccaneer bands.

The attack was organized as a government-sponsored business venture, complete with investors and hired buccaneers. In March 1689 a French admiral, Baron Jean de Pointis, arrived in Saint Dominique to lead the expedition, and brought with him a squadron of ten French warships. Buccaneers supplied a further seven ships, while governor Du Casse commanded his own squadron in the pay of the colony. The expedition was, therefore, composed of over 30 ships and 6,500 men, including French soldiers and artillery.

Baron de Pointis quickly fell out with the buccaneers, who were only persuaded to continue their involvement by Du Casse. Written contracts were drawn up detailing how the booty would be divided, and the expedition sailed by the end of the month. It arrived off Cartagena on April 13, 1689, and the defenses were surveyed.

The city was situated at the base of a narrow peninsula between the sea and an inshore bay, and gun batteries and reefs prevented any direct assault. Forts guarded the Boca Chica passage that allowed access to the bay, and landward defenses extended north of the city and east along the peninsula. An inlet of the bay, which could only be crossed via the fortified island of Imanie, acted as a moat to the north of the city. The only weak points were that the garrison was well under strength, and many of the fortifications were poorly designed to support each other.

A second share of the booty

The French fleet stormed and captured the forts guarding the entrance to the inland bay, then anchored their fleet in its sheltered waters. Artillery to bombard the city was landed and, on April 30, a breach was made in the Cartagena's walls. An attack led by Du Casse and the buccaneers was repulsed, and so the bombardment continued.

Since there was clearly no hope for the defenders, on May 6, 1689, Cartagena surrendered. The French entered the city and formally agreed to sack only half the wealth of the city and its inhabitants. This civilized system was regulated by Baron de Pointis, and Du Casse and the buccaneers felt they were being swindled. When the French were ready to leave on May 29, de Pointis handed over only a fraction of the share that the buccaneers expected from the enterprise.

As the French navy sailed off, the buccaneers decided to help themselves to their fair share by sacking Cartagena for a second time. They returned to the city on June 1, imprisoned and tortured the population, and grabbed what booty they could. This was divided between the buccaneers, and the raiders returned to Saint Dominique.

While this was happening, an English fleet arrived and chased the French fleet, which escaped during a gale. Turning back, the English then pounced on the returning buccaneers, capturing several of their ships and most of the Cartagena plunder. Baron de Pointis returned to France with an immense haul for the French king, but kept a substantial share for himself. King Louis XIV sent a substantial cash award to the buccaneers for their efforts, but the only real winners from the operation were the

king, the admiral, and their investors.

The operation was one of the last conducted by the buccaneers in the Caribbean. Many turned to legal privateering for profit, while others, particularly the English, preferred to abandon legality altogether and turn to piracy.

above: *When the French had departed, the buccaneers felt cheated of their proper share, and returned to Cartagena to extract even more plunder from the unfortunate townspeople. "The Sack of Cartagena." Oil painting by Howard Pyle.*

left: *Baron de Pointis, the French commander of the joint military and buccaneer force that attacked Cartagena. After the fall of the city, the buccaneers felt he had swindled them of their agreed share of the booty.*

Tortuga and Port Royal

BUCCANEER HAVENS FOR THE FRENCH AND ENGLISH

During the 1600s, an island and an island port became notorious centers for the Caribbean buccaneers. In both locations, what started as officially sanctioned operations turned into something far less savory.

right: *Engraving of a pirate catching a turtle on the eponymously named island.*

Tortuga lies off the northwestern coast of Hispaniola (modern Haiti) and was named because of its turtle shell shape. (The French name of *Isle de la Tortue* means "Turtle Island.") It first served as a refuge for French cattle hunters (boucanniers) who were trying to evade Spanish troops and, by 1620, a small settlement was established.

In the 1620s French hunters turned to piracy for extra income, attacking passing Spanish ships. Spanish punitive attacks on the island throughout the 1630s failed to drive out these early buccaneers and, by 1642, the French government appointed a governor, Jean le Vasseur, who constructed a fortress to guard the harbor. He then broke ties with France, and made the island a haven for new buccaneers. He even repulsed a Spanish attack, which encouraged more French

buccaneers to seek refuge on Tortuga.

Subsequent French governors continued this autonomous policy of providing a haven for buccaneers, who could protect the island better than the French navy. A major Spanish assault destroyed the colony in 1654, but the Spanish withdrew the following year to defend Hispaniola against the English.

In 1656, Englishman Elias Watts acquired a commission as governor of Tortuga and recruited English and French buccaneers and settlers. This began the main buccaneering period, a phase that would last for two decades. A French governor expelled Watts in 1659 and Tortuga returned to French control.

During the 1660s, French settlements spread along the northern and western coasts of Hispaniola, creating the French colony of Saint Dominique. It looked to the Tortuga buccaneers for protection and paid for the privilege. Tortuga continued as a buccaneer haven until the early 1670s, by which time Petit Gloave in southwestern Saint Dominique had replaced it as the main buccaneer haven, principally because it provided better markets for the sale of

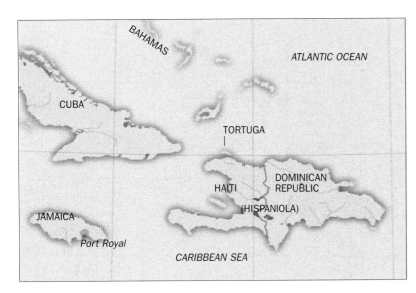

contraband. Buccaneers and pirates used the island on a smaller scale until the early 18th century.

Port Royal—Sodom of the New World

When the English captured Jamaica in 1655, they found an easily defended natural harbor on its southern shore. A peninsula enclosed a deep bay, and the English quickly established a fortified port they named Port Royal. The English governor feared a Spanish invasion, so he lured English buccaneers away from Tortuga by offering a safe haven.

Port Royal was well located for raids on the Spanish Main and provided a ready market for stolen contraband. Soon dozens of buccaneer ships were based in the port, and after peace was declared with Spain in 1660, governors continued to encourage attacks on the Spanish as a means of aggressive defense.

Buccaneering reached a peak in the 1660s when profits from raids made Port Royal a thriving, lawless boomtown of 6,000 people and brought huge profits to land-owners and investors alike. A visiting preacher claimed, "This town is the Sodom of the New World" and "its population consists of pirates, cutthroats, whores, and some of the vilest persons in the whole of the world."

Morgan's sack of Panama led to the arrest of Governor Modyford and Morgan, and the new governor was sent from England with a brief to end buccaneer activities. As buccaneers turned to full-blown piracy and attacked English ships, the Jamaican authorities were forced to protect their business interests. Pirates were convicted and executed and an anti-piracy law was passed in 1681. This effectively drove the pirates off to seek other havens in the Bahamas or the Carolinas, and Port Royal became a commercial rather than a buccaneering port by the mid-1680s. By that time its population equaled that of Boston and the town boasted more bars, brothels, marketplaces, warehouses, and wealth than any other American port.

A massive earthquake struck the town in June 1692. The northern section that included most of the docks slid into the sea and a tidal wave swept over the town. Over 2,000 people were killed in the disaster. Many saw the catastrophe as the judgment of God on "that wicked and rebellious place, Port Royal."

below: *Port Royal, Jamaica, as painted by Paton Richard (1717–91). The artist shows Port Royal at a time well after its catclysmic destruction in 1692. The town, although far smaller than the buccaneer original, has recovered as a port, and the beginnings of Kingston can be seen on the distant shore of the bay.*

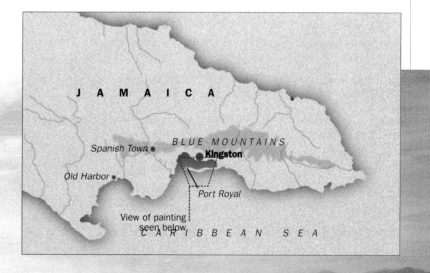

The Golden Age of Piracy

At the end of the 17th century there took place the greatest outburst of piracy in the history of seafaring. Ironically called "the Golden Age of Piracy," the era lasted 40 years, from around 1690 until about 1730. Although the worst affected areas were the Caribbean and the Atlantic seaboard of America, pirates ranged further afield, particularly off the West African coast and the Indian Ocean. The age produced many of the most famous pirates; legends in their own time. Characters such as Blackbeard and Bartholomew Roberts now seem larger than life. The outbreak was the result of circumstances; the end of a long war, ports full of unemployed sailors, and lack of legal employment. Slowly, judicial and naval pressure curbed the piracy boom, and by 1730 it was all but over. Although later outbreaks of piracy occurred, this short era remained lodged in popular and romantic culture as the Golden Age of Piracy. To the victims of pirate attacks, there was nothing "golden" about it.

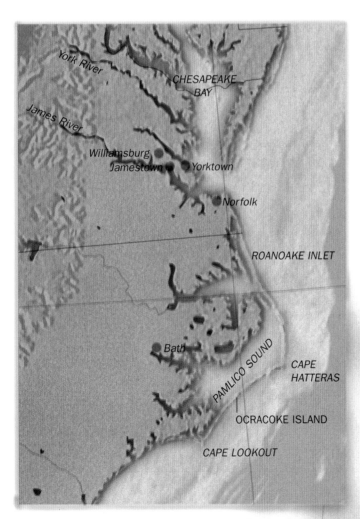

PACIFIC OCEAN

Boston

New York

VIRGINIA

NORTH
CAROLINA

SOUTH
CAROLINA

Charleston

ATLANTIC OCEAN

BAHAMAS

NEW PROVIDENCE

GULF OF MEXICO

LEEWARD ISLANDS

Havana

CUBA

HAITI   DOMINICAN   PUERTO RICO
         REPUBLIC   ST. KITTS
ISLA DE JUVENTUD   (HISPANIOLA)
(ISLA DE PINOS)
                                                  MARTINIQUE

JAMAICA
                                        BARBADOS

                                        WINDWARD ISLANDS

Veracruz

CARIBBEAN SEA
                                        Curaçao

Cartagena

Panama City

THE GOLDEN AGE OF PIRACY

While piracy has existed in some form for as long as mankind has traveled by sea, one short period has remained in the popular imagination as being the "classic" pirate era. This was known as "the Golden Age of Piracy," which lasted a mere 40 years (1690–1730) at the most generous reckoning. For various reasons, there was a huge outbreak of piracy in the waters of the Caribbean and the American Atlantic seaboard.

The prey were the merchant ships that plied from Europe to the American colonies, or that carried slaves from West Africa to the Caribbean, then returned to Europe carrying rum and sugar. Unlike the pirates of fiction, these maritime criminals never expected to plunder cargoes of gold and silver, but preyed on the everyday commerce of the Colonial Americas.

The worst of these pirate excesses was limited to an eight-year period, from 1714 until 1722, so the true Golden Age cannot even be called a "golden decade." This is the era that has been portrayed by writers of fiction such as Robert Louis Stevenson and J.M. Barrie, painters such

right: *A classic preoccupation of pirates—digging a hole to bury the treasure, and yet in this era, the plunder was rarely gold.*

below: *A fearsome engraving of the notorious Blackbeard.*

as Howard Pyle, and in scores of Hollywood pirate movies. Everyone can conjure up an image of an archetypal pirate from the Golden Age. As has already been discussed, the reality of piracy was obscured by contemporary writers who romanticized their exploits, so there is little wonder that the modern perception of them is often highly inaccurate.

This huge and seemingly spontaneous outbreak of piracy developed from a number of stimuli. First, the end of the buccaneering era in the Caribbean—where, during the 1680s, England and France had encouraged lucrative attacks on their Spanish neighbors—forced ex-buccaneers to look elsewhere. An increasingly anti-piratical policy by the Jamaican government drove a number of these former buccaneers toward piracy, and many crossed the Atlantic to prey on shipping along the slave coast of West Africa and, later, in the Indian Ocean.

Unemployment boosts piracy

Second, a fresh outbreak of war between England and Holland on one side and France on the other provided an opportunity for privateering contracts. After Spain joined the allied side, many former English and Dutch buccaneers sought

1664	1690–1730	1700	1701	1703	1707	1714	1716
The Dutch lose New Amsterdam to the English, who rename it New York.	"The Golden Age of Piracy."	Black "Jolly Roger" flags first flown from pirate ships.	"Captain" William Kidd is executed for piracy.	St. Petersburg, Russia, is founded by Peter the Great.	The Act of Union joins England, Scotland, and Wales to form the United Kingdom of Great Britain.	End of the War of the Spanish Succession. New Providence becomes a base for pirates.	Blackbeard arrives in the Bahamas and joins the pirate crew of Benjamin Hornigold.

Letters of Marque from French colonial governors. This period of warfare continued, with only a short intermission, for over two decades, and created opportunities for immense profits to be made from privateering.

Third, in 1714, peace brought ruin to America's seafaring community. The end of the war left thousands of former privateersmen with the options of unemployment, poorly paid service in merchant ships, or a career in piracy. Many chose the latter course, but most still balked at crossing the lines of their old privateering contracts (the Letters of Marque) to attack ships of their own nationality.

The political situation in the American colonies and the Caribbean seemed to help these pirates. The lack of strong government in many American colonies made the Atlantic seaboard a hunting ground for pirates. The obvious benefits of illicit trade between pirates and townspeople were balanced against the disruption of shipping and rising insurance prices, but for at least a decade most colonial governors welcomed the contraband that pirates brought to their ports to sell. Slowly, as their own economic position was able to take advantage of a large peacetime increase in maritime trade, these same colonial governors clamped down on piracy in their waters, and judicial and military pressure was employed to end the outbreak.

By 1730 this era of rampant pirate activity had ended. Although later outbreaks of piracy occurred, this short period would remain lodged in popular and romantic culture as the Golden Age of Piracy. The romantic name was coined by contemporary writers such as Captain Johnson. Pirates became a popular source of escapism, with their activities fully and often completely inaccurately reported in newspapers of the period. This popular image played on the notorious cruelty of many of these pirates, but failed to describe the misery and brutality of their lives, and the inevitability that they faced an early death through battle or execution.

below: *Not only men—Anne Bonny raided Spanish ships in the Caribbbean before her capture in 1720.*

1717	1718	1719	1720	1722	1725	1739	1740
Stede Bonnet turns to piracy. Woodes Rogers is made Governor of Bahamas.	Charles Vane sails fireship toward Rogers. Howell Davis fakes legitimacy to cover piracy.	Daniel Defoe publishes *Robinson Crusoe*.	Calico Jack, Anne Bonny, Mary Reade, and their crew go to trial.	Bartholomew Roberts is shot. Englishman Samuel Bellamy dies in the wrecking of his ship.	Danish sailor Vitus Bering discovers the straits separating Russia and the Americas.	Smuggler and highwayman Dick Turpin is executed.	Decline of the Spanish treasure fleet system; officially ended in 1778.

Flying the Jolly Roger

THE ORIGIN OF PIRATE FLAGS

Jack Rackham

Christopher Condent

During the 17th century in the Caribbean, buccaneers fought under the national flag of their mother countries. Sometimes other flags were flown, either designed to intimidate the enemy or to act as identification; often flown with a national flag. While the origin of buccaneer flags remains unclear, their purpose was evident: to intimidate victims by conjuring up images of dread.

Red was the preferred color for buccaneer flags, a color traditionally meaning that no quarter would be given and that battle would be a fight to the death. It implied that the defender's rapid surrender was the only alternative to slaughter. Some privateer captains created their own designs based on these red flags to add extra menace to what were already alarming banners. These emblems became known collectively as the "Jolly Roger," derived from the French phrase *Jolie Rouge* (pretty red), an ironic reference to buccaneering flags.

Pirate or buccaneering flags with a black field were a direct derivative of the red warning flag and were pigeon-holed under the same collective name of *Jolie Rouge*. The first reported instances of black pirate flags date from the early 18th century, the first example being recorded in 1700. Within 15 years, pirates frequently used black flags and, by 1714, they were a clearly recognized symbol.

The idea of flying a red or black flag was to intimidate the enemy into immediate surrender to avoid costly and potentially deadly fights. But if the flag's objective was to signal a vicious reputation so that the victim would give up quietly, it was counter-productive if the reputation was like that of the French buccaneer L'Olonnais; victims knew that they would be killed anyway, so nothing would be lost by resisting.

Edward England

Christopher Moody

Walter Kennedy

Henry Every

Stede Bonnet

Deception by foreign flag

When Howell Davis took to piracy, his ship lacked a Jolly Roger, so they flew "a dirty tarpaulin, by way of black flag, they having no other." The victim instantly recognized the meaning of the makeshift flag. In 1718, Charles Vane flew the English flag from one mast and a black pirate flag from another, and two years later Edward England flew a black flag from his mainmast, a red flag from his foremast, and the English flag from his ensign staff.

Pirates clearly flew national flags in order to give the appearance of being privateers, and privateers only attacked ships of their own nation's enemies. During the occasional times of peace during the late 17th and 18th centuries, when all privateering commissions were considered void, this meant nothing. Edward England flew an English flag while he was attacking a British East Indiaman. Clearly flags meant little until the intent of an unknown sail was determined.

Even though a sighted ship might be flying a recognizable national flag, it might not be that of its own nation. Ships often held a variety of national flags in an attempt to avoid attack in hostile waters, or to confuse or deceive an enemy until it was too late for them to escape. Privateers, buccaneers, pirates, and even men-of-war flew foreign flags and banners, in order to entice an enemy within range of their guns. As long as these flags were replaced with the appropriate national emblem, this was seen as a legitimate *ruse de guerre*, although pirates obeyed no rules and could fly whatever flag they pleased! The best policy in time of war or in pirate waters was to assume that all shipping was hostile, and sail away as quickly as possible.

PIRATE FLAGS

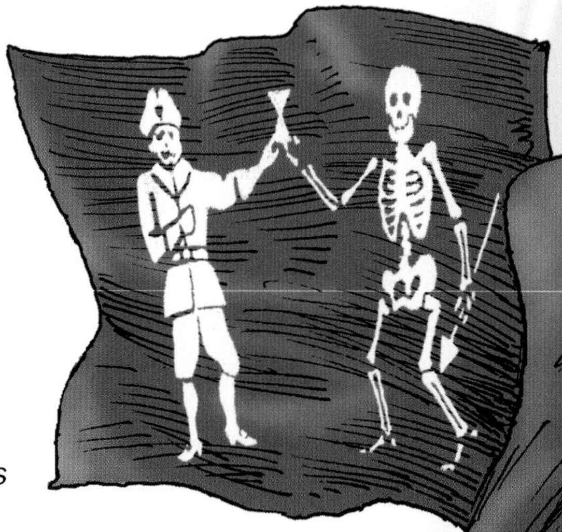

Bartholomew Roberts

Bartholomew Roberts

ABH AMH

Emanuel Wynne

Richard Worley

The symbolism of the Jolly Roger

The point of the Jolly Roger was to intimidate victims into surrender without fighting. Not only did it save pirate lives, it also meant that the ship could be captured intact—a far more valuable prize than one badly damaged by artillery fire. However, if the flag said more and offered a clue as to the identity of the pirate who flew it, it was easier to terroize victims through a reputation for mercilessness when crossed.

Specific designs helped to identify particular pirates, so victims would know who they were up against. If a ship drew close and unfurled a flag associated with Bartholomew Roberts or Blackbeard, the victim would be well advised to surrender immediately. Although the images used on pirate flags varied, common themes are to be found in almost all known examples. In the early 18th century, the symbolism behind most common images was widely known and easily recognized: images from gravestones, allegorical paintings, church carvings, and even tradesmen's signs. These images usually included suitably threatening messages: a skull and crossed bones or a skeleton, representing death; an hourglass to show time running out; or a sword to indicate a tough fight. In the early 18th century, everybody knew what these images were meant to convey.

The first reference to a black Jolly Roger was in 1700, when French privateer turned pirate Emanuel Wynne reportedly flew a black flag decorated with a skull, crossed bones, and an hourglass. It has been argued that black as opposed to red was flown to show that the ship was no longer a privateer but a pirate, but this seems unlikely, and privateers probably flew black flags as well as red ones.

Thomas Tew

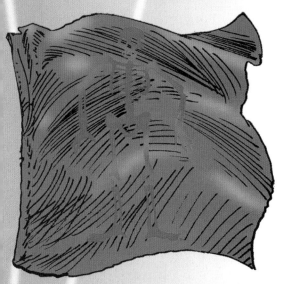

Edward Low

Blackbeard

Modifying the Jolly Roger

What is known is that following 1700 additional emblems on the basic red or black flags were increasingly associated with piracy, and different symbols were associated with individual pirate captains. Symbolism could sometimes take the form of a specific threat, aimed at a particular group of people. The pirate Bartholomew Roberts harbored a grudge against the islands of Barbados and Martinique, so as he cruised their waters during the late summer of 1720, he created flags designed to intimidate the islanders. One showed a pirate figure, presumably representing Roberts, standing on two skulls. Under one skull were the letters "ABH," meaning "A Barbadian's Head," and the second was labeled "AMH"—"A Martiniquan's Head." The threat was clear, and sailors from these two islands could expect no mercy if they offered any resistance.

The premier symbol was the skull, representing death (and threatening it to those who saw it). It was often used in conjunction with crossed bones, another symbol of death, or crossed swords. Both symbols were popular images on 17th- and 18th-century gravestones.

While death played a strong part in this symbolism, the way it was used varied. Some records of pirate flags show dancing skeletons, meaning dancing a jig with death, synonymously playing with death, or not caring about fate. This was also the symbolism behind raised drinking glasses, the image referring to a toast to death in store—those flying this flag didn't care about their fate. Other popular symbols included spears, swords, wings, initials, and hearts. Sometimes several images were combined. Bartholomew Roberts flew a flag showing a pirate holding an hourglass standing beside a skeleton holding a spear. Blackbeard used a flag showing a skeleton holding an hourglass with a spear and a bleeding heart next to it. The symbolism of these versions of the Jolly Roger was unequivocal: resistance will result in death.

Edward Teach: Blackbeard

THE MOST NOTORIOUS PIRATE OF THEM ALL

Nicknamed after the long, dark beard he sported, Blackbeard appeared as a demonic figure. Despite his reputation, he was not the worst pirate of his day, but a fiery appearance and a spectacular end ensured his place in the pirate hall of fame.

If you ask someone who they consider to be the most notorious pirate of all time, the answer will invariably be "Blackbeard." Others caused far more mayhem, captured richer cargoes or more ships, but this one pirate has come to represent the genre more than any other. The enduring popularity of Blackbeard most probably stems from his appearance. In 1717 a victim described him as "a tall, spare man with a very black beard which he wore very long." Blackbeard tied his beard up with black

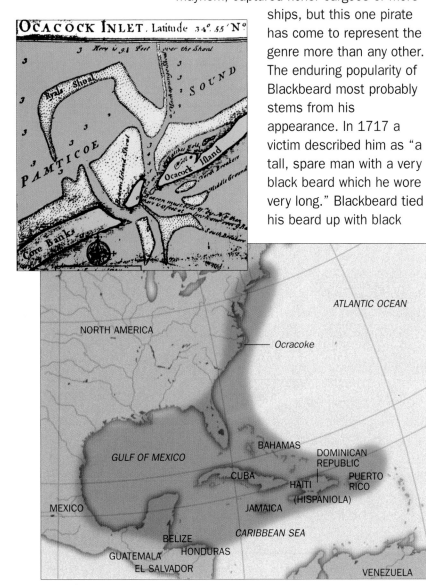

ribbons, and wore a sling over his shoulders that held three brace of pistols. The demonic image has been appended to by Johnson and others, claiming burning pieces of slow match stuck out from under his hat.

"Blackbeard" was the nickname given to Edward Teach, a seaman born in Bristol, England. He reportedly served onboard a British privateer based in Jamaica, but following the peace of 1714 found himself unemployed. He arrived in New Providence in the Bahamas in 1716, by then a thriving pirate haven, and joined the crew of the pirate Benjamin Hornigold.

By late 1717, Teach was given his own sloop to command and demonstrated he was a charismatic leader. Teach captured a French slave ship that he rearmed with 40 guns and renamed *Queen Anne's Revenge*. Teach decided to cruise on his own, and at first based himself at New Providence and captured several prizes. The imminent arrival of Governor Rogers meant that Teach had to find a new base.

In January 1718 he sailed to North Carolina and established a lair on Ocracoke Island, near the settlement of Bath Towne, which provided a market for plunder. A bribe to the colony's governor ensured safety from prosecution. By March, Teach was cruising in the Gulf of Mexico, where he captured several prizes, including the sloop *Revenge*, which belonged to the pirate Stede Bonnet.

Blackbeard's demise

On his return northward along the Atlantic coast in May, Teach decided to blockade the port of Charleston, South Carolina. Standing off the entrance to the harbor, Teach took eight vessels, and captured a number of prominent local citizens in the process. These he ransomed; the demands included a chest of medical supplies (it was rumored that Teach had contracted a form of venereal disease). The pirates returned to Ocracoke but lost *Queen Anne's Revenge* on a sandbar. In Bath Towne, Teach sold his stolen ships and cargo, bought a house, and was even granted a pardon by the governor.

Resentment was growing over this brazen display of lawlessness. When Charles Vane visited Teach in October 1718 and a week-long bout of festivities was held, many colonists feared that the Carolinas would become a new pirate haven. In Virginia, governor Alexander Spotswood decided to take action. He hired two sloops and manned them with a hand-picked Royal Naval crew commanded by Lieutenant Maynard.

On November 22, 1718, Maynard arrived off Ocracoke at dawn. As luck would have it, many pirates were in Bath Towne, so Teach, aboard the sloop *Adventure*, was outnumbered. He escaped through an unmarked channel, while the sloops ran aground. According to Maynard, Teach shouted, "drank Damnation to me

and my men, whom he stil'd Cowardly Puppies, saying he would neither give nor take Quarter."

The sloops broke free with the rising tide and continued the pursuit. Teach fired grapeshot into the pursuing sloop, *Ranger*, that killed several of her crew, including the midshipman in charge. A shot from Maynard's sloop cut Teach's jibsheet, and forced the pirates to run aground. Maynard had hidden most of his men, so Teach decided to board the sloop. As he came alongside, Maynard's crew rose from their hiding places and a brutal hand-to-hand fight began.

Maynard and Teach fought each other, and the pirate was wounded, then killed by a naval crewman. The remaining pirates were either killed or captured. Maynard rounded up the pirates in Bath Towne, then returned to Williamsburg, with Blackbeard's decapitated head hanging from the bowsprit of his sloop. The surviving pirates were tried; in March 1719, 13 were hanged in Williamsburg.

above: *Artist's impression of Blackbeard's last fight against Lieutenant Maynard of the British Royal Navy. The wounded pirate was eventually dispatched by a Scots sailor wielding a broadsword.*

far left: *Ocracoke Inlet, the hideout of Blackbeard. Narrow entrances and uncharted sandbars made it difficult to sneak up on the pirate base.*

"Calico" Jack Rackham and the Female Pirates

CUTTHROATS OR PIONEER LIBERATED WOMEN?

Although "Calico" Jack was a lesser pirate, his capture made him famous when it was discovered that two of his crew were women. Their trial created a media sensation, as the public savored every detail of their scandalous lives.

above right:

"Calico" Jack Rackham, as depicted in Johnson's "A General History of Pirates."

Almost as famous as Blackbeard are the two female pirates, Anne Bonny and Mary Reade. Their trial in 1720 caused a sensation, the excitement stemming from the revelation that they had lived as men for years. Their fellow pirate, "Calico" Jack Rackham was a small-time pirate, whose subsequent notoriety arose more for his unusual choice of crew than his mediocre exploits.

Calico Jack was typical of the pirates whose small sloops preyed on coastal shipping. Although his roots are obscure, by 1718 he had arrived on New Providence and served with Charles Vane, becoming his deputy when elected as quartermaster. When an argument arose with Vane, the crew chose Rackham as the new captain. Vane was put ashore, and Rackham continued the cruise.

It has been claimed that Rackham lost his sloop while the crew was ashore and the pirates were surprised by two naval sloops. Whatever the circumstances, by May 1719 Rackham had returned to New Providence to plead for a pardon, which was granted as part of a widespread pirate amnesty. While there, he met Anne Bonny.

Bonny was the illegitimate daughter of an Irish lawyer from South Carolina. She married a seaman, James Bonny, and ran off with him. When he turned to piracy she joined him in New Providence, where she was wooed by Jack Rackham. The arrangement is unclear, but there is evidence that when Rackham returned to sea both Anne and James Bonny accompanied him.

By August it was decided that unemployment ashore was less preferable than a criminal life at sea, so Rackham stole the sloop *William* and returned to piracy, with Anne and, possibly, James Bonny accompanying him. For the next

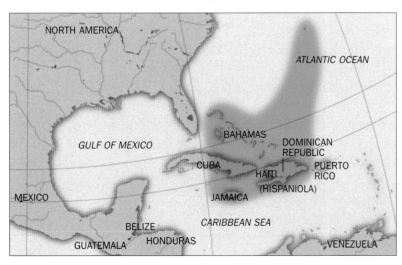

15 months, Calico Jack and his crew cruised off the coast of Cuba, capturing several small vessels.

Sensational trial of Reade and Bonny

The account of Mary Reade's life comes from Charles Johnson's pirate book, and was almost certainly fictional. Reade was apparently born in England, and her impoverished mother "bred her daughter dressed as a boy" in order to benefit from a stipend from a relative. As a teenager, Reade worked as a boy in domestic service, escaped to serve on a warship, then ran away and joined the British army. She fell in love and married a soldier, and when he died, she took passage as a seaman bound for the West Indies. Her ship was captured by pirates and, after serving with them for a while, she accompanied them to New Providence. She accompanied Rackham when he sailed on his pirate cruise in August 1719.

In late 1720 Rackham's luck ran out. While at anchor off the western tip of Jamaica he was surprised by a government sloop. Most of the nine men onboard the pirate sloop were drunk or asleep after celebrating the taking of a prize. According to testimonies the women roused them, and the *William* cut her anchor cable and tried to escape. After a chase she was overtaken by the pursuers, led by Captain Barnet.

The pirates' sloop was boarded and, reputedly, Anne Bonny and Mary Reade were the only members of her crew to offer resistance, the rest being too drunk to defend themselves. The women were overcome, and the pirates were taken to Port Royal to stand trial. The capture caused a sensation and turned the female pirates into notorious celebrities.

The excitement stemmed from the revelation that they had lived as men for years, escaping the traditional restrictions imposed on the lives of contemporary women. In other words, not only were they female pirates, but they had broken the rules of society. In court it was reported that "they were both very profligate, cursing and swearing much, and very ready and willing to do anything." Victims testified that they wore men's clothing in action, but otherwise dressed as women.

Anne and Mary were condemned, but then reprieved when it was discovered that both were pregnant. Subsequently, Mary died in a Jamaican prison in 1721, but Anne's fate is unknown. Calico Jack Rackham and the male pirates were hanged on November 27, 1721.

below: *Anne Bonny and Mary Reade, who dressed as men when engaged in piratical acts. At other times, they wore contemporary women's clothing. The revelation that there were female pirates caused a sensation.*

Bartholomew Roberts

THE LAST GREAT PIRATE OF THE GOLDEN AGE

Roberts was perhaps the most successful pirate of the period, and ranks with "Blackbeard" as being the most colorful. By the time he was killed in action in 1722, Roberts had captured hundreds of ships on both sides of the Atlantic, and amassed a fortune in plunder.

above right:

Bartholomew Roberts, as depicted in Johnson's "A General History of Pirates." When he died he wore the same cross around his neck as shown here; a gold cross decorated with emeralds and hung from a gold chain.

Bartholomew Roberts was one of the most successful pirates of all time. In a 30-month period he captured more than 400 prizes and terrorized the waters of the American colonies, the Caribbean, and the coast of West Africa. Roberts—born John Roberts in southern Wales—was the mate on a slave ship when it was captured by Howell Davis in June 1719. Davis was killed in an ambush on Principé, off the coast of Guinea, and Roberts was elected captain. He changed his name to Bartholomew Roberts, and soon earned the nickname "Black Bart."

He sailed for Brazil, where he attacked a Portuguese convoy and captured several ships, although he was deserted by colleagues who sailed off with his original sloop, the *Rover*. Roberts renamed his surviving sloop *Fortune* and headed north,

capturing ships on the way. Selling the ships and cargo in New England in early 1720, he proceeded to haunt the fishing grounds of Newfoundland, capturing over 170 vessels. Exchanging a prize for a French ship, which he armed with 28 guns and renamed *Royal Fortune*, he sailed back down the American coast, and captured even more vessels.

He reached the Caribbean in the summer of 1720, capturing 15 French, British, and Dutch vessels in rapid succession. Roberts tried to cross the Atlantic to West Africa, but was foiled by the weather. Back in the West Indies by September 1720, he started a six-month rampage through the Leeward Islands, attacking St. Kitts and Martinique, and captured at least one hundred ships. One of these was a 52-gun warship carrying the governor of Martinique. Roberts hanged him from the yardarm of his own ship, then tortured and killed most of the French crew. He also renamed this latest prize the *Royal Fortune*—one of several craft he gave that name—and converted her into a powerful pirate ship.

In April 1721 Bartholomew Roberts crossed the Atlantic to West Africa, where he captured several slavers, including the

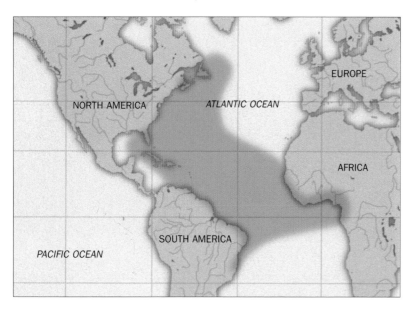

A New and Exact Map of
GUINEA
Divided into ye GOLD, SLAVE and IVORY
COAST &c. with their several Kingdoms, and ye
adjacent Countries. By H. Moll Geographer.

Onslow—another ship he renamed *Royal Fortune.* On this occasion, one slaver that refused to pay a ransom had his ship burned, along with its human cargo.

Escaping into the line of fire

The deadly spree came to an end on February 10, 1722, when the British warship *HMS Swallow* caught up with Roberts off Cape Lopez, in modern Gabon. Five days previously, Captain Challoner Ogle of the *Swallow* had captured Roberts's consort, the 32-gun *Great Ranger.* The pirates were at anchor after a night of celebration, following the capture of several prizes the previous day.

The *Swallow* arrived at dawn, and Roberts ordered his ship to head toward Ogle's, hoping to sail past him and out into the open sea. As the ships passed, the *Swallow* fired a broadside of grapeshot at close range. Roberts was killed instantly. His crew threw his body overboard to avoid the corpse being captured. The ships continued to exchange broadsides in a running battle, but the surviving pirates surrendered after three hours.

Two other pirate vessels were captured, and the three produced a large haul of gold dust valued at over 14,000 English

pounds. In what was the largest pirate trial and execution of the era, the survivors were tried at Cape Coast Castle, in West Africa. Of these, 54 were hanged, 37 were sentenced to penal servitude or prison, while the remainder were acquitted; 70 African pirates were sold into slavery.

Bartholomew Roberts was one of the most successful and colorful pirates of all time. He was an unusual character for this age, described as tall, good-looking, teetotal, and always well dressed. He possessed a ruthless skill in the piratical arts of intimidation and seamanship, and was highly regarded by his crew. During his

brief career, Roberts carved out a reputation that would never be surpassed for its achievements or its bloodthirstiness.

Samuel Bellamy

THE STORY OF THE *WHYDAH*

Bellamy's run-of-the-mill career holds more interest because in the 1980s his ship, *Whydah*, was discovered and salvaged, giving us a tantalizing glimpse into a pirate's shipboard life of the early 18th century. He drowned in the shipwreck off Cape Cod, and the few crewmen who survived the disaster were executed.

right: *Fragments of cannons were recovered from the wreck of the Whydah. Here a researcher begins cleaning the end of a gun near the touch hole.*

Sam Bellamy was born in Devonshire in England, a county with a strong seafaring tradition. The early days of his pirate career are unclear, but it has been suggested that the catalyst was found while he was a seaman, working on the salvage of a Spanish shipwreck. He argued with the project leaders, so Bellamy and a small group decided to turn pirate. Given the date—if this event happened—Bellamy was probably involved in attacks on the camps of salvors working on the wrecks of the Spanish 1715 treasure fleet, off Florida's east coast. These raids were led by the pirate Henry Jennings, so Bellamy may have served with him.

By 1716 Bellamy had reached New Providence, where he sailed with the pirate Benjamin Hornigold, whose crew included Edward Teach (Blackbeard). Hornigold had a degree of conscience, and his small pirate squadron fell apart in August 1716 when he refused to attack British vessels. Bellamy and Blackbeard decided to go their own way, and Bellamy was elected captain of Hornigold's former sloop, the *Mary Anne*.

For the rest of the year, Bellamy cruised off the Virgin Islands accompanied by another vessel commanded by the French pirate Olivier La Bouche. The partnership proved moderately successful, and Bellamy and his consort captured several ships throughout the fall and winter of 1716–17. Like many pirates, Bellamy wanted a larger flagship than a sloop, so when he moved into the captured square-rigged ship *Sultana*, he handed control of his former sloop to his quartermaster, Paul Williams.

The three pirate vessels continued their voyage until early 1717, when a storm

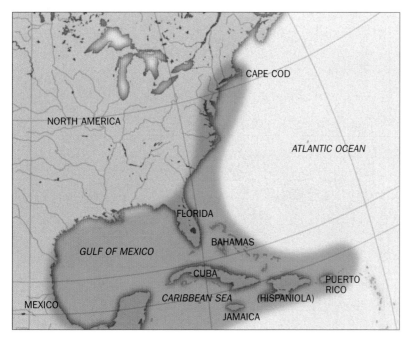

separated the two British pirates from their French colleague. In February or March 1717, Bellamy and Williams captured the *Whydah*, a British slave vessel returning home on the last leg of her triangular slave-trading voyage. She carried money, sugar, and indigo, and the rich prize was quickly adapted to become Bellamy's new flagship.

Formidable but not invincible

Whydah was a 300-ton (272-tonne) ship-rigged galley, and was quickly adapted to carry the 28 guns moved aboard from other ships, turning her from a slaver into a formidable pirate ship. Bellamy and the *Whydah*'s former captain became friends, and it is said that the pirate let the slave captain go free, and even gave him the *Sultana* in which to sail home.

In two ships Bellamy and Williams sailed north along the Atlantic coast of the American colonies, capturing four more vessels off Virginia. One of these was added to the pirate squadron, which continued its cruise northward. In April 1717 they were hit by a sudden storm that drove them northward past New York and toward the New England coast. As it subsided the pirates decided to sail back south to Rhode Island, where the local governor reputedly took a lenient view of pirate activities, so long as his colony could profit from them.

The pirates never made it. After taking several prizes in Massachusetts waters, tragedy struck. On the night of May 17, in

a heavy fog, the *Whydah* struck a sandbar three miles (4.8km) south of the village of Wellfleet, on Cape Cod, Massachusetts. One of the prize vessels sailing with the flotilla ran aground further to the south.

Whydah was capsized by the Atlantic surf, and of her crew of 146 pirates, all were drowned apart from two, who were captured as soon as they reached the shore. Samuel Bellamy was lost in the shipwreck. The two *Whydah* survivors were tried in a Massachusetts court, together with seven pirate survivors from the wrecked prize ship. Two were acquitted and the remaining seven hanged in Boston.

A postscript to the story was written when the wreck of *Whydah* was recovered in 1984 by the wreck hunter Barry Clifford. Finds included coins, weapons, and even the ship's bell, which marked the last resting place of Samuel Bellamy. These objects are now on display in a museum in Provincetown, on Cape Cod.

above: *The hilt of a sword still looks remarkably intact.*

below: *Everything Bellamy needed to fire a cannon—the round shot, followed by wadding.*

85. A - F

Charles Vane

AN UNLUCKY AND UNPOPULAR PIRATE

Vane was a contemporary of "Blackbeard," but unlike Teach, he was unpopular, and was removed from command by "Calico" Jack Rackham in a demonstration of pirate justice. Constantly dogged by misfortune, Vane eventually met a grisly fate.

below: *Charles Vane, depicted in Johnson's "A General History of Pirates." A competent captain, his lack of popularity with his crew proved his undoing.*

Charles Vane was a British pirate who is first mentioned serving in the crew of Henry Jennings. During 1716, Jennings and his crew attacked the camps of Spanish salvors, recovering sunken treasure from the wrecks of the 1715 treasure fleet disaster along Florida's eastern coast. Jennings was originally based in Jamaica, but Spanish political pressure forced him to escape to New Providence, the pirate haven in the Bahamas.

By July 1718 Vane sailed on his first independent cruise, using New Providence as his base. When the British sent governor Woodes Rogers to New Providence in August 1718, Vane was faced with a dilemma. Vane had just captured a French square-rigged ship—he would have to give up his plunder or flee. He set the French vessel on fire and sailed it straight for Rogers' flagship. As it tried to avoid the fireship, Vane and his pirate crew sailed, firing at the flagship and jeering at it. Vane escaped amid the smoke and confusion. Meanwhile, Jennings accepted an offered pardon, and turned his back on piracy.

Evading pursuit, Vane and his unrepentant pirates escaped to the Carolinas. He captured four vessels but clashed with a pirate called Yeats, who Vane had placed in charge of one of the prizes. Yeats abandoned Vane, providing the first indication that there was rancor between Vane and his crew. Vane gave chase, but abandoned the pursuit when Yeats evaded him, possibly by sailing into Charleston harbor and giving himself up in return for a pardon.

A number of armed vessels were sent after Vane and his pirates by colonial governors during late August and early September 1718, but he evaded them all. Off North Carolina's Ocracoke Island, Vane and his crew met Edward "Blackbeard" Teach, and the two pirate crews celebrated with a week-long bacchanalian party.

Ejected by "Calico" Jack

By October 1718 Vane was cruising off New York, where he captured two small ships off Long Island, but no other

potential prizes were spotted until late November. A heavily armed French warship was spied and evaded. An argument arose, where the quartermaster, "Calico" Jack Rackham, accused his captain of cowardice. The crew demonstrated the extent of Vane's lack of popularity by voting Rackham in as captain in his place. It seems that Vane was given a small captured sloop and sent on his way with the few crew who remained loyal to him, including the former mate, Robert Deal.

Starting from scratch again, Vane and about 15 crew sailed south toward the Caribbean. Sailing southwest through the Florida Straits, they rounded Cuba's western tip and cruised between Jamaica and the Yucatán peninsula. In November the pirates captured a sloop, which was given to Deal, and two small local craft, which were abandoned. In the Gulf of Honduras the two pirate sloops captured two small Jamaican vessels, one being the sloop *Pearl*. The ships were released after being plundered.

After wintering on the small Honduran island of Baracho, in February 1719 the two pirate sloops set off for the Windward Passage between Cuba and Hispaniola, but after only a few days at sea a hurricane struck. The two sloops lost contact with each other and Vane's vessel was wrecked on a reef. Only the captain and a single seaman survived. Stranded on a small uninhabited island in the Gulf of Honduras for several months, the two men survived by eating turtles and fish before being rescued by a passing ship.

A chance meeting between the rescuer and another ship led to Vane being identified as a notorious pirate, taken prisoner, and shipped to Port Royal, Jamaica to stand trial. Vane's protégé, Robert Deal, had survived the hurricane only to be captured by a warship, brought to Jamaica, and executed. Both Vane and his one surviving crewman were found guilty and hanged in November 1720.

above: *Ocracoke, September 1718— Vane and Blackbeard hold a week-long party, complete with women and rum brought in from nearby towns.*

above opposite: *Pirates holding a trial—Vane may have faced such when his crew voted him out.*

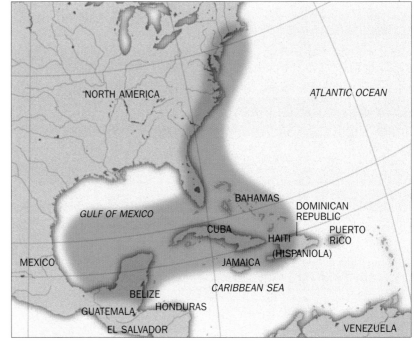

Stede Bonnet

THE GENTLEMAN PIRATE

Stede Bonnet abandoned a comfortable life as a respected plantation owner in Barbados and turned to piracy. The aptly nicknamed "gentleman pirate" even bought his own pirate ship and hired his own crew!

right: *Stede Bonnet, the "gentleman pirate," as depicted in Johnson's "A General History of Pirates." He turned to piracy more from boredom than necessity, but his former social standing failed to spare him from hanging.*

According to Johnson, Stede Bonnet was a major in the island militia and "a gentleman of good reputation in the island of Barbados, was a master of a plentiful fortune, and had the advantage of a liberal education." If this is true, it is amazing that a successful and established plantation owner would suddenly turn to piracy. Unfortunately, no archival record of him can be found, although at his trial the judge described him as an esteemed man of letters.

Whatever the background of Bonnet or his reasons for turning to a life of piracy, during the spring of 1717, he set sail aboard his own 10-gun sloop called *Revenge*, together with a crew of 70 seamen. He sailed for the Atlantic coast of the American colonies and captured and plundered several ships off the Virginia Capes, then off Long Island, New York, and by August 1717 he was off South Carolina, where he took two more small vessels.

At some stage he met Edward Teach (Blackbeard), probably during his cruise off the Carolinas. Although it has been hinted that Bonnet was captured by Teach, this remains unclear, although a Boston paper of November 1717 reported that he was a virtual prisoner on Blackbeard's ship. It appears that one of Teach's men was put

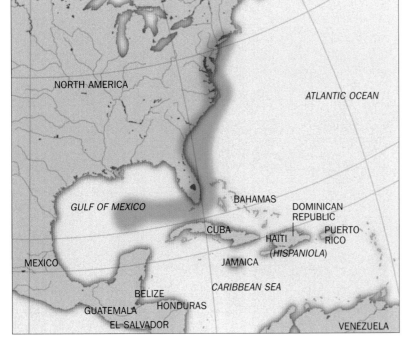

in charge of *Revenge*, while Bonnet accompanied Teach in *Queen Anne's Revenge*. Bonnet must have sailed with Teach during his cruise in the Caribbean and the blockade of Charleston in May 1718, but on the return to Ocracoke, Bonnet was set free, along with his ship.

Hearing that Britain was at war with Spain, Bonnet approached the governor of North Carolina for a pardon, which was granted. He set off for St. Thomas, in the Virgin Islands, to act as a privateer, with a Letter of Marque entitling him to attack Spanish shipping legally. He still bore a grudge against Teach and tried to track him down off Ocracoke during June 1718, acting as a pirate turned pirate-hunter. He failed and, instead of sailing to St. Thomas, he reverted to piracy.

A new chance at success

In order to disguise himself he changed the name of his sloop to the *Royal James* and adopted the identity of Captain Thomas. He captured three prizes off Virginia, then another six vessels. Keeping two of them, Bonnet sailed into the Cape Fear river for repairs and captured a local ship to provide the necessary timber.

The city authorities at Charleston in South Carolina were still smarting from their attack by Blackbeard a few months earlier, and when they heard pirates were moored within reach they acted.
A local ship owner, Colonel William Rhett, was authorized to attack the pirates with two armed sloops, the *Henry* and the *Sea Nymph*. While they were about to sail, pirate Charles Vane was sighted off the city; the Carolinean sloops gave chase, but he escaped.

Colonel Rhett returned to his earlier mission and sailed up Cape Fear during the evening of September 26, 1718. Bonnet retreated up the river but ran aground and was forced to fight. After a five-hour battle the pirates surrendered. The prisoners were taken to Charleston and imprisoned.

Bonnet escaped, but was quickly recaptured and tried. His escape prevented any chance of bargaining for a pardon, and

Judge Trot refused to show leniency. Only three of the 33 prisoners were acquitted. The condemned men included some who had only joined the pirates weeks before.

Stede Bonnet, the gentleman turned pirate, was found guilty and hanged on White Point near Charleston in November 1718, along with 30 of his crew. Following their humiliation by Blackbeard, the resentment felt by the citizens of Charleston after Blackbeard's attack helped to seal Bonnet's fate.

above: *Bonnet was hanged in Charleston in November 1718. He is shown clutching a bunch of nosegay, as a sign of repentance.*

Howell Davis

THE MASTER OF DECEPTION

The mentor of the more successful Bartholomew Roberts, Davis terrorized the West African slave coast. A master of disguise, he frequently passed himself off as a law-abiding pirate-hunter—his luck ran out when a local governor called his bluff.

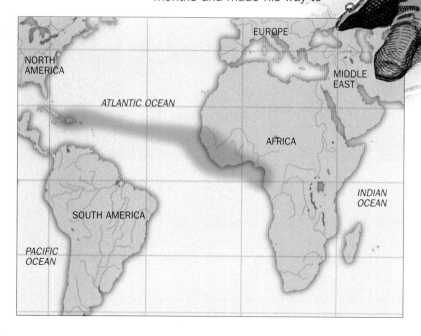

right: *The Welsh pirate Howell Davis, as shown in a 19th-century illustration. He is shown storming the fortifications of a slaving fort, but in reality, he captured a fort on the West African coast by deception.*

Howell Davis was reputedly born in Milford Haven, a seaport in southwest Wales. In 1718 he served as the mate on the slave ship *Cadogan* of Bristol when it was captured by pirates off the West African coast. Led by Edward England, these pirates killed the slaver captain and some crewmen, but Davis and others elected to join the pirate band.

According to Johnson's *General History*, Davis was given the *Cadogan* as a prize and tried to sail to Brazil, but the crew rebelled and sailed for Barbados instead, where Davis was imprisoned on suspicion of piracy. He was released after three months and made his way to New Providence, known as a nest of pirate activity. When he arrived he discovered that the new governor, Woodes Rogers, had dispersed the pirates, forcing many to renounce their former career.

In late 1718 Howell Davis took passage on the *Buck*, a sloop bound for the West Indies crewed by ex-pirates, and, when it lay off Martinique, he encouraged the 35-man crew to return to piracy. Davis was elected as their captain during a council of war, the decision aided by "a large bowl of punch." The sloop based itself in a cove in eastern Cuba and cruised eastward to the Virgin Islands and Hispaniola, where Davis captured two French ships. The second

NORTH AMERICA

EUROPE

ATLANTIC OCEAN

MIDDLE EAST

AFRICA

SOUTH AMERICA

INDIAN OCEAN

PACIFIC OCEAN

prize was a 24-gun ship, vastly superior to the *Buck*, but Davis reputedly used deception to capture her by pretending that his earlier prize was a well-armed pirate ship and the sloop just her light escort. The French crew were intimidated enough to surrender.

He looted the two prizes then returned them to their French crews, and headed east across the Atlantic in the smaller and faster sloop. Stopping in the Cape Verde Islands off the West African coast, he persuaded the local Portuguese governor that he was a legal British privateer. After getting provisions for the ship, Davis sailed the waters of the islands, and at Maio captured several ships at anchor in the harbor, including the 26-gun ship that he made his new flagship and renamed *Saint James*.

The luck runs out

Howell Davis crossed to the mouth of the Gambia river with his two vessels, where he deceived the commander of a Royal African Company slaving fort. He pretended he was a legitimate privateer, and then captured the fort's governor during a welcome dinner and held him to ransom. Continuing the cruise, Davis met a ship commanded by the French pirate La Bouche, the old colleague of Sam Bellamy. Together with a third pirate, they cruised in consort for a few weeks until a drunken argument forced them to go their separate ways.

On his own again, Davis captured four English and Dutch slave ships, each containing a rich cargo of slaves, ivory, and trade goods. Since by then the *Buck* had become unseaworthy, Davis abandoned it for one of the slave ships, the *Rover*, which he converted into a 32-gun pirate ship. The pirates moved south, and off the Gold Coast (Ghana) they captured a slave ship whose crew included the Welshman Bartholomew Roberts. Roberts joined Davis and went on to become one of the most successful pirates of the Golden Age.

Davis captured another rich Dutch slaver, which he pressed into service to replace the rotten *Saint James*. The pirates sailed to Principé, a Portuguese island off the coast of Guinea. Davis tried to convince the local governor that the *Rover* was a privateer engaged in an anti-piracy patrol. Davis even captured a French ship that entered the harbor on the grounds that it had traded with pirates.

This time around the governor was not so easily fooled. The day before the pirates planned to depart, Davis and a band of his crewmen were ambushed and killed by Portuguese militia, following up a report that they planned to kidnap the governor. The remaining crewmen elected Bartholomew Roberts as their captain, who went on to bombard the fort and town before escaping. Davis was a colorful character, and his frequent use of deception shows that he was an intelligent and charming man.

above: *Howell Davis, as depicted in Johnson's "A General History of Pirates." Like the picture on the left-hand page, the artist chose to depict his capture of a Gambian slaving fort on the engraving.*

Pirate Weapons

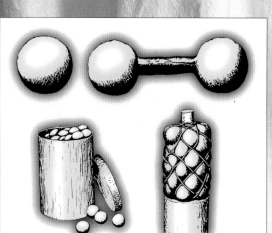

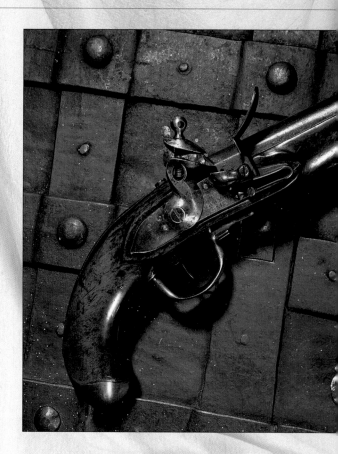

left: Artillery shot from the top left, clockwise: roundshot, with its longer range, was used to smash hulls and masts; at closer ranges, the double-cannon ball and chain shot could bring down sails and rigging; while grapeshot was an anti-personnel weapon.

Pirates preferred to capture a victim without a fight—usually sheer intimidation worked. Poorly armed merchant ships surrendered rather than risk the deaths that usually followed an unsuccessful defense against pirates. Once within range, the pirate vessel would usually hoist a Jolly Roger and force surrender by firing a gun across the victim's bows. Any form of resistance could lead to slaughter.

The victim was often ordered to lower her boats and then ferry over a pirate prize crew. Pirate ships were heavily armed, and in some cases they felt that it was worth their while attacking less compliant and more powerfully armed opponents. Gauging the risks was part of the pirate captain's job. Charles Vane paid the price of shying away from a fight, while Edward England relished the prospect, but paid the price for leniency toward the men he vanquished.

If the pirate ship had to fight its victim, the preferred method was by boarding it, which reduced the chance of damage to the prize through gunfire. In a hand-to-hand fight pirates were usually the better armed, and more numerous than their opponents. When the ships were alongside each other, the pirates threw grappling hooks, pulling the two ships together. Once the pirates swung aboard, a fierce hand-to-hand fight would ensue.

Firearms were popular boarding weapons, and included muskets, blunderbusses, and pistols. Blackbeard is reported to have carried three pairs of pistols, as well as a sword and a knife. The most popular edged weapon was the cutlass. A cheap, clumsy, but effective cutting weapon, it was the maritime blade of choice. Naval officers and pirate captains often favored the more gentlemanly smallsword, designed to be thrust with the point. Half-pikes, axes, knives, and even belaying pins were used in a desperate hand-to-hand fight. Another weapon was the grenade (or "grenadoe"), which could cause mayhem on the decks of a small ship.

top: *With its short barrel, this Belgian flintlock pistol would have been easily stuffed into a belt.*

above: *In the packed melee of hand-to-hand combat, swords would be replaced by shortswords or stabbing daggers.*

Arming for effectiveness

The ferocity of hand-to-hand fighting at sea is captured in this account of Blackbeard's last fight: *"Maynard and Teach themselves begun the fight with their swords, Maynard making a thrust, the point of his sword went against Teach's cartridge box, and bended it to the hilt. Teach broke the guard of it, and wounded Maynard's fingers but did not disable him, whereupon he jumped back and threw away his sword and cut Teach's face pretty much; in the interim both companies engaged in Maynard's sloop, one of Maynard's men being a Highlander, engaged Teach with his broad sword, who gave Teach a cut on the neck, Teach saying, Well done lad; the Highlander replied, If it be not well done, I'll do better. With that he gave him a second stroke, which cut off his head, laying it flat on his shoulder."*

Gunnery was used only as a last resort. Even small trading vessels carried artillery pieces (guns or cannons; a cannon referred only to a specific size and type of ordnance). The frequent warfare of the 17th and 18th centuries meant that arming a vessel was vital, and also meant that most sailors were skilled in firing them.

A four-wheeled truck carriage used a simple elevating system and wooden spikes to aim the gun at sea, and equipment such as worms, rammers, and sponges were kept beside the guns, ready for action when required. A four-pounder, the typical gun size on a pirate sloop, could fire a roundshot about 1,000 yards (914m). In addition to roundshot, which damaged the hull, chain shot (or bar shot) was fired at the enemy's rigging, which tore apart the sails and made it impossible to escape. At close range, grapeshot was used, designed to cut down the enemy crew.

Knowing what ammunition to load and when to load it was vital to success in sea warfare and reduced damage to the potential prize. Parsimonious with their ordnance, pirates used gunfire sparingly; in most cases chasing shots or warning shots were sufficient to halt the prize, ready for capture and boarding.

Woodes Rogers

THE BAHAMIAN GOVERNOR

Finding that the business of privateering in the English Channel was drying up, Woodes Rogers sailed for more exotic climes in the Pacific. The privateer then turned pirate hunter and set his sights on cleaning up the pirate haven of New Providence.

right: *Woodes Rogers in earlier and less respectable days directs crewmen to frisk Spanish ladies for their jewelry after successfully taking the port of Guayaquil in Ecuador in 1709. Rogers was unusual in that he attacked the Spanish on the Pacific seaboard of the Americas, only turning to more traditional waters for British privateers when he turned pirate hunter and became governor of the Bahamas.*

Woodes Rogers was born in Poole, on England's southern coast. His father—a merchant and a ship owner—moved the family to the seaport of Bristol, where Woodes later married the daughter of a naval officer. In time, Woodes took his father's place in the business. Part of the shipping business owned privateering vessels that preyed on French shipping in the waters of the English Channel and the Caribbean.

As prizes became harder to capture, Rogers looked elsewhere to find a profit. Emboldened by tales of buccaneering activity in the Pacific during the late 17th century, he proposed cruising the Pacific coast of South America. The family teamed up with other backers to fit out two 300-ton (272-tonne) privateers, the *Duke* commanded by Rogers and the *Duchess* commanded by Stephen Courtney. The former buccaneer and scientist William Dampier served as pilot due to his experience of the coast. Rogers was probably considered the rich owner rather than a sea captain, but he proved an excellent commander and a skilled seaman, and his crew came to respect him.

The two ships rounded Cape Horn during January 1709 and, in February, they anchored in the waters of Juan Fernandez Island, only to find the castaway Alexander Selkirk, who had been marooned there for four years. He was the figure on whom Robinson Crusoe was based.

Keeping away from land, the privateers sailed up the South American coast and captured several Spanish prizes as they headed north. In May, Rogers turned his sights on the city of Guayaquil, Equador, which he captured and held to ransom. The privateers cruised on up to the Californian coast, aiming to ambush the annual Manila galleons sailing from the Philippines to Mexico. In January 1710 they attacked two galleons and captured one but were driven off by the second, larger galleon.

The ships continued sailing west, to arrive in Bristol in October 1711 after circumnavigating the world. Rogers made a fortune on the enterprise and published an account of his travels, but financial mismanagement at home forced him to declare bankruptcy. From 1713 he commanded a slave ship sailing between Indonesia and Africa.

Governor Rogers

In 1717 government pressure forced the landowners of the Bahamas to appoint Rogers as the new governor of the islands. Rogers and the British government knew the islands were a haven for lawlessness, and the establishment of any kind of authority would be an extremely hazardous undertaking. Apart from a naval escort that left soon after its arrival in New Providence, Rogers and

his financial backers paid for their enterprise out of their own pockets.

The new governor arrived in August 1718, escorted by three small Royal Naval warships, a frigate, and two sloops. Only Charles Vane resisted the arrival, sending a fireship against the frigate and firing on it as he escaped. The worst pirates had already left or would sneak away over the next few days. The rest promised to give up piracy in return for a pardon, and even cheered Rogers when he stepped ashore. Over 600 were pardoned, including Benjamin Hornigold and Henry Jennings, and some even helped Rogers to defend the island against Spanish or pirate attack by forming a militia and an anti-piracy squadron.

When the naval squadron left, many former pirates departed to revert to their old ways, but a mass-hanging of turncoat ex-pirates in December 1718 and a bungled Spanish attack the following year helped to unite the colony. By 1721, with no further support forthcoming from Britain, Rogers and his family returned to London, where he was imprisoned for debt. He was freed after a lengthy appeal and a salary was paid to him that allowed his return to New Providence for a second term. His attempts to improve the agricultural production of the islands came to nothing, and he died there in 1732.

Despite all his other achievements, Woodes Rogers is best remembered as a pirate hunter. Almost single-handedly, he cleaned up the Bahamas pirate haven and greatly contributed to the end of the Golden Age of Piracy.

New Providence

HOME OF NOTORIOUS PIRATES

Just about every famous pirate of the Golden Age used New Providence as a base at some point in their career, until privateer turned pirate hunter Captain Woodes Rogers was appointed governor, with a mission to clean up the island.

In 1716 the pirate Henry Jennings sailed into the anchorage off the village of Nassau, the main settlement on the island of New Providence in the center of the Bahamas. What he found was a perfect haven for pirates, with a harbor deep enough for small ships but too shallow for warships, a good supply of food and water, and high hills to provide lookout points. A number of pirates had already discovered the anchorage, and for a few hectic years in the second decade of the 18th century it was the most bustling hotbed of pirate activity in the Americas.

New Providence contained no native population by the late 17th century. The land area was about 60 square miles (155km^2), barely enough to support a small settlement. Most land-owners lived on Eleuthera, further to the east. Until the arrival of the British-appointed governor in 1718, governors were appointed by these land-owners.

Following the closing of Port Royal to buccaneers, a handful settled on New Providence during the 1680s, but their settlement was destroyed by a Spanish punitive expedition in 1684. Other English buccaneers moved there in 1698 from Tortuga. Pirates occasionally used the islands as a marketplace during the next decade, despite frequent Spanish attacks.

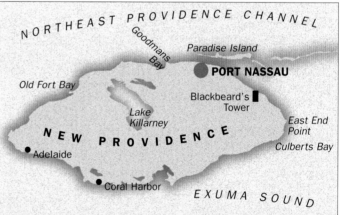

By 1704 the settlement at Nassau was all but abandoned, and the governor abandoned the fort there. The end of the War of the Spanish Succession in 1714 meant that many privateers turned to piracy, and New Providence became a natural haven for them.

It was close to major trade routes, and favorable winds allowed an easy passage to these hunting grounds. The natural harbor noted by Jennings allowed the safe anchorage of hundreds of small ships. It offered fresh water, timber, and a number of wild animals. This refuge became

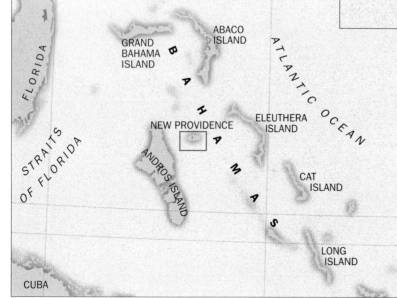

increasingly popular with pirates, and as the capital of the British Bahamas lacked a governor, there was no central authority to curb the growth in pirates using the port.

Rogers breaks up pirate ranks

By 1717 over 500 pirates used the island as a base, serving in a score of ships, mainly sloops and brigantines. The patrons of the makeshift shanty taverns of Nassau would have read like a veritable pirates "Who's Who" in late 1717 and early 1718, men like Benjamin Hornigold, Charles Vane, Henry Jennings, "Calico" Jack Rackham, Edward Teach (Blackbeard), and Samuel Bellamy.

Traders and merchants accompanied the pirates, and the settlement of Nassau blossomed into a freewheeling market in contraband goods, slaves, and liquor. The few shacks of Nassau town were augmented by a village of tents constructed from sails and spars. Shipwrights earned a wage repairing ships or converting them into pirate ships, while armorers repaired guns and swords, and remounted artillery on new carriages. The island economy thrived through trade with

the pirates, until news of the pirate haven reached the authorities in London.

The British Government decided to break up the pirates' nest and restore its authority. The newly appointed governor of the Bahamas, Captain Woodes Rogers, arrived in August 1718, escorted by three Royal Naval warships. Many of the pirates fled. Charles Vane fired on the governor; other pirates such as Jennings, Hornigold, and Rackham gave up their piratical careers, at least for a while. Rogers even appointed Hornigold as a pirate hunter, and a mass pirate hanging in December 1718 showed that the governor was serious.

Legal authority was there to stay, and the days of New Providence as a pirate haven were over. Without piracy, the island returned to being a Bahamian backwater. Although Rogers continued to try and develop the Bahamas, New Providence never regained the economic vibrancy of its pirate heyday. Rogers died in Nassau in 1732. Today, Nassau thrives on its piratical history, and museums, bars, and restaurants all over New Providence bear testimony to the strong links the island has with its past.

above: *Rogers was successful in turning New Providence from piracy. Here he is seen in a painting by William Hogarth with his family, as his son proudly shows his father a plan of burgeoning Port Nassau (visible in the background). In reality, events proved less happy for the new British acquisition.*

PERSIAN
GULF

STRAIT OF HORMUZ

Muscat

GULF OF OMAN

ARABIA

Jedda Mecca

RED SEA

Mocha

GULF OF ADEN

AFRICA

ZANZIBAR

SEYCHELLES

COMORO
ISLANDS

RANTER BAY

ST. MARY'S ISLAND

MADAGASCAR

MAURITIUS
RÉUNION ISLAND

St. Augustine Port Dauphin

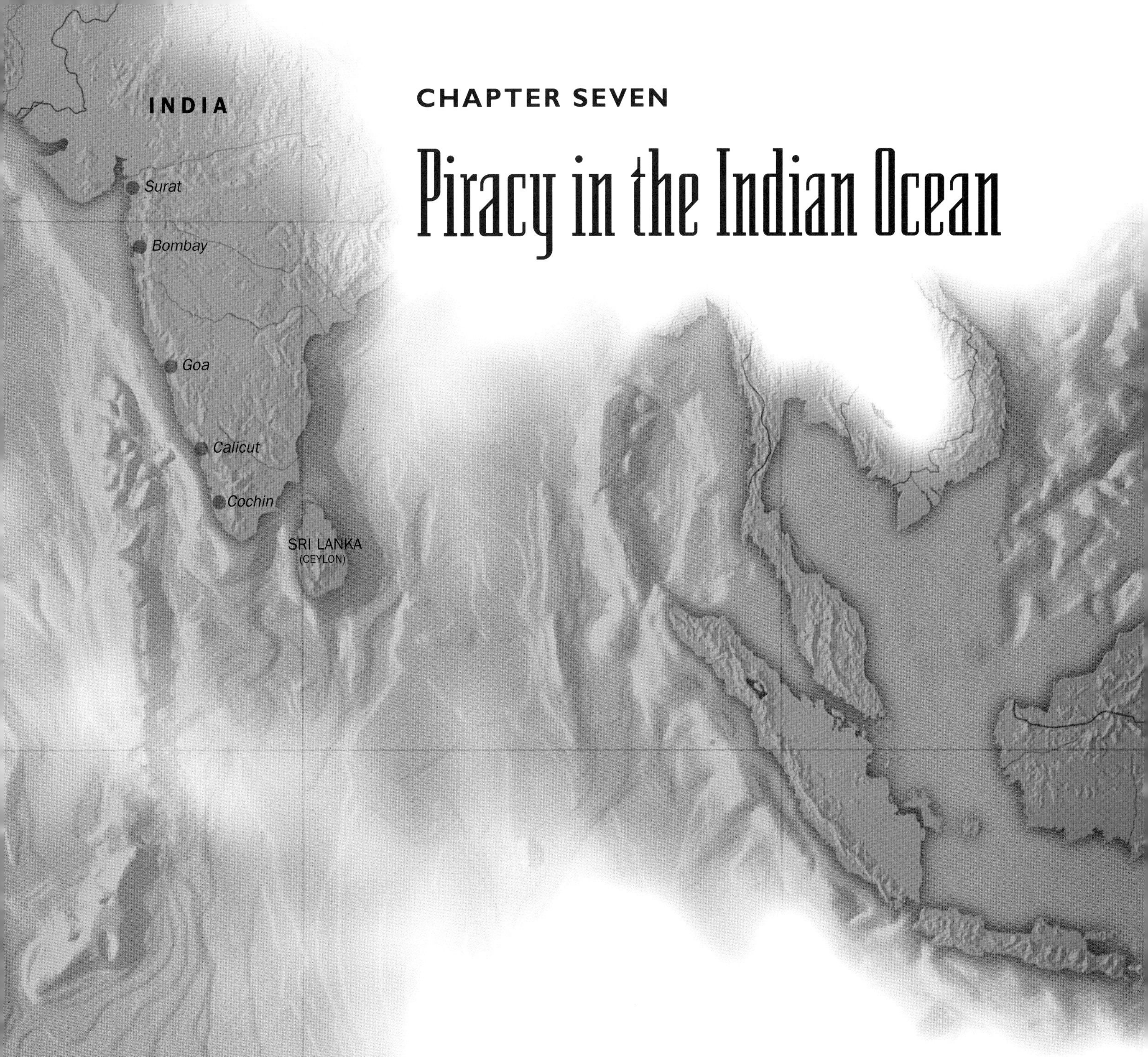

Surat

Bombay

Goa

Calicut

Cochin

SRI LANKA
(CEYLON)

INDIAN OCEAN

CHAPTER SEVEN

Piracy in the Indian Ocean

During the last decades of the 17th century, pirates from Europe and the Americas entered the warm waters of the Indian Ocean and found it a perfect hunting ground. Indian and Arab ships sailed along the ocean's northern shores carrying a wealth of potential plunder. The richest prizes afloat were to be found in Indian waters, and of these the most lucrative were the East Indiamen, trading ships that brought the wealth of the East to the markets of Europe. Pirates who preyed on the ships that crossed this rich ocean included such notorious characters as Henry Every, William Kidd, and Thomas Tew. Their ranks also included the less well known but far more successful Angria family of pirates from India. For a period of 30 years the Indian Ocean was a hotbed of piratical activity, producing some of the most enduring pirate legends.

ollowing the return of Portuguese navigator Vasco da Gama from India in the late 15th century, a new sea route was opened between India and Europe, via the African coast. As a consequence, Europeans expanded their sphere of influence into the Indian Ocean in the 16th century, which meant that the Arab monopoly of land caravans was challenged by faster and more cost-effective maritime trade routes.

During the 16th and early 17th century the Portuguese dominated these sea routes, but by the mid-17th century Dutch and English merchant ships also made regular voyages. The traders brought European cloth, manufactured goods, and precious metals to exchange for spices, silk, and porcelain. Mercantile companies flourished, so that by the end of the 17th century the English East India Company had established itself in India, and their Dutch rivals controlled Far Eastern business through trading settlements in Indonesia. The Portuguese had lost their monopoly and found themselves restricted to a minor role.

The end of buccaneering in the Caribbean led to an increase in the number of pirates looking elsewhere for rich pickings. One such area was the west coast of Africa, where the slave trade was in its heyday. By 1690 a Portuguese monopoly along the slaving coast had been broken open, allowing an influx of English and French slavers. The English even operated the barbaric trade through the medium of a government-sanctioned organization, the Royal African Company.

Pirates became an increasingly prevalent threat along the West African coast, despite naval patrols and the fortification of slave-trading stations. It was only a matter of time before these pirates from the Americas and Europe ventured around the Cape of Good Hope and into the warm waters of the Indian Ocean.

A sea of pirate potential
Piracy was no new phenomenon to the region. Long before the first trading contacts between Europe and India, piracy was commonplace in many parts of the Indian Ocean. Pirates operated along the western coast of India and along the coast of Arabia and Persia. The Indian Moghul Empire patrolled the waters of the northern Indian Ocean with heavily armed warships and war galleys, while Arab ports maintained their own naval patrols. These measures were insufficient to quash the constant piratical activity, and the arrival of European and American

below: While pirates never made others walk the plank, abandoning crew members or captains on deserted islands or stretches of coast was a more common form of punishment— "Marooned." Oil painting by Howard Pyle.

1498	1591	1592–98	1595	1600	1602	1645	1646
vasco da Gama becomes the first person to make a return voyage from Europe to India.	Spanish and Portuguese mercenaries destroy the Songhay Empire of West Africa.	Korea is devastated by Japanese invasion.	The East Indies are colonized by the Dutch.	The English East India Company is formed. Rum is invented by the Spanish in Barbados.	The Dutch East India Company is formed.	Abel Tasman discovers New Zealand while circumnavigating Australia.	The Bahamas are colonized by the English.

pirates exacerbated the situation.

By 1690 the great Moghul Empire was gripped by internal disputes and warfare, and its control of the region's sea lanes was becomingly even less effective. Although Indian and Arab maritime trade thrived, the ability to protect shipping declined. This was the situation that faced the first pirates to round the Cape of Good Hope, and they saw it as a golden opportunity.

Pirates such as Henry Every and Thomas Tew preyed on this shipping with great success and, for about 20 years, European pirates controlled the waters of the Indian Ocean. The large island of Madagascar became an ideal pirate base. It was well placed to intercept both local shipping and that of the European East Indies traders, some of the richest prizes afloat.

Attacks on the East India Company's ships by pirates such as William Kidd and Edward England caused an outcry in London that led to the introduction of maritime convoys and an increase in naval patrols. By 1720 the pirate threat from European and American rovers had passed, only to be replaced by one that was even more difficult to contain. Political turmoil in India allowed adventurers to

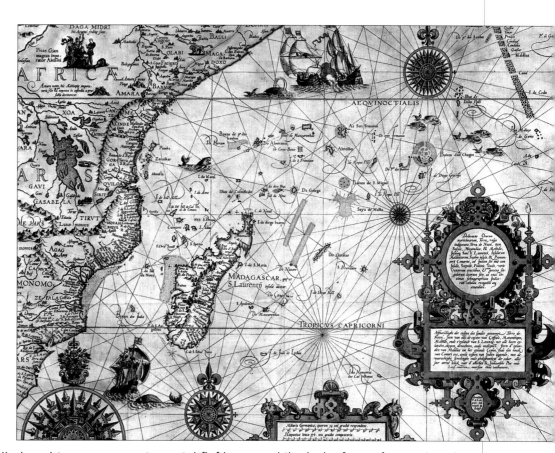

carve out coastal fiefdoms, and the lack of coordinated or centralized political control in India meant that these adventurers were free to turn to piracy.

For the first half of the 18th century, pirates on India's west coast attacked local shipping and vessels of the East India Company with impunity, protected from reprisal by strong fortifications and a fleet of trained pirates. It was only when the East India Company launched a full-scale invasion of these fiefdoms that the scourge of piracy was eliminated from the Indian Ocean.

above: *The Indian Ocean, with the island mass of Madagascar to the left of center. The island provided pirates with a secure base from which to attack ships sailing between India and Europe.*

PIRATE PROFILE

Thomas Tew

THE PIRATE WHO BOUGHT HIS PARDON

A legitimate sea captain from Rhode Island, Tew was a privateer turned pirate. By buying off the right people, he was able to return to the American colonies and socialize with the cream of society. The call of piracy remained, and in 1694, Tew sailed on one last piratical voyage, bound for the Indian Ocean.

Born in Newport, Rhode Island, to a respectable and prosperous family, Thomas Tew moved to Bermuda in 1690 to become a privateer. Britain was at war with France, and those that preyed on French shipping bound for Canada enjoyed a profitable business. Tew joined a

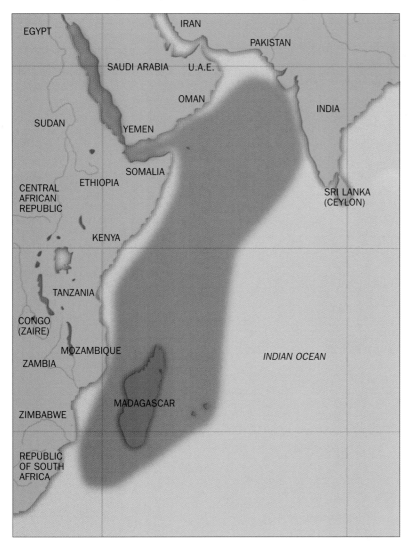

consortium to buy a sloop called the *Amity*, and they fitted her out for a privateering cruise. The consortium appointed Tew captain and he was granted a Letter of Marque by the island's English governor that allowed him to attack French vessels on the high seas and French slaving stations on the African coast.

In 1691 he left Bermuda with another local privateer, bound for Goree on the West African coast. Their target was a French settlement, which would be attacked in conjunction with the Royal African Company of London. The two ships became separated in a storm and, now alone, Tew gathered together the crew and proposed they turn to piracy. It was said he argued that it was better to risk your life for plunder than for government. His crew agreed.

The *Amity* set course for the Cape of Good Hope, then entered the Indian Ocean. Tew stopped briefly at Madagascar before sailing north and into the Red Sea. In the Straits of Bebelmandeb he fell upon an Arab merchant ship, which was captured without any pirate casualties. The haul was impressive; enough to ensure a share of 3,000 English pounds per head, with a larger portion reserved for Tew and his Bermudan backers.

In late 1693 the *Amity* again stopped in Madagascar and, according to Johnson's *A General History of Pirates*, Tew met the French pirate, Misson. They founded the colony of Libertaria, a form of pirate Utopia. Johnson described it as a fortified harbor, with a marketplace, houses, and docks. The society at Libertaria was an egalitarian one, where all men were regarded as equal. However appealing, there is no evidence that either Misson or Libertaria ever existed, and Johnson's

(Map labels: EGYPT, IRAN, PAKISTAN, SAUDI ARABIA, U.A.E., OMAN, INDIA, SUDAN, YEMEN, SOMALIA, SRI LANKA (CEYLON), CENTRAL AFRICAN REPUBLIC, ETHIOPIA, KENYA, TANZANIA, CONGO (ZAIRE), MOZAMBIQUE, ZAMBIA, INDIAN OCEAN, MADAGASCAR, ZIMBABWE, REPUBLIC OF SOUTH AFRICA)

literary purpose may have been to underline the leveling nature of pirate society.

The true story

What is known is that by April 1694 Tew had returned to Newport, Rhode Island, where he paid off his crew, sold the *Amity*, and went to live ashore. During his sojourn in New England, Tew visited New York and met Benjamin Fletcher, the English governor. Fletcher described Thomas Tew as "agreeable and companionable." After several months, Tew decided to return to the Indian Ocean for another cruise, and Fletcher willingly provided Letters of Marque and, possibly, financial backing.

In November 1694, Tew left in a new ship that he had also named *Amity*, accompanied by two other privateers turned pirates: Thomas Wake and William Want. Want had served with Tew on the previous voyage and was apparently a trusted associate. Tew stopped again in Madagascar, and for the next few seasons cruised independently, in association with his two fellow New Englanders, or as part of a pirate squadron. It has also been claimed that he operated alongside Henry Every.

Certainly by 1696 he was regarded as a notorious pirate. In the warrant issued by King William III to Captain William Kidd in January of that year, Thomas Tew (written as "Too") was specifically named as a pirate and, as a pirate-hunter, Kidd was told to seek him out.

Tew's activities are unclear during this period, but it was probably in June 1695 that he entered his old hunting ground of the Red Sea, where he attacked an Arab vessel. Unlike previous prizes, it put up resistance, and Tew was hit by a cannon ball that ripped open his abdomen,

mortally wounding him. His crew were captured and, although their fate has not yet been uncovered, they were undoubtedly executed by the victors.

Tew was one of the archetypal romantic pirates: dashing, successful (for a time), and able to cheat the gallows through death in action. Like his contemporary Henry Every, Tew's career served to encourage others to follow in piratical footsteps.

above: *Mixing with the cream of colonial society— in this picture by Howard Pyle, the affable Thomas Tew fascinates New York's Governor Fletcher with tales of his adventures.*

William Kidd

THE UNLUCKIEST PIRATE

Captain Kidd is known less for piratical success than for his fate. Kidd was an energetic privateer who was given secret funding to engage in semi-legal privateering. When he turned to piracy the powerful backers turned against him. What followed was the most famous pirate trial in history.

above right: *The only known portrait of William Kidd, probably painted when he was a prosperous privateering captain.*

William Kidd is best remembered as a failure, a pirate who was caught, tried, and executed for his crimes. He only made one privateering voyage tainted by piratical acts, and took only one significant prize. This was enough to cause his arrest and trial, which was surrounded by a major political scandal. His deeds were completely overshadowed by the notoriety surrounding his case.

Kidd was born in Scotland, possibly in Greenock. Although details are vague, he almost certainly spent 20 years as a seaman before his first historical appearance in 1689. In that year he served on a privateer operating in the Caribbean. Kidd helped to steal the vessel and sailed it to Nevis. Elected as captain, he renamed the ship *Blessed William*, probably after the new Protestant English king, William III. Soon after, the crew decided to turn pirate and abandoned Kidd.

He traveled to New York, where he married and possibly engaged in more privateering. In 1695 Kidd sailed to England, hoping to win more lucrative privateering contracts. In London he met Richard, Earl of Bellamont, the new Governor of New York and Massachusetts. Bellamont talked Kidd into a scheme involving semi-legal privateering, where Kidd would captain a newly built privateer and his actions would produce a healthy profit for Bellamont and other financial backers, mostly government politicians.

The 300-ton (272-tonne), 34-gun privateer *Adventure Galley* was purchased and fitted out in London with oars as well as sails, hence its name. A Letter of Marque was signed by William III, allowing Kidd to attack pirates and any French he encountered in the Indian Ocean. It was implied that the backers would turn a blind eye to the occasional piratical act if it produced a profit, a small recompense as

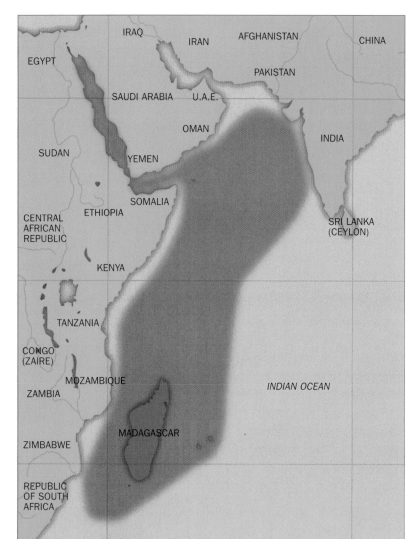

left: *The Adventure Galley was built at the Deptford shipyards in London in 1695. As an ocean-going vessel she was unusual in having oars. The cutaway drawing shows the below-decks construction.*

the fiscal constraints of the contract meant that Kidd would otherwise see little profit. The restrictive terms strongly influenced Kidd's future actions.

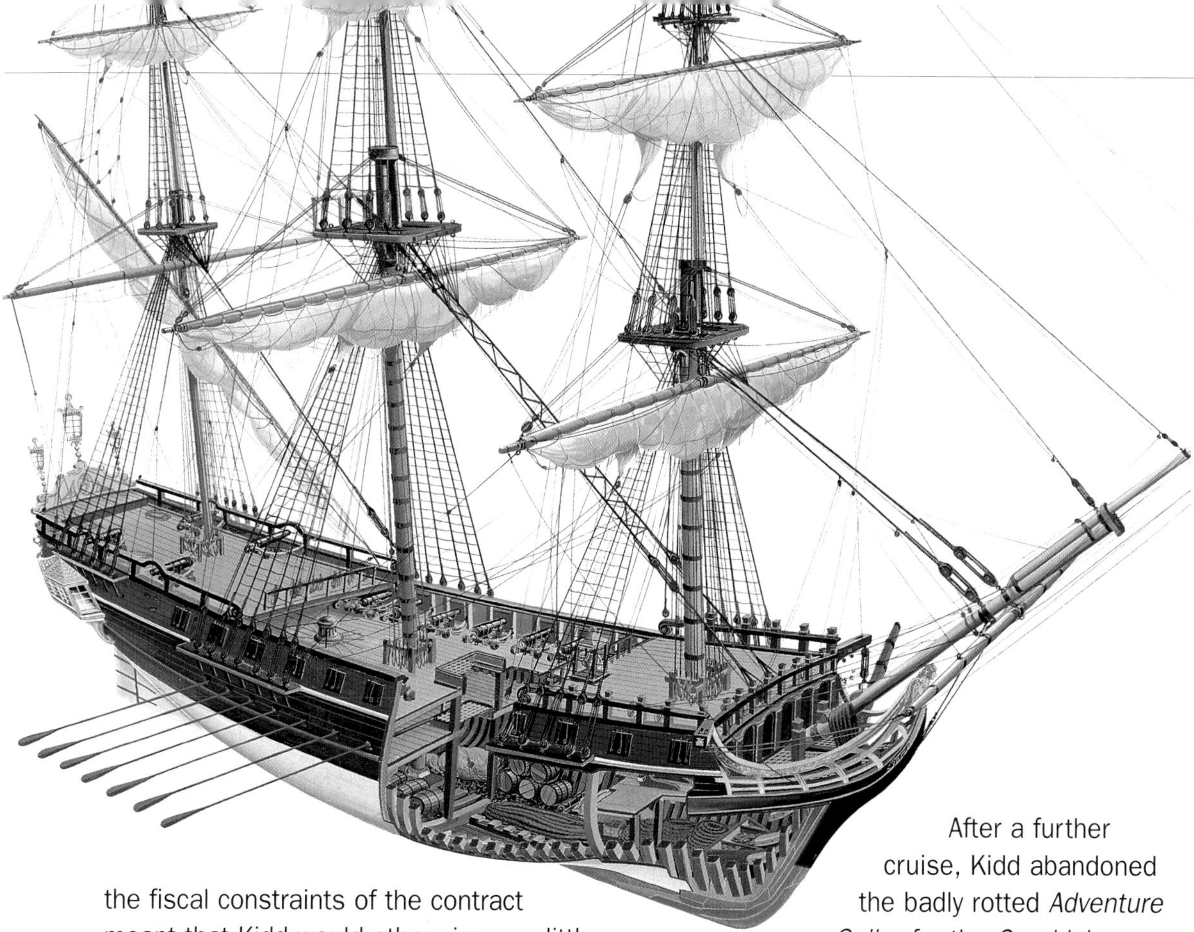

A series of failures

Adventure Galley sailed for New York in May 1696 to sign on a crew of experienced privateers, then crossed the Atlantic to the Cape of Good Hope and the Indian Ocean. In April 1697 Kidd stopped at Madagascar, where he quickly decided to turn to pirate rather than hunt them down as arranged. In August he attacked an East India Company ship in the Red Sea but was driven off. Another unsuccessful skirmish with Portuguese warships sapped the morale of his crew and, after snapping up a small Anglo-Indian prize, Kidd withdrew to the Laccadive Islands for repairs.

He returned to sea in November 1697, but avoided a fight with another East Indiaman. Another evasive encounter resulted in an argument between Kidd and the gunner, William Moore. It ended by Kidd hitting the seaman with a bucket, killing him. After capturing three small prizes off the Indian coast, in January 1698 Kidd captured the *Queddah Merchant* with a lucrative cargo. The East India Company forced the government to brand Kidd as a pirate—a pardon was now impossible.

After a further cruise, Kidd abandoned the badly rotted *Adventure Galley* for the *Queddah Merchant*, which was renamed the *Adventure Prize*. Kidd gave up the cruise and sailed to Boston, where he tried to arrange a pardon with Governor Bellamont. Instead, Bellamont had him arrested and sent to London to stand trial. Rumors that Kidd buried his plunder on Long Island before sailing to Boston may be accurate, although Bellamont probably recovered the goods after Kidd was arrested.

In early 1700, Kidd was thrown into prison in London. While the opposition tried to make Kidd name his political backers and testify against them, his backers conveniently "lost" all the incriminating documents and so prevented a political scandal. To avoid further embarrassment, Kidd was speedily tried, convicted of the murder of William Moore, and hanged at Execution Dock in London's Wapping on May 23, 1701. His body was then hung in a cage on the banks of the River Thames, as a warning to would-be pirates. A victim of miscalculation and intrigue, Captain Kidd is perhaps one of the unluckiest pirates of his era.

below: *"Captain Kidd." Watercolor by Howard Pyle. The artist's pirate is a more demonic figure than the one opposite.*

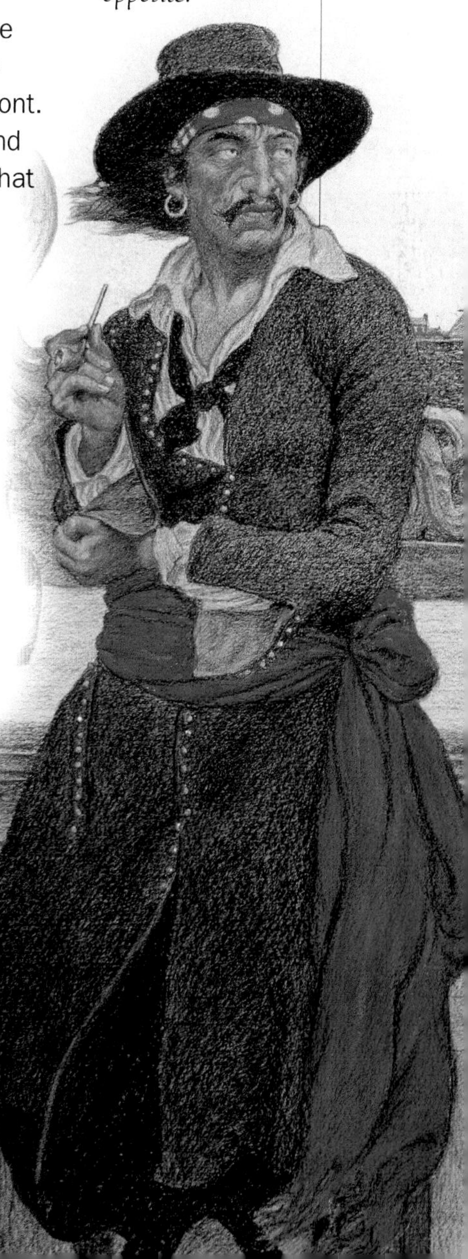

Henry Every

THE PIRATE WHO KNEW WHEN TO STOP

A rare breed among pirates, Henry Every knew when to change his ways. After capturing what was probably the richest pirate plunder in history, Every disappeared without trace to live off his loot.

above right:

Henry Every, as depicted in Johnson's "A General History of Pirates." He is shown as a great pirate "nabob," complete with slave and his own pirate fort.

H enry Every (or Avery) is often seen as the ultimate successful pirate: he captured the richest prize of his day, eluded the authorities, and lived to tell the tale. He became the subject of a play, *The Successful Pyrate*, and provided inspiration for others. Above all, unlike Thomas Tew and other contemporaries, he knew when to stop.

Every's early life remains shrouded in mystery, although he has been described as an unlicensed slave-trading captain of the

early 1690s. Until the end of that decade the Royal African Company held a monopoly on this profitable trade, but interlopers who broke slave-trading laws could reap immense profits. By 1694 Every had apparently abandoned slave trading, and—although rumors of an early privateering career based in the Bahamas have no proven basis—by June he was serving as first mate on a privateer named the *Charles*, licensed by the Spanish to operate against the shipping of the French colony of Martinique, in the West Indies.

When the captain was drunk, Every led a mutiny and the crew took over the ship, renaming her the *Fancy*, with Every as her new captain. The *Fancy* was an ideal pirate ship, designed as a fast privateer and armed with 46 guns. The pirates crossed the Atlantic to the African coast, then rounded the Cape of Good Hope and entered the rich waters of the Indian Ocean. North of Madagascar, Every captured four vessels, including a French pirate vessel, and returned home with his spoils.

The three other prizes were English. Every wrote an astonishing letter, which he gave to a London-bound ship, and it was

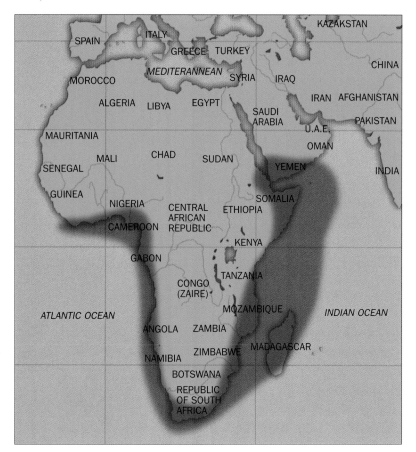

published in the newspapers. In it, Every claimed that he had no hostile intentions toward English or Dutch ships, but hinted that "my men are hungry, stout and resolute, and should they exceed my desire I cannot help myself." It was probably designed to be a bargaining point if ever he was captured, and he concluded with the phrase, "as yet an Englishman's friend, Henry Every."

Ransacking the Indian treasure fleet

In 1695 he sailed up the African coast and into the Red Sea, where he found many other pirates. Every forged an alliance and formed them into a pirate squadron powerful enough to intercept the well-armed Indian treasure fleets that sailed between India and the Middle East. The pirates lay in wait for the annual treasure fleet that was due to return to India from Arabia and that would be carrying gold, silver, and jewels, which had earlier been exchanged for Indian or Oriental silks and spices.

When they saw the pirates, the Indian ships fled. Nightfall covered their escape, but Every was fortunate that when dawn broke he found two of the Indian treasure ships within reach. The smaller of the two, *Fateh Mohammed*, was quickly overcome, but the larger *Gang-i-sawai* only surrendered after a brutal fight. The survivors were tortured and killed to reveal hidden caches of treasure, and women were raped, a brutality fueled by the religious and racial differences between the pirates and the Indians.

Every and his crew found they had captured the fleet's main treasure ships, owned by the Grand Moghul himself, containing over £600,000 of gold, silver, and jewels (approximately $105m today). Each pirate in the fleet received a share of over £1,000 ($176,000), with a larger share going to Every and his own crew.

The allied pirate fleet disbanded and the *Fancy* sailed back to the Caribbean.

In the Bahamas, the governor offered Every protection (in return for a bribe), and the crew were paid off and dispersed. Many returned to England, where several were caught and hanged, but Every sailed for Ireland, then vanished. His subsequent life remains a mystery, but it was thought he was able to retire into obscurity with his wealth. Known as the "Arch Pirate" or by his nickname of "Long Ben," Every is the only pirate who survived to live off his ill-gotten gains. As such, he was one of the most successful pirates of them all.

below: *Henry Every is shown with his ship the Fancy in the background, locked in her fight with the Moghul treasure ship Gang-i-sawai. Its capture resulted in one of the greatest pirate hauls in history.*

Edward England

THE SOFT-HEARTED PIRATE

Driven from the Bahamas when a British governor arrived, Edward England sailed to the Indian Ocean. Although a brave and skillful, he made the mistake of being soft-hearted toward his enemies. For his kindness, his crew marooned him on a deserted island.

Although fierce in battle and a skilled ship captain, Edward England's weaknesses went against the vicious standards of his profession. He was a moderately successful pirate but lost his ship and crew for showing leniency to the sailors he captured. He ended his days starving to death in the slums of Madagascar, a miserable end to a chivalrous man.

Like many pirates, his origins are obscure, but he was probably born in Ireland as Edward Seegar. As a seaman, he served on a trading sloop based in Jamaica and pursued a legitimate career as a sailor. This ended in 1717, when his vessel was captured by the pirate Christopher Winter.

above right:

Edward England, shown with the battle between his ship the Fancy and the East Indiaman Cassandra in the background. Following a brutal fight, the Captain of Cassandra beached his ship and his crew escaped.

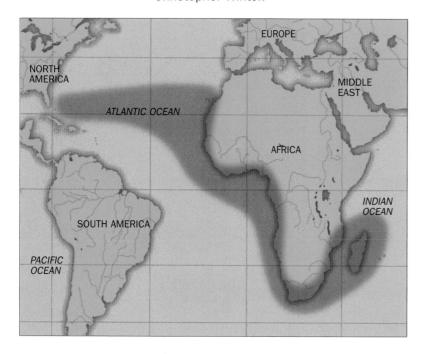

The pirates returned to New Providence in the Bahamas with their prize and, electing to join them, Seegar changed his name to England in an effort to cover his tracks. He served under Winter until July 1718, when Governor Woodes Rogers arrived in New Providence to drive out the pirates. England escaped in a captured sloop and set out on his own piratical career with a new crew.

England crossed the Atlantic and cruised off the West African coast from the Azores to the Cape Verde Islands and captured several prizes. One of these was a larger vessel called the *Pearl*, which England took as his own flagship, while keeping the sloop as an auxiliary vessel. The pirates continued their cruise off Africa, sailing off the Guinea coast, capturing dozens of prizes. One, the sloop *Victory*, was given to John Taylor, one

of England's crewmen.

The pirates rounded the Cape of Good Hope and sailed into the Indian Ocean, seeking out the rich maritime traffic between India and Europe. Probably in Madagascar they put ashore to careen their vessels and "liv'd there very wantonly for several weeks, making free with the Negroe women." England and Taylor went on to cruise in consort off the northwest coast of India. Again, England moved into one of his prizes, a 34-gun square-rigged ship called the *Fancy*.

A hard-won victory turned sour

England and Taylor returned to Madagascar via Johanna Island, northwest of Madagascar, which was a popular pirate rendezvous. Approaching the harbor on August 27, 1720, England found three ships, one Dutch and two English East Indiamen. The two smaller ships raised anchor and escaped, but *Cassandra*, the more heavily armed East Indiaman, bought time for them by sailing out to engage the *Fancy*. While John Taylor in the *Victory* pursued the fleeing vessels, Edward England in the *Fancy* engaged the *Cassandra*, captained by a Scot called James Macrae, in a brutal sea battle. They apparently pounded each other with broadsides at close range, and the engagement lasted several hours. Both captains and crews displayed enormous determination and bravery, but in the end the better armed pirate ship was clearly getting the best of the engagement. Captain Macrae ran his badly battered ship onto the beach and led his surviving crewmen ashore.

The pirates sent a boat to capture the *Cassandra* and found a cargo reputedly valued at 75,000 English pounds, a sizable fortune in 1720. Macrae and his crew hid ashore for ten days then, short of food and water, they gave themselves up. It was a gamble, since although the *Cassandra* had suffered 37 casualties, over 90 pirates were killed on the *Fancy*. The pirates might have been celebrating for days, but they might also have been seeking revenge for their lost shipmates. After a lengthy argument between England and John Taylor, England's lenient nature won out, and he set Macrae and his crew free.

In retaliation, Taylor fomented rebellion among the pirate crew and led a successful revolt against England, who was removed from his position. They marooned him on a small island off the coast of Madagascar, along with three loyal supporters, in early 1721. The castaways eventually reached Madagascar, where England was reduced to begging for food, and where he died soon afterward.

133

Kanhoji Angria

THE DYNASTY OF INDIAN PIRATE KINGS

An African pirate who established a pirate kingdom on India's west coast, Angria and his son preyed on the English East India Company for over 30 years, terrorized the port of Bombay, and extorted protection money from everyone who crossed their path.

above right:

For pirates, an East Indiaman was a more valuable prize on the voyage east because it would be laden with gold and silver to buy cargo, which was more difficult to handle and sell if captured on the homeward trip.

At the start of the 18th century the Indian Moghul Empire was in disarray as it fragmented under political and military pressures. Into the vacuum came a dynasty of pirate rulers who, for half a century, challenged both the English East India Company and fellow pirates from Europe and America.

Kanhoji Angria was an African Muslim who gained control of a long stretch of India's western seaboard to the south of Bombay. From coastal strongholds and small offshore islands, he sent large fleets to attack coastal shipping and, where possible, to capture East Indiamen. The Angrian fiefdom attracted adventurers from India and from Europe, and by the 1720s the region played host to hundreds of well-armed pirate craft, whose captains owed allegiance to the Angria family.

Kanhoji Angria established island bases off Bombay—headquarters of the East India Company—and for years terrorized the Indian and British shipping that used the port. His next step was to extort protection money, and even East Indiaman captains were forced to pay the pirates to gain safe access to Bombay.

In 1712 Angria's ships captured the private yacht of the East India Company's Bombay governor and forced him to pay a humiliating ransom to retrieve his vessel. However, the deal also included group protection money for all East India Company ships, and so for the next four years Angria restricted his attacks to Indian shipping.

The activities of Angria and his pirates were considered a major embarrassment to the British, so when a new company governor was appointed in January 1716, British policy changed. Governor Charles Boone ordered that naval resources should gather for an assault on the pirate nest, and in return Angria began to harass British shipping once more. Two company

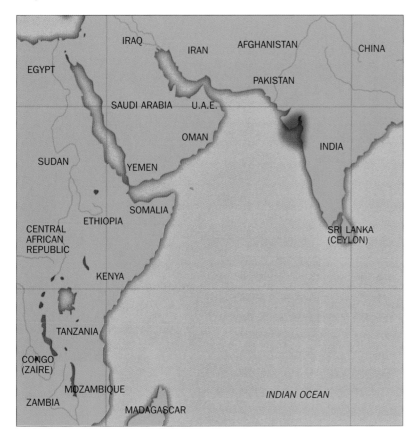

EGYPT
IRAQ
IRAN
AFGHANISTAN
CHINA
PAKISTAN
SAUDI ARABIA
U.A.E.
OMAN
INDIA
SUDAN
YEMEN
SOMALIA
ETHIOPIA
CENTRAL AFRICAN REPUBLIC
SRI LANKA (CEYLON)
KENYA
TANZANIA
CONGO (ZAIRE)
MOZAMBIQUE
INDIAN OCEAN
ZAMBIA
MADAGASCAR

attacks on Angria's island strongholds near Bombay were repulsed, and in late 1716 Angria even blockaded the port, forcing Boone to pay another humiliating ransom.

The Angria clan's continued success

In late 1717 another major British attack on Angria's strongholds was repulsed by gunboats, and the situation reached a stalemate. A Royal Naval squadron was sent to attack Angria in 1721, in conjunction with Portuguese land forces, but they were driven off. (This may be explained partly by the charges of bribery that were later leveled at the British naval commander on his return home.) When Kanhoji Angria died in 1729, his pirate realm was considered unassailable; the perfect pirate haven.

He was succeeded by his two sons, Sumbhaji and Mannaji, who divided their father's territory; Sumbhaji controlled the island strongholds to the north near Bombay, and Mannaji ruled the southern land-based portion. The inevitable power struggle left Sumbhaji in control of everything except a small coastal enclave, which he left to his Mannaji.

Sumbhaji Angria continued his father's policy of harassing shipping around Bombay, although the East India Company was growing stronger and warships frequently escorted their merchant vessels. In 1736 he captured the East Indiaman *Derby*, filled with gold, the richest Indiaman prize ever taken.

When Sumbhaji died in 1743, he was succeeded by his half-brother Toolaji Angria, who stepped up the harassment of British commerce. He attacked East Indiaman convoys and drove off or captured escorting warships and took merchant ship prizes. To the British in the 1750s, the situation was intolerable and, following an alliance with the Indian Maratha Confederacy, an overwhelming land and sea assault was launched on the Angrian strongholds. The pirate strongholds fell one by one, until by February 1756 only Angria's main fortress at Vijayadurg remained, and it too was stormed after a devastating bombardment. Toolaji Angria was captured and imprisoned, his pirate fleet was destroyed, and his treasury shipped to Bombay.

The Angrian pirate dynasty was probably more successful than any other pirate or buccaneer group of the 17th and 18th centuries, and maintained a secure pirate haven for half a century. In the process they repeatedly humiliated the British East India Company, and hindered the spread of British control in India. As such the Angria family are regarded with some national affection in India today.

below: *The Angrian pirates were every bit as cruel as their European counterparts—only more inventive. This book illustration shows the captain of a captured prize being "roasted" on a griddle.*

Madagascar

A PIRATE UTOPIA?

Lying astride the rich trade routes between India, the Middle East, and Europe, the large island of Madagascar was an ideal base for pirates. For a quarter century from the 1680s onward, Madagascar would be a thriving pirate haven, and reputedly was also the home of a social experiment called Libertaria.

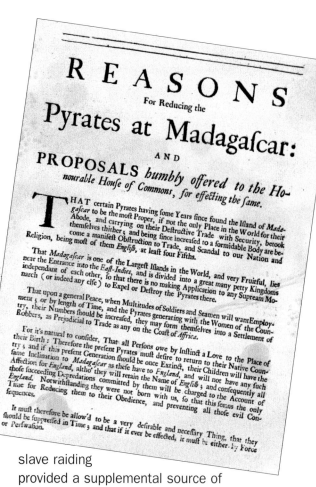

right: *By the first decade of the 18th century, the use of Madagascar as a pirate base became a political issue. Proposals were made to reduce pirate numbers through offers of pardons and by military action.*

This large island, approximately 250 miles (402km) off the East African coast, was ideally located for pirate attacks on the rich shipping of the Indian Ocean. It served as a pirate base throughout the Golden Age of Piracy (1690–1730), where the vastness of the island's interior and the multiplicity of hidden anchorages made the sea raiders feel invulnerable. The island is over 300 miles (483km) wide at its broadest point, and over a thousand miles (1,609km) long; the distance from modern Washington DC to Miami. The native population was scattered and sparse enough for the pirates to disregard them as a threat, and the wildlife and fruit plentiful enough to feed everyone.

Pirate participation in tribal warfare and slave raiding provided a supplemental source of income for Europeans with firearms. Madagascar also provided the first sheltered anchorages in the Indian Ocean after rounding the Cape of Good Hope, so it was a popular watering place for ships bound for India. This meant rich pickings, and the chance of capturing an East Indiaman as a prize. It was also within easy range of the Red Sea, where Arab and Indian maritime traffic yielded a substantial haul of booty.

As the buccaneering era ended in the Caribbean basin in the 1680s, former buccaneers ventured into the Indian Ocean and used bases in northern Madagascar to prey on Indian shipping. By the 1690s pirates were arriving in Madagascar in increasing numbers; men such as Henry Every, William Kidd, Thomas Tew, and Edward England.

Recognized pirate anchorages were established at Ranter Bay (now the Baie d'Antongil), St. Augustine's Bay, and St. Mary's Island, all on the island's east coast, and as well at the nearby but more remote anchorages at Réunion island and Mauritius to the east, and Johanna Island

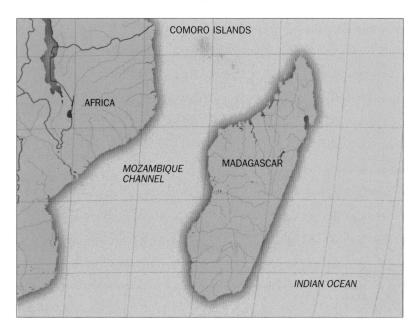

COMORO ISLANDS

AFRICA

MOZAMBIQUE
CHANNEL

MADAGASCAR

INDIAN OCEAN

in the Comoro archipelago to the northwest. St. Mary's Island, in particular, was easily defended, and it was reported that by 1700 the island provided a home for 17 pirate vessels and 1,500 pirates.

Misson's ultimate pirate haven

By 1705 the Madagascar pirates were considered too well entrenched to attack, so the English parliament discussed ways to reduce the threat. Convoy systems were organized, and squadrons of warships patrolled near the main pirate havens. Slowly, these reduced pirate activity in the region; many pirates moved elsewhere or settled on the island and took up farming. Some even went into service with the Angrian pirates of India's west coast. By 1711 it was reported that only 60 or 70 pirates remained on Madagascar.

In *A General History of the Pirates* Charles Johnson relates the tale of French pirate Captain Misson, who established a utopian pirate republic on Madagascar that he called Libertaria. The settlement described by Johnson was an early leveling and egalitarian community, in which pirates and other inhabitants supported the rights of the people, made and enforced their own laws, and

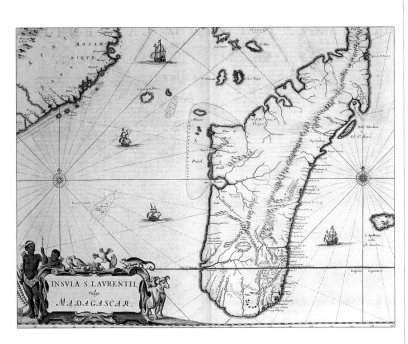

enshrined the concept of liberty. In effect, Libertaria was indeed a utopia built on socialist principles, before the phrase had been invented. Its principal settlement boasted wharves and markets, bars and fine stone houses, and was protected from attack by well-placed stone forts. Wounded pirates were cared for, so that they could die in peace and security, captured slaves were freed, while religious freedom was enjoyed by all.

Unfortunately, neither Captain Misson nor Libertaria existed, and historians such as Christopher Hill argue that Johnson's chapter was a political essay disguised as a pirate history. As such, it traces its roots back to the English Revolution of the mid-17th century and the oppressively harsh conditions faced by early 18th-century seamen.

The reality of pirate life in Madagascar was completely different. Edward England died as a starving beggar in one of its east coast pirate havens, and a report from St. Mary's Island in 1711 stated that the pirates lived in squalor, "most of them very poor and despicable, even to the natives." This was a far cry from any description of a pirate utopia.

above: *During the late 17th and early 18th centuries, Madagascar played host to a band of pirates who used the island as a base. Their main settlement was in the northeast corner of the island mass.*

left: *A pirate and a Madagascar woman in a 19th-century engraving. After piracy ceased to be a lucrative occupation on the island, many pirates either returned to an honest means of living or settled on the island and took local wives.*

Bringing the Pirates to Justice

Most pirates knew that they could not evade justice forever. Although a few notorious pirates such as Henry Every were never caught, most felt the full force of Admiralty law. If caught, pirates could expect a swift trial and a speedy execution. For some, their fate was even worse.

right: *The British frigate HMS Saint Michael was one of many naval ships pressed into service to bring war to the Atlantic pirates. Although she was built in 1669 and would have been long in the tooth by the beginning of the 18th century, the anti-pirate war was so intense that naval authorities were obliged to press older and second-rate ships into the line.*

The excesses of the so-called Golden Age of Piracy (1690–1730) caused a public outcry and an increasingly firm anti-pirate stance by regional governments, major national powers, and navies. In the early part of the "age" several colonial governors along the American Atlantic seaboard and in the Caribbean islands regarded pirates as a useful source of income, bringing captured produce to their markets.

What changed the mind of these colonial leaders was the economic boom that developed following the end of almost constant warfare in 1714. It opened up European and American markets and increased maritime trade almost threefold within 15 years, but a large number of former privateers turned to piracy. When piracy began to hinder the economic development of the American colonies and cut into the profit margins of European merchants and investors, the climate changed.

On both sides of the Atlantic, a growing clamor for anti-piracy legislation and maritime security led to a major clamp-down on piratical activity. A fresh breed of governors, such as Woodes Rogers in the Bahamas and Alexander Spotswood in Virginia, led the way by establishing anti-pirate naval patrols and maintaining a tough judicial line when pirates fell into their hands.

While many of these naval patrols were financed and manned by the colonies themselves, the maritime powers of the world also contributed heavily to this repression of piracy. Britain's Royal Navy was the leading maritime power in the early 18th century and, together with the navies of France, Spain, and Holland, its patrols helped to extinguish piracy in Caribbean waters, then later from the American Atlantic coastline, the west coast of Africa, and the Indian Ocean. A host of major pirate figures fell foul of the patrols, including Blackbeard, Bartholomew Roberts, Stede Bonnet, and "Calico" Jack Rackham.

Caging the dead to protect the living

Apart from increased naval patrols on the high seas and in threatened coastal areas, the institution of convoy systems helped to curb the pirate threat. Convoys were adopted for a number of years by the British in the Indian Ocean and by most nationalities in the Caribbean, where they used the system created by the Spanish treasure fleets. By making piracy too difficult and too dangerous, the occurrences of pirate attacks lessened dramatically.

While a physical naval presence and an increasingly strict anti-pirate policy served to eliminate most pirates from the world's oceans by 1730—with the notable exception of the Far East—a major contribution to the eradication of piracy was the psychological effect this activity had. Most pirates during the Golden Age knew that their run of luck could not go on forever. With the occasional exception of men who knew when to retire or accept a pardon and start a new life, such as Henry Every, almost every pirate met death in battle or on the gallows. The pirate's life was nasty, brutish, and short, and by emphasizing the near certainty of a grisly end ther aurhorities gained a powerful and effective psychological deterrent aimed at seamen who might otherwise have considered a career in piracy.

The policy of hanging pirates *en masse*, and then suspending the bodies of leading pirates in cages to rot away, provided a clear demonstration of the fate that would befall anyone who turned to crime on the sea. Sited as they were at the entrances to ports like London, Charleston, and Port Royal made these cages clearly visible to all passing ships and sailors. The decaying bodies of William Kidd, Jack Rackham, and Charles Vane were a graphic piece of anti-pirate propaganda.

The whole process of the trial and execution of pirates, as well as the frequent grisly abuse of their corpses, was well documented, and attracted a widespread and morbid interest among contemporary observers. The procedure also followed a set pattern, which was designed to obtain the maximum propaganda value from the judicial process and so add to the effectiveness of the deterrent.

The Trial and Execution of Pirates

If convicted, pirates faced almost certain death by execution, which was carried out by different methods according to the customs of the country in which the pirate was tried. No method was pleasant; most were grisly.

below: *The gallows at Wapping, London, where pirates were hanged "above the low water mark."*

Pirates who were caught during the late 17th and early 18th centuries faced the prospect of a highly publicized trial and, if found guilty, almost certainly faced execution by hanging. In England this process took place in a particular manner, explained below, that was later exported throughout the British colonies in the Americas, the West Indies, India, and West Africa. Similar systems were adopted by France and Spain, although certain aspects, such as the type of execution and the increased use of lifetime sentences in slavery, differed from the English judicial model. For example, the Spanish used the garrote, while the French made extensive use of penal service in their colonies.

During the late 17th century it was common that only pirate captains and ringleaders were executed, but throughout the Golden Age of Piracy mass executions of entire crews were frequent, and acted as a warning to others. The largest execution held took place in 1722 at Cape Coast Castle, in West Africa. The crew of Bartholomew Roberts was tried *en masse*, and 54 pirates were executed.

In most countries, trials were conducted according to Maritime or Admiralty law. In England, condemmed pirates were taken from their prison in London to Execution Dock in Wapping, on the banks of the River Thames, where a wooden gallows was built on the foreshore above the low water mark (i.e. within the boundaries of Admiralty law's authority).

After a brief prayer from a chaplain or priest, the pirate was allowed a last speech, and then hanged. The body was left for a day-and-a-half to be washed by the tides "as Admiralty law proscribes," and then buried in an unmarked grave or hung in an iron cage to rot, as a warning. From 1701, Admiralty Courts were established in the English American and Caribbean colonies to oversee all trials involving crimes committed "below the high water mark," extending Admiralty authority, and these followed the same pattern.

A catalog of executions

From 1716 onward, these colonial courts supervised a string of mass pirate executions. Some of the more prominent executions in the Americas included:

Jack Rackham and nine pirates in Kingston, Jamaica (November 1716); 13 pirates from Blackbeard's crew in Williamsburg, Virginia (March 1718); Stede Bonnet and 30 pirates in Charleston, North Carolina (October 1718); eight pirates captured by Woodes Rogers in New Providence, Bahamas (December 1718); Charles Vane and one fellow pirate in Kingston, Jamaica (March 1722); Charles Harris and 25 pirates in Newport, Rhode Island (July 1723); 11 pirates from the crew of George Lowther on Saint Kitts (November 1723); William Fly and two pirates in Boston, Massachusetts (July 1726).

The corpses of more prominent pirates were used as a form of grisly propaganda. Following the "tide washing," the corpse was cut down, tarred, bound in chains, and placed inside an iron cage. This was then hung from a gallows, often located at the entrance to a port, like the shore of the River Thames near London or at Gallows Point outside Port Royal, Jamaica. The body was left to rot inside its cage, a process that sometimes took up to two years, depending on the climate.

This was the fate that befell William Kidd's corpse, "whose body was visible for years after his execution." The sun, rain, and frost rotted the body, and seagulls pecked out its eyes, but the tar and cage kept the bones in place, "as a great terror to all persons from committing ye like crimes." Pirates later said they would sooner die in battle than "be hanged up drying, like Kidd." Without doubt, as a grisly piece of propaganda, it was an effective deterrent to would-be pirates.

By 1730 all of the most notorious pirates and their crews had been hunted down and either killed in action or executed after public trials. The Golden Age of Piracy was effectively ended through a combination of naval patrols and harsh judicial punishment.

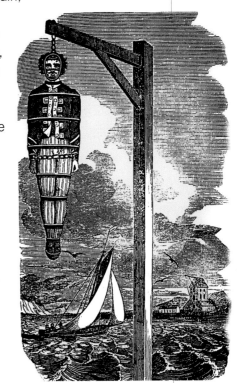

above: After William Kidd was hanged, his body was tarred, and then suspended in a cage on the banks of the Thames Estuary. The body served as a threat to others that they would meet the same fate if they followed in Kidd's footsteps.

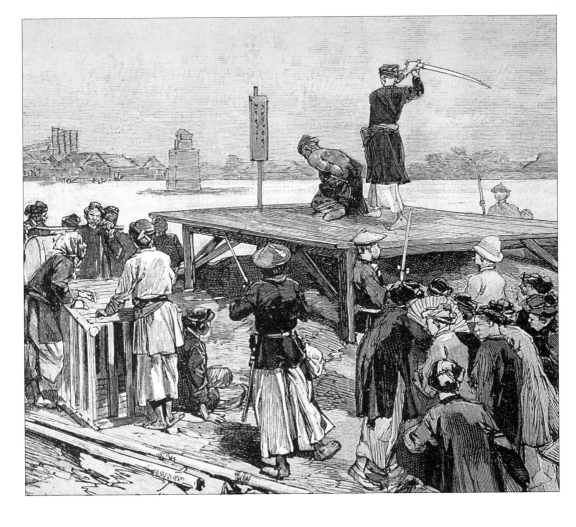

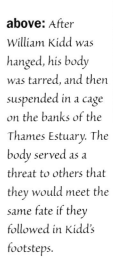

left: Execution styles varied. This illustration shows a pirate of the China Sea facing death by beheading—more merciful than many occidental methods.

CHAPTER EIGHT

The Privateering Era

For centuries privateers were really only legitimized pirates, and their number included Sir Francis Drake and Sir Henry Morgan. Privateering became widespread during the 18th century, when the Atlantic and Caribbean were plunged into a near-constant state of warfare between European powers. The American Revolution provided an opportunity for Colonial seamen to harass British shipping and to reap large financial profits. The War of 1812 fueled this need for privateering, and Americans, using purpose-built vessels, were singularly successful. Privateers needed a war to maintain their legal right to attack shipping, and peace made privateers redundant. Those that refused to stop their attacks became pirates, unprotected by any government.

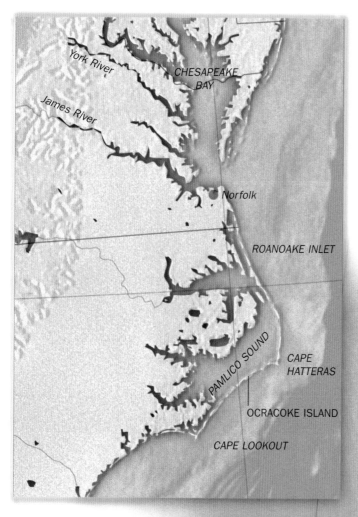

PACIFIC OCEAN

MAINE

Halifax

NEWFOUNDLAND
GRAND BANKS

Salem
Boston
MASSACHUSETTS
NEW YORK
Newport
CAPE COD
LONG ISLAND

New York

PENNSYLVANIA
NEW JERSEY

Baltimore
Washington DC

VIRGINIA

NORTH
CAROLINA

SOUTH
CAROLINA

ATLANTIC OCEAN

Charleston

GEORGIA

New Orleans

FLORIDA

BAHAMAS

GULF OF MEXICO

LEEWARD ISLANDS

Havana

CUBA

DOMINICAN
REPUBLIC
PUERTO RICO
ST. KITTS

HAITI

ISLA DE JUVENTUD
(ISLA DE PINOS)

(HISPANIOLA)

MARTINIQUE

JAMAICA

BARBADOS

WINDWARD ISLANDS

MEXICO

Veracruz

CARIBBEAN SEA

Curaçao

Cartagena

Panama City

THE PRIVATEERING ERA

Privateering was essentially piracy legitimized by the privateer's government. It allowed him to attack the shipping of his nation's enemies at a minimal cost to the government involved. A Letter of Marque was issued that authorized a privateer captain to plunder enemy shipping, and, in return, profits were divided between the owners, the crew, and the government. It was a system that worked well for everyone, apart from the country whose shipping was being attacked.

The word "privateer" was first recorded in the 17th century, but officially-sanctioned pirates had existed for centuries. Sir Francis Drake was a privateer, as was Sir Henry Morgan. While privateering was conducted in European as well as American waters, the regions of the American Atlantic seaboard and the Caribbean proved particularly fertile hunting grounds. Colonial privateers were active against the French from the 1680s, particularly during Queen Anne's War (1701–13), and when peace was declared many privateers turned to piracy.

The great age of privateering began on the resumption of war with France and Spain in the 1740s, and Letters of Marque were issued to hundreds of Colonial privateers. Their main hunting ground was the Caribbean, although they also ventured into the Atlantic. Shipping in the 18th century carried a range of cargoes in American waters. Sugar was shipped either ground or as molasses, while colonial cotton plantations and linen factories ensured a steady textile trade, and spices grown in the Americas were popular in Europe markets. The slave trade still carried its miserable cargo from Africa to the Americas throughout the century. Rum was shipped to Colonial America and England, while gin and wine were imported from Europe. Other European imports included manufactured goods, tools, and weapons. The large variety and volume of maritime trade ensured rich pickings for pirates and privateers.

Enemy turns ally

Following the rebellion of the American colonies in 1775, the United States saw privateers as a means of striking back at the British. While the Royal Navy maintained an overwhelming naval superiority, small privateers could avoid these powerful fleets and cause havoc among British merchant shipping. They

below: *The best privateers were small, fast vessels such as cutters and sloops. "The Privateer Fly." Oil painting by Francis Holman.*

1686	1701–13	1725	c.1730	1739–48	1747	1756–63	1768
Treaty of Whitehall forbids conflict in New World between British and French; privateers flourish.	Queen Anne's War (War of the Spanish Succession).	Danish sailor Vitus Bering discovers the straits separating Russia and the Americas.	End of the "Golden Age of Piracy."	King George's War (War of the Austrian Succession).	John Paul Jones born, a privateer who failed to kidnap Earl of Selkirk in British waters.	Seven Years' War between England and Prussia defeat Austria, France, Russia, and Sweden.	Captain James Cook explores the Pacific Ocean.

were also a lucrative source of revenue, since over 3,000 British ships and their cargoes were captured and brought into American ports during the period.

Apart from long-range raiding by naval commanders, such as John Paul Jones, the Continental Navy was largely unsuccessful in the war and posed no serious threat to the maintenance of British sea power in American waters. However, British naval mismanagement and the temporary superiority of a French fleet helped to seal the fate of the British cause in America during late 1781. The war demonstrated that privateering on a massive scale could provide the US government with an effective commerce-raiding fleet and a healthy source of income, so American policy continued to be supportive of privateering.

The War of 1812 proved the value of this policy, as American ship-owners launched a series of "super privateers," ideally suited to their role of state-sponsored piracy. American privateers continued to hunt down British shipping in the Atlantic, but these ships had the range to extend raids into European waters, the Pacific Ocean, and the Indian Ocean, causing extensive damage to British commerce. The rise of independence movements in Latin America during the second decade of the 19th century led the rebel governments of Mexico and South America to issue hundreds of Letters of Marque, authorizing privateers to attack Spanish shipping.

At the end of the Napoleonic Wars, and with peace declared between Britain and America, the Caribbean was filled with unemployed privateers. While almost all American and European privateers obeyed instructions and curtailed their activities when peace was declared, many Latin American privateers did not, and even expanded their attacks to include non-Spanish shipping. The former enemies united in order to combat what was turning into a new wave of piracy. During the 1820s the British and American navies cleared the seas of these privateers turned pirates, and so ended centuries of piracy, buccaneering, and privateering in the waters of the Americas.

above: *During wartime, privateers tied down valuable naval resources by forcing rival maritime powers to use warships to escort convoys and to hunt down privateers. "HMS Hibernia fighting a privateer, 1814." Oil painting by an unknown artist of the British School.*

1769	1775	1788	1789	1791	1798	1805	1812–15
James Watt patents the steam engine.	Beginning of the American Revolution.	English prisoners arrive at Botany Bay for Australia's first penal colony.	George Washington is made the first United States President.	The Constitution Act divides Canada into French- and English-speaking territories.	The Dutch East India Company goes bankrupt.	The French-Spanish navy is defeated in the Battle of Trafalgar.	War of 1812 between the US and Britain.

French Privateers

War between France and Britain during the 18th century usually led to naval disaster for France. Her only real chance of success was to encourage French privateers to prey on British shipping. For some Frenchmen, such as Robert Surcouf, privateering was a way to settle old scores and generate wealth and advancement.

opposite:

Boardings were uncommon in privateering actions; capturing a victim by threat was considered preferable. "Captain William Rogers capturing the Jeune Richard, 1807." Oil painting by Samuel Drummond.

For much of the 18th century the British Royal Navy carried out a series of large fleet actions against French and Spanish opponents and was consistently victorious. Maintaining a close blockade of enemy coasts and eliminating enemy maritime trade proved to be a winning strategy that led to Britain's complete dominance of the world's oceans by 1800. Faced with this overwhelming history of naval achievement, opponents were forced to rely on raiding commerce to damage their British enemies, rather than through fleet actions. Privateering became a favorite French solution during their frequent wars with the British, and the combination of French settlements in the Caribbean and the vulnerability of British maritime trade in the area made it a particularly attractive option. The 1686 Treaty of Whitehall deemed that conflict in the New World would not lead to war between the two nations, and in effect sanctioned privateering, whether the two countries were at war or not.

The French islands of the Lesser Antilles provided perfect privateer bases during the War of the Austrian Succession (1739–48). French privateers operating in the Caribbean and out of Canadian bases preyed on British shipping, and both the French and Spanish crowns issued Letters of Marque by the hundred. The French fortress of Louisburg protected the French Canadian privateers and provided a safe base from which to attack the shipping of the American colonies.

During the Seven Years' War (1756–63) French privateer raids were so dangerous that they influenced British strategy, which included the decision to capture the privateer havens of Louisburg, Martinique, Guadeloupe, and Dominica. France supported the Americans in their revolution against Britain after 1778, and French privateers benefited from a Royal Navy weakened by cutbacks and inefficiency. British losses from Spanish and French privateers during the Revolutionary War amounted to an estimated 5 percent of her mercantile fleet.

In British-controlled waters

The French port of Dunkirk had been a privateer base for centuries. It served over 60 French privateers sailing under French

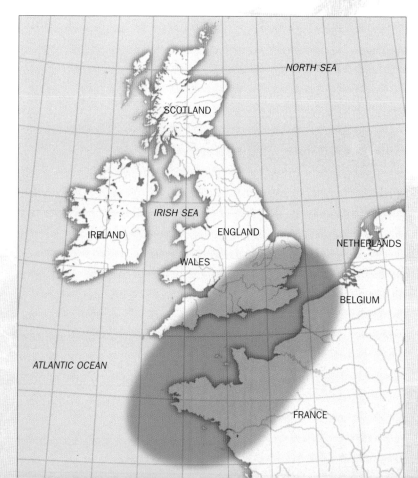

NORTH SEA

SCOTLAND

IRISH SEA

IRELAND

ENGLAND

NETHERLANDS

WALES

BELGIUM

ATLANTIC OCEAN

FRANCE

or American Letters of Marque during the war, and Dunkirk privateers were responsible for the capture of hundreds of British prizes in the waters of the English Channel and the Irish Sea.

The French Revolutionary and Napoleonic War began in 1796, and the French found their harbors blockaded and their navy in poor condition. As the British maintained a strong naval presence in the Caribbean, French privateers looked elsewhere for the opportunity to harass British shipping.

The most successful of these was Robert Surcouf, a privateer from the Breton port of St. Malo. Although denied a Letter of Marque, Surcouf sailed for the lucrative waters of the Indian Ocean. There he captured several British ships, including the richly laden East Indiaman *Triton*. He took his prizes to Martinique, where, since Surcouf lacked a privateer's license, they were confiscated. He sailed to France and was promptly issued with one.

Surcouf returned to the Indian Ocean and captured more prizes, including the *Kent*, another East Indiaman. Returning to France during the brief peace of 1802–3, the now-wealthy privateer turned St. Malo and other small ports into French privateer havens, and continued to harass British shipping for the remainder of the Napoleonic Wars. The emperor even made him a baron.

French privateers also captured hundreds of neutral American vessels, and prompted America to fight a "Quasi War" in 1798 to drive off their attackers. British shipping suffered even more from these French privateers—mercantile losses exceeded 2,000 ships during the first six years of the Napoleonic Wars.

The British also used privateers during the wars with France and the American Revolution. By 1809, when Britain and Spain made peace, the owners of these privateers were complaining that French shipping had been so devastated that there were no prizes to be had. War between Britain and the United States in 1812 would make privateering profitable again, but this time it was the Americans who would be the principal beneficiaries.

American Privateers

MARITIME DEFENDERS OF NEW-FOUND LIBERTY

The American Revolution gave American seamen an opportunity to raid British merchant shipping, and their successes drove the new nation to greater heights in the War of 1812, which proved to be a boon to the privateering industry.

With the outbreak of American revolution in 1775, the Continental Congress and individual colonies began commissioning privateers. Although the Continental Navy accomplished relatively little during the eight-year war, the large number of American privateers at sea captured over 3,000 British merchant ships. These successes were repeated during the War of 1812 (1812–15), when purpose-built long-range privateers proved particularly effective at harassing British shipping.

As early as April 1775 rebel whaleboats captured a British schooner off Martha's Vineyard, near Boston and, by early 1776, larger and better-armed privateers were cruising in the Atlantic and the Caribbean, while smaller ships concentrated on harassing British and Canadian fishing fleets off Newfoundland. As well as valuable cargoes, captured British supply ships provided much-needed muskets and powder for George Washington's Continental Army.

Unlike naval crews, privateersmen received no pension or pay—their only source of income was prize money. Immense profits could be made; the Salem privateer *Rattlesnake* alone took prizes worth over $1,000,000 in a single cruise. Ports such as Salem, Boston, and Baltimore grew rich as a result of their privateer fleets, although French ports and colonies also provided safe privateer havens.

The British slowly introduced a convoy system for protection, but thousands of British ships sailed unescorted. Although most ships were armed, the heavier armament and larger crew of the privateer gave it the edge in action. Shipping losses were part of the reason for the erosion of Britain's will to continue the struggle, following the defeat of her army at Yorktown in 1781.

The War of 1812 was largely a naval conflict, and a boon to the privateering industry. Ship owners were eager to repeat the privateering successes of the American Revolution and within two months over 150 privateers were at sea. Many were poorly

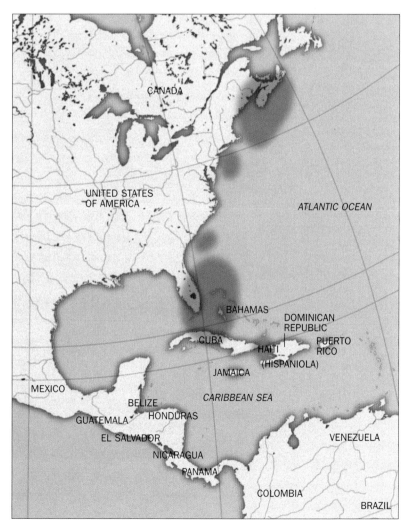

armed initially, relying on boarding rather than gunfire to capture vessels. Many British merchant ships were also unarmed, and the vast size of the British merchant fleet meant that prizes were plentiful.

Victories of specialized craft

American owners began to build specialized vessels, designed from the keel upward as privateers. Some of these, like the heavy schooners *Paul Jones*, *Saratoga*, *Yorktown*, and *Revenge*, were able to carry over 150 men and an armament capable of engaging British frigates, if the need arose.

Baltimore was the main privateer port on the Atlantic seaboard, and her schooners were renowned for their speed and easy handling. Taking advantage of the lessons learned during the American Revolution, leading shipwrights developed these new privateers in the Baltimore yards. One of their products was the 350-ton (318-tonne) privateer *America*, armed with 20 guns and carrying a crew of 120. She took 40 prizes from the British during the war that returned her owners a profit of over $600,000.

The most successful privateer of the War of 1812 was the Boston brig *Yankee*, whose 40 prizes totaled over $3,000,000. Other purpose-built heavy privateers such as the schooners *Prince of Neufchatel*, *Chasseur*, and *Lyon* contributed to the growing toll on British merchant shipping. The best of the specialized privateer schooners of the War of 1812 were as well designed for speed as later clipper ships or trans-Atlantic racing yachts, and were a tribute to the designers who created them.

In 1814, over 500 privateers operated from American ports. When France surrendered that year, Britain turned her attention to America. A blockade was established and by the end of the year American maritime commerce was at a standstill and privateering had virtually ceased. Losses from privateering led ship owners on both sides of the Atlantic to demand an end to the war, and peace was finally declared in 1815.

The war was a privateer's godsend. Over 1,300 British ships were captured during three years of war—although British privateers also harried American shipping. It was the last great surge of American privateering, and apart from attacks by Confederate raiders during the American Civil War, state-sponsored piracy became a thing of the past.

below: *An American privateer and a British warship engage in battle.*

John Paul Jones

PIRACY IN THE NAME OF CONGRESS

One of John Paul Jones's first acts of piracy against the British — kidnapping an earl—was foiled due to the the intended victim's absence. Little else this American naval officer did failed, and yet it took a hundred years before America hailed him a hero.

right: *To Americans struggling for independence, John Paul Jones was a naval officer—to the British he was a rapacious pirate.*

The inclusion of an American national hero in a catalog of pirates may be surprising. Although the colonists regarded him as a naval officer, to the British he was a Scotsman who attacked the merchant shipping of the British crown. He was therefore considered a pirate.

Born as John Paul in southwest Scotland in 1747, he sailed to Virginia in 1760 to join his elder brother. He became a

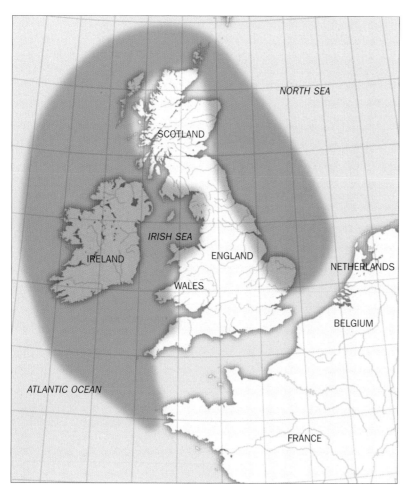

seaman, and within seven years he was the captain of a West Indies merchantman. Some unrecorded incident led him to flee back to America, where he changed his identity, adding "Jones" to his name.

In 1775 John Paul Jones became a lieutenant in the new Continental Navy and commanded a number of ships before he was given the 18-gun *Ranger*. Hopes for a more prestigious command failed to materialize, and a disillusioned Jones sailed for Brest in France in early 1778, with orders to harass British shipping.

Jones set out in April 1778 and headed north into the Irish Sea. He landed at the northern English port of Whitehaven, where he burned shipping in the harbor and destroyed a small fort. After, he stopped on the Scottish coast near Kirkudbright. Plans to kidnap and hold for ransom the Earl of Selkirk, who lived nearby, were foiled by the nobleman's absence. Jones made off with the family silver instead. He later had a change of heart and returned it to Lady Selkirk, but the British still considered it piracy. Further up the Scottish coast Jones was met by the small

British 20-gun brig *Drake*, which he captured and brought back to Brest.

Jones was given the command of a new ship, a converted French Indiaman which was renamed *Bonhomme Richard*. In August he put to sea again, in company with French privateers, and captured three British merchant ships off the coast of Ireland and northern Scotland. By early September he was in the North Sea, but had become separated from all but one of his French consorts. He tried to repeat his earlier raids by landing on the Scottish coast at Leith, near Edinburgh, but bad weather forced him to abandon the attack.

A crippling close-fought battle

John Paul Jones continued to cruise down the British coast. On September 23, 1779, off Flamborough Head, he met a British convoy escorted by two warships. Jones steered for the 50-gun *Serapis* while his French consort *Pallas* engaged a British 20-gun sloop. Jones was suspicious of the French artillery his ship carried, so he resolved to fight the British ship at close quarters. A boarding attempt failed, and the ships began a gunnery duel at point-blank range.

The American ship was getting pummeled, and Captain Pearson of the *Serapis* asked Jones, "Has your ship struck?"[†] Jones replied, "I have not yet begun to fight," and the slaughter continued. Jones maneuvered his ship alongside the British warship, and his withering musket fire devastated its decks. A hand grenade exploded part of the *Serapis*'s magazine and Pearson eventually conceded defeat. Both ships were shattered; the *Bonhomme Richard* eventually sank and the *Serapis* limped toward a friendly port. Jones entered the history books as the most successful American naval commander of the Revolutionary War.

In France, Jones was fêted as a hero, and his deeds were even honored by a ballad that popularized him as an American "pirate." Jones went on to serve in the Russian navy and fought against the Ottoman Turks in the Black Sea. Discredited by charges of assaulting an underage girl, he left Russia for Paris, where he died a broken and almost forgotten man in 1792. The British still regarded Jones as a pirate, or at best a privateer, and even the American Congress appeared to deny him the respect he deserved. It was a century before his remains were brought home to his adopted land and John Paul Jones was awarded the status of a national hero.

[†] *To "strike" the ship's flag was a signal of surrender.*

below: *John Paul Jones commits the Bonhomme Richard to attack the British warship Serapis, off Flamborough Head in 1779.*

CHAPTER NINE

The Last Pirates

New Orleans
Barataria

Galveston

Tampa Bay

GULF OF MEXICO

Havana

ISLA DE JUVENTUD
(ISLA DE PINOS)

GULF OF HONDURAS

YUCATAN

COZUMEL

Veracruz

MEXICO

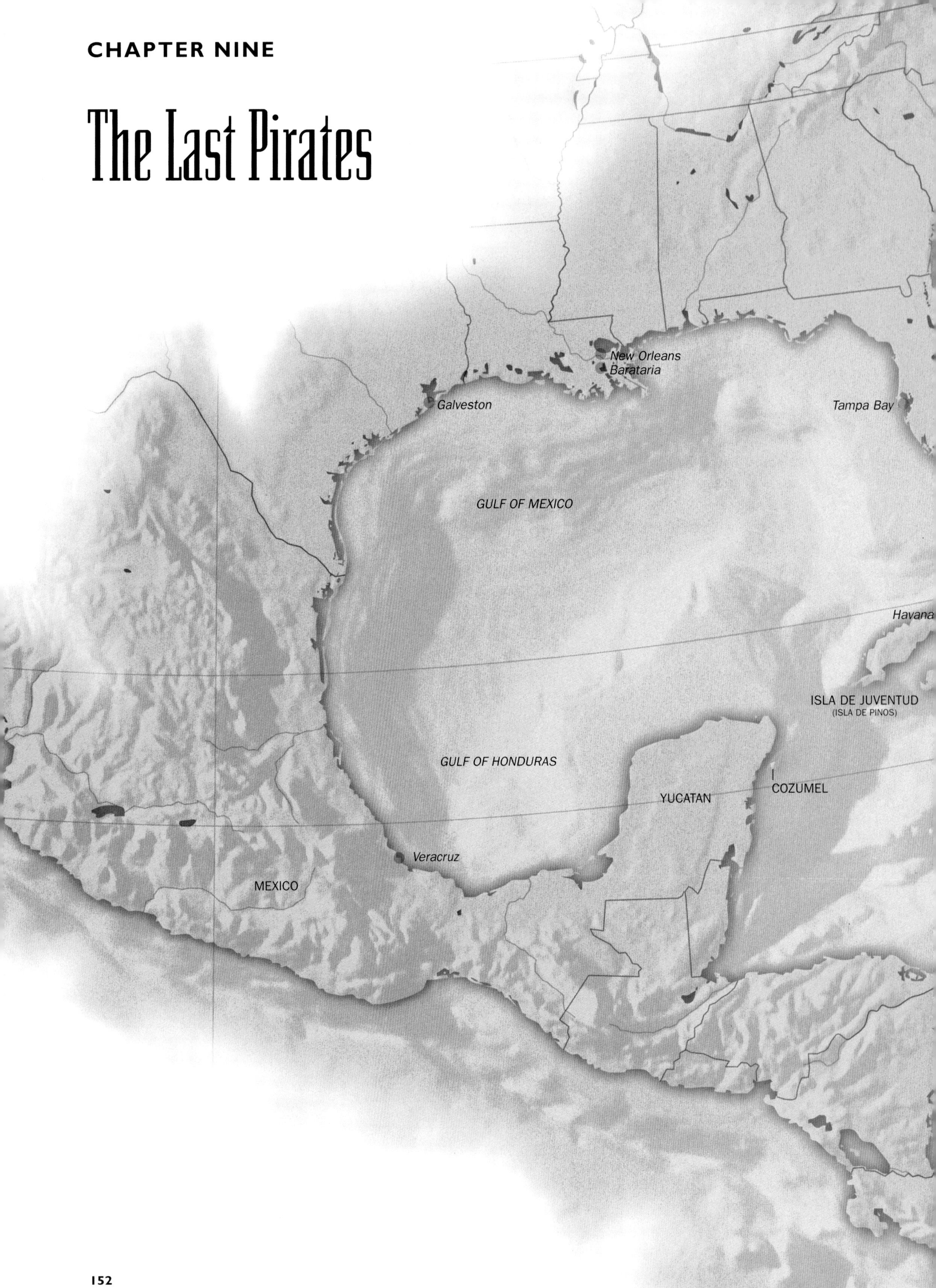

The end of the Napoleonic Wars and the Wars of Liberation in Latin America left American waters filled with privateers. These brutal men were used to pillaging on the high seas for a living, and hundreds of them turned to piracy. For a decade from 1815, a new wave of piracy swept the Caribbean and devastated shipping. This mayhem was checked and finally ended by the aggressive naval actions of Britain and the United States, who fought a campaign against the pirates. By the late 1820s the era of the last pirates was over. Apart from a few isolated examples of brutal robbery on the high seas, the waters of the Atlantic were once more safe from piracy.

St. Augustine

FLORIDA

BAHAMAS

NASSAU

LONG ISLAND

LEEWARD ISLANDS

KEY WEST

ANGUILLA

ST. THOMAS

ANTIGUA

ST. KITTS NEVIS

CUBA

GUADELOUPE

TORTUGA

DOMINICAN
REPUBLIC

PUERTO RICO

HAITI

DOMINICA

Santiago de Cuba

(HISPANIOLA)

MARTINIQUE

CAYMAN
ISLANDS

WINDWARD ISLANDS

ST. LUCIA

JAMAICA

GRENADA

TOBAGO

CARIBBEAN SEA

ISLA DE BLANCA

TRINIDA

ISLA DE MARGARITA

CURAÇAO

THE LAST PIRATES

Although piracy could never be completely stamped out, after the "Golden Age" there was nothing more than the occasional isolated incident in American or Caribbean waters for almost a century. Then in 1815, after the end of the Napoleonic Wars and the War of 1812, thousands of privateers found themselves without work. Many turned to piracy, operating from remote harbors in places like Cuba and Puerto Rico.

Although a number of them, such as Jean Laffitte, were American, the majority came from the Spanish-speaking regions of the Caribbean and South America. For them, the catalyst was the long string of wars fought between Spain and her former New World colonies. These Latin American Wars of Liberation erupted in 1808, when Spain was fully occupied by the Napoleonic French invasion that devastated the Iberian peninsula.

By 1826 Mexico, Peru, and Chile were independent states, Central America had founded its own state, and Simon Bolivar's rebel army had liberated Ecuador, Colombia, and Venezuela. Cuba remained under Spanish control, but it was plagued by guerrilla fighting. All these emerging states had hired privateers to fight on their behalf against Spain. This meant that by 1820 there were hundreds of privateers operating in the Caribbean, and many were not content to restrict their attacks to Spanish shipping.

With the end of the Napoleonic Wars, the oceans were once more considered to be safe for commerce. The growing demand for materials driven by the Industrial Revolution in Europe (and the emergent industry of America) meant that ship owners were riding a wave of extraordinary demand for their cargoes. Consequently, the Caribbean and American shipping lanes were filled with a greater amount of vessels than had ever been seen before.

Petty robbery by violent thieves

Many of the new pirates were small-time robbers, content to attack ships that carried little in the way of plunder. Captain Lander of the American brig *Washington* reported that in an attack in 1822 Hispanic pirates stole $16, food, cooking equipment, clothing, and a compass. This was not robbery on a grand scale, but these pirates frequently murdered their victims to prevent anyone identifying them later. While men like Bartholomew Roberts plundered wealthy cargoes and spared the crew during the Golden Age of Piracy, in the 1820s sailors were often massacred for the clothes they wore.

At this time the United States of America was a growing mercantile power, so American shipping was particularly vulnerable. Between 1815 and 1820 hundreds of American vessels were attacked and plundered, and marine insurance rates soared. Stories of excessive brutality and murder were commonplace.

From 1820 onward, major efforts were made by the US Navy and the British Royal Navy to stamp out piracy in the Caribbean. Aggressive naval patrols and raids on known pirate havens gradually brought the situation under control. Pirates like Jean Laffitte were driven from the seas, and although a few notorious pirates remained at large, by the late 1820s the threat of widespread piracy had receded.

This did not mean that the seas were completely safe. A number of particularly brutal pirates remained, and their attacks were the final examples of piracy in Atlantic waters. In 1828 the Portuguese pirate Benito de Soto attacked the British ship *Morning Star* in the South Atlantic. He killed her captain and raped female passengers before abandoning his sinking victim. He was subsequently recognized by survivors in Gibraltar, where he was tried and hanged.

right: *As merchant shipping became more wary of the "new" brutal pirates, they were forced into all kinds of deceptions. In "Pirates try to lure a merchantman dressed as women," the armed and ready villains lie on deck hidden from the crew of the passing vctim. Oil painting by Augustus Baird.*

1796	1798	1803–15	1805	1812–15	1812	1815	1820s
Ceylon (Sri Lanka), India, is conquered by the British.	The Dutch East India Company goes bankrupt.	The Napoleonic Wars.	The French-Spanish navy is defeated in the Battle of Trafalgar.	The War of 1812 between the US and Britain.	French pirates Jean and Pierre Laffite are caught, charged, and escape.	Wellington defeats Napoleon at the Battle of Waterloo.	Efforts by the US Navy and British Royal Navy virtually eliminate piracy in the Caribbean.

In 1832, the American vessel *Mexican* from Salem was captured by the pirate ship *Panda*, commanded by Pedro Gibert. The prize was looted, the crew locked below decks, and the ship set on fire. The crew managed to escape and extinguished the fire. Gibert was later caught by the British, then extradited to Boston, where he was tried and hanged.

Although shocking examples of pirate brutality, these were isolated cases. In the waters of the Americas and the Atlantic, piracy had become a thing of the past, and so it came to be viewed with a romanticism it never deserved.

1820	1821	1825	1827	1833	1834	1836	1837
The US Navy clears pirates from Galveston Bay on Gulf of Mexico; Cuba is the new haven.	President Monroe establishes anti-pirate squadron, commanded by David Porter.	The first ever passenger railway in use, in England.	Portuguese Benito de Soto takes over slave ship on which he serves and turns against the Spanish.	"Don" Pedro Gibert captured by British navy; at trial, he faces American sailors he left to burn.	The analytical engine, a mechanical computer, is invented by Charles Babbage.	Mexicans beat the Texan army at the Alamo.	Queen Victoria is crowned.

Jean Laffite

THE PIRATE HERO OF NEW ORLEANS

Lafitte, a small-time pirate who operated from a lair in the bayous south of New Orleans, was saved from the noose by his support of the Americans during the Battle of New Orleans in 1815. Afterward, the national hero set off to find a new place to pursue his bloodthirsty career.

above right:

Laffite leads his men in clearing the decks of a captured prize.

As with many pirates, the details of Jean Laffite's early years are vague. He was born around 1780 in France, traditionally in the southern city of Bayonne, although Haiti has also been identified as his birthplace. By 1809 he and brother Pierre lived in New Orleans. They ran a blacksmith business that also acted as a cover for a smuggling operation involving slaves and stolen goods.

From 1810 Jean Laffite acted as the leader of a group of pirates, privateers, and smugglers based in Barataria Bay, south of New Orleans. Over the next few years Laffite's pirates raided shipping in the Gulf of Mexico, concentrating on Spanish ships and slave traders, while Laffite supervised the sale of the plunder.

As slave trading was outlawed in Louisiana, plantation owners attended secret auctions near Barataria, where the slaves and plundered goods were traded to merchants of the nearby city. This operation became too well known, and the Governor of Louisiana arrested the Laffite brothers in November 1812 on charges of piracy and illegal trading. Released on bail due to the efforts of New Orleans's best lawyers, the Laffite brothers escaped and the trading continued, but this time they hid the auctions deep in the Louisiana bayous. The governor put a price of $500 on Jean Laffite's head in 1813, and the pirate responded by posting bills offering $5,000 for the head of the governor!

In 1812 disagreement over maritime heavy-handedness led to a war between Britain and the United States. An American invasion of Canada was repulsed, and then after a series of successful frigate actions, the fledgling US Navy found itself blockaded in its home ports by the superior British fleet. The British raided the American coast in Maryland and even captured Washington D.C. and burned the White House.

From informer to victim to ally

At New Orleans, the British wanted to repeat their success, since an attack would severely disrupt the booming trade of the Mississippi river. In September

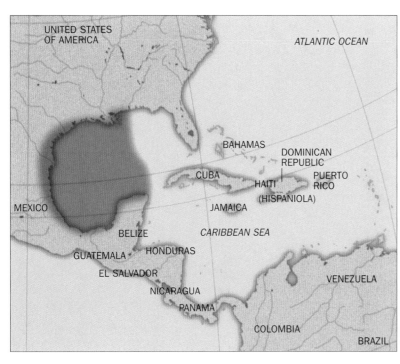

1814 British officers offered Laffite a pardon and financial reward if he would help them to attack New Orleans. Instead, Laffite informed the State authorities—his actions were probably more influenced by the threat to his lucrative New Orleans market than patriotism.

He was rewarded with a surprise visit by the State's small naval force, the schooners *Carolina* and *Louisiana*. The warships entered Barataria Bay and captured most of the pirate fleet as it lay at anchor. Laffite and his colleagues hid in the bayous until the navy left, then reclaimed their settlement.

However, Lafitte's fortunes changed when, in December, a British attack was considered imminent. General Andrew Jackson, having arrived in the city, placed the region under military control. He offered Laffite and his crew a truce in return for their help in defending New Orleans by manning guns landed from the two warships. Early in January a British force disembarked east of the city and were bloodily repulsed in the resulting Battle of New Orleans (January 8, 1815).

Laffite's pirates were rewarded with an official pardon issued by President Madison a month later. While many seized the opportunity to give up piracy, the Laffite brothers chose to continue. The area around New Orleans was too tightly controlled by the military to allow a resurgence of piracy, so the brothers stole a vessel and sailed to Texas. The region was a lawless frontier area between America and Spanish Mexico and provided the pirates with refuge.

Jean Laffite's pirate attacks resumed and by 1817 he held Galveston as his new secure port. Criminals flocked to Galveston and within a year it supported 20 pirate schooners and a thriving market in slaves and contraband. In the following two years Laffite made the mistake of attacking several American ships, and an outcry led to the dispatch of a naval expedition.

In 1820 a force spearheaded by Captain Biddle in the brig *USS Enterprise* bombarded and destroyed Galveston. Laffite escaped capture, but his subsequent life is unknown. Although it is considered likely he died in Mexico, rumors persisted that he survived and returned to the United States under an assumed name.

below: *Captain Biddle in the USS Enterprise opens fire on the pirate schooners crowding Galveston harbor.*

"Don" Pedro Gibert

THE LAST OF THE AMERICAN PIRATES

Pedro Gibert was one of the very last of the pirates to plague the Atlantic seaboard of America. In 1832 he captured an American ship bound for South America, and when his crew asked what to do with their prisoners, he told them: "Dead cats don't mew!"

Claims that Pedro Gibert was the son of a Spanish nobleman appear unfounded, and he was probably born somewhere in South America around 1800. He became a seaman and, by 1830, he commanded a schooner called the *Panda*. He had previously served as a privateer in the service of Colombia, preying on Spanish shipping during South America's struggle for independence.

In the early 1830s Gibert relied on the less glamorous trades of smuggling and slave trading. He adopted the title of "Don," which, according to the testimony of his fellow pirates, implied a noble lineage. Gibert established a secure base in a stretch of one of the inshore lagoons on Florida's east coast, probably, near St. Lucie Inlet.

At some point he decided to try piracy. Cruising in the waters of the Florida Straits on September 20, 1832, he spotted the American brigantine *Mexican*, *en route* from Salem, Massachusetts, to Buenos Aires in Argentina. As the *Panda* approached, Gibert hoisted the Colombian flag, but Captain Isaac Butman decided not to take any chances and turned away. The *Mexican* was armed with two small guns mounted amidships, but when the ammunition was brought up it was found that the roundshot was too large for the guns. Her only chance was to flee, but in the chase that followed the *Panda* proved to be faster. Just before the *Mexican* was overhauled by the pirates, Captain Butman hid the $20,000 in coins he was carrying, money intended to pay the crew and purchase cargo.

The pirates boarded the *Mexican*, locked up the crew, then ransacked the ship. Gibert beat and tortured the captain and some of his crew, and forced them to reveal the location of the ship's hidden paychest. Gibert returned to the *Panda* with the chest and the rest of the plunder.

Crawling from the fire
When his men asked what they should do with the prisoners, Gibert told them, "Dead cats don't mew. You know what to do." For some reason the crew decided not to kill

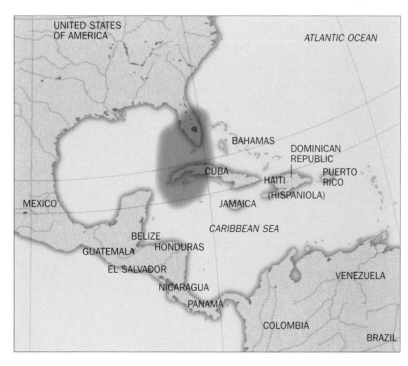

the crew outright, but locked them below deck. The pirates lowered the sails, cut the rigging, and set fire to the ship.

They returned to the *Panda* and sailed off, leaving the *Mexican*'s crew to burn to death. Somehow, one of the victims squeezed through a hatch and freed his fellows. Captain Butman led the fire-fighting and got the blaze under control, but cannily left part of the fire smoldering. As the *Panda* disappeared over the horizon, the pirates continued to see smoke rising over their victim. Once they were gone, the *Mexican*'s crew doused the decoy fire and saved what they could of their sails, charts, and navigational equipment. Butman sailed back north, eventually reaching New York. Gibert was now a wanted man.

The *Panda* remained near Florida for a few months, possibly engaged in smuggling between Florida and Cuba. By March 1833 she was off the West African coast. Although slaving was illegal in British territories, an illicit trade continued, and Gibert hoped to secure a human cargo.

Instead of finding slave traders, he met the Royal Navy. A British warship on patrol came upon the *Panda*, and her sailors boarded the schooner. Gibert and his crew were arrested as slave traders, but managed to escape when the warship returned to her home port. The runaways were soon rounded up and shipped to England.

Once the true identity of the prisoners became known, Gibert and 11 fellow pirates were extradited to the United States to stand trial for piracy. In a Boston courtroom they faced the *Mexican*'s crew who they had left to die. The outcome was inevitable. While two pirates were acquitted, six received long custodial sentences, and Pedro Gibert and three of his crewmen were sentenced to death. Gibert and his companions were hanged in 1835, the last pirates to be executed in the United States of America.

above: *Gibert's pirates from the Panda (left) row toward the Mexican in 1832. Thomas Fuller, the Mexican's 19-year-old mate, was a key witness in Gibert's trial.*

Benito de Soto

THE BRUTAL CAPTAIN OF THE *BLACK JOKE*

One of the last pirates, Portuguese-born de Soto was accused of horrendous cruelty; locking passengers and crew of a captured ship below decks, he scuttled it to hide the evidence. But he found there was no such thing as the perfect crime, and his past returned to haunt him.

right: *De Soto's small ship the Black Joke attacked the Morning Star in mid-Atlantic, locked the prisoners on board and scuttled her to hide the evidence of their crimes.*

Benito de Soto was a Portuguese seaman who served on an Argentinian brigantine slave ship. In 1827 the ship was anchored off the coast of Angola in southwest Africa. As she set sail with her slaves, de Soto and the mate took over the ship. The crew's loyalties were divided, and 18 sailors refused to participate in the mutiny. De Soto had them put into an open boat and cast adrift. The boat was said to have capsized while trying to land and its crew drowned. As the mutineers celebrated, de Soto removed a potential rival by shooting the mate dead in a staged argument. De Soto was duly elected captain, and promptly renamed the ship the *Black Joke*.

De Soto sailed the *Black Joke* to the Caribbean, where the slaves were sold in Spanish colonial markets. The pirates sailed south and attacked Spanish ships in the Caribbean, before passing the line of the Lesser Antilles. Every vessel they encountered was sunk without ceremony and the crew killed. The progress of the pirates was marked only by a string of missing ships.

They began a leisurely pirate cruise down the Atlantic coast of South America, but finding few prizes, the pirates sailed into the mid-Atlantic to straddle the busy maritime trade route between Europe and the Cape of Good Hope. Sailing ships swung well out into the South Atlantic to take advantage of trade winds, almost reaching the coast of Brazil before turning southeast for the coast of South Africa. This meant that de Soto was likely to encounter lucrative prizes returning from India and the Far East carrying spices, opium, or tea. There was also the possibility of encountering ships returning

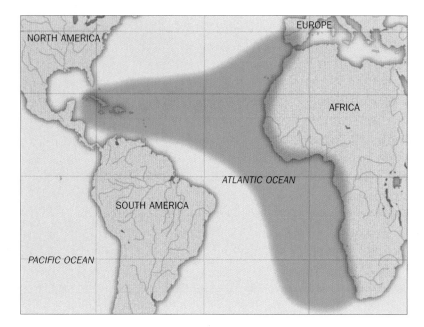

NORTH AMERICA

EUROPE

AFRICA

ATLANTIC OCEAN

SOUTH AMERICA

PACIFIC OCEAN

to Europe from South America. As more ships disappeared, a concerned maritime world correctly assumed that pirates were operating in the South Atlantic. Homebound East Indiamen were ordered to wait at St. Helena for a naval escort to convoy them into safer waters.

A fateful encounter

On February 21, 1832, de Soto in the *Black Joke* came upon the bark *Morning Star*—a three-masted ship, two square-rigged sails and a rear third with a gaff sail—returning home from Ceylon to England. The smaller and faster pirate ship ranged alongside the *Morning Star* and fired into her at point-blank range. A number of passengers and crew were wounded or killed. De Soto ordered the bark to heave to, then demanded that her captain be sent over in the ship's boat. He took offense at the time the English captain took to comply, and when he arrived onboard the *Black Joke*, de Soto cut him down with a cutlass. "Thus," he is said to have cried, "does Benito de Soto reward those who disobey him."

The pirates crossed over to the *Morning Star* and boarded her. In an orgy of destruction they killed some of their male prisoners and raped the female passengers. The prisoners were locked inside the *Morning Star*'s hold, then she was looted and holed. After scuttling the bark, the pirates returned to their own ship and sailed off.

The crew managed to free themselves, man the pumps, and save their vessel from sinking. They were rescued by a passing ship the next day—for the first time there were survivors to testify to de Soto's crimes. Part of the *Morning Star*'s crew were wounded soldiers returning home from India, and their treatment, combined with the brutal rape of the women, made de Soto the most notorious criminal on the high seas.

De Soto and the *Black Joke* sailed across the Atlantic and headed north toward Europe. On reaching Spain the pirates sold their plunder, but the sloop was wrecked off the Spanish coast near Cadiz. De Soto and his crew traveled to Gibraltar, where they hoped to find a replacement ship. Unfortunately for them, the wounded soldiers from the ill-fated *Morning Star* had also reached Gibraltar, and Benito de Soto was recognized by one of his victims. He was taken to Cadiz, where he was tried, sentenced, and hanged.

below: *Following the capture and execution of Benito de Soto in Cadiz, the pirate's head was stuck on a spike, a grisly warning to other mariners who considered piracy.*

Barataria, Galveston, and Cuba

PIRATE LAIRS ON THE GULF OF MEXICO

Barataria near New Orleans was a perfect pirate base until a strong United States naval presence made it unsafe. So the pirates moved to Galveston, beyond the authorities' reach, and to ports along the Cuban coast. The United States declared war and swore to destroy the "pirate nests."

The last wave of piracy that swept the Caribbean basin resulted from the end of legitimate wartime privateering opportunities, and thrived on the region's political instability. Many pirates needed reliable markets for the sale of their plunder, and this usually meant large cities, preferably in regions that supported a slave economy. Slaves continued to be a regular form of plunder, although the export of slaves to many countries of the Americas was considered illegal. Pirate havens also had to be remote from areas of authority, a factor often incompatible with the requirement of a ready market. A handful of areas provided the special needs of the last American pirates.

The most notorious of these was Barataria, the bay south of New Orleans that provided a base for Jean Laffite. Barataria Bay was an inlet to the west of the Mississippi delta, linked to the river by a network of small rivers, canals, and hidden backwaters. The pirates used the island of Grand Terre as a base, aided by the local Cajun population, who provided guides to the bayous and alligator-infested lagoons that provided security from attack.

The same waterways gave easy access to New Orleans and its market for plunder. Slaves captured by the pirates were sold to local plantation owners in hidden locations near New Orleans, while informants warned Laffite if they were in danger of attack. The alarm system failed when the pirate base was located by two warships, and although the pirates evaded capture, their haven ceased to be safe.

Laffite moved to Galveston in Texas, which, for a few years, became a new safe pirate haven. Texas was a frontier region, operating outside the authorities of Spain or Mexico on the one hand and the United States and Texan rebels on the other. While the four powers struggled for political control, piracy thrived along the remote Texan coasts. There were several pirate havens, including Matagorda Bay and the Sabine estuary, although by 1817 the small town of Galveston became the supreme pirate base on the Gulf of Mexico.

Texas to Cuba then inland

While Galveston Bay provided an escape route inland if Galveston Island was attacked, the town itself became a bustling and cosmopolitan market for pirates, frontiersman, and Mexican traders. This success also invited the attention of the United States navy. Attacks on American shipping from pirates based in Galveston provided the excuse to destroy the town, and it was captured and burned in 1820. The Texan coast continued to shelter pirates, but regular naval patrols made the region an unsafe for them.

From 1820, the center of pirate activity moved to Cuba's northern coast. Spanish colonial officials turned a blind eye to pirate attacks, and even actively encouraged piracy as a source of revenue. Corruption was rife and pirates, such as Charles Gibbs, bought political protection by giving local authorities a share of their plunder. American consuls reported that the Spanish mayors in the ports of Matanzas and Caibarién were in league with pirates, as was the governor of the western province of Pinar del Rio. All of these places lay close to the busy shipping lane of the Florida Straits.

America countered the threat of Cuban piracy with a two-pronged attack. Naval forces patrolled the coast and a diplomatic initiative forced the Spanish authorities to crack down on officials who condoned piracy. By December 1823, when President

Monroe announced his Monroe Doctrine, he noted "the cooperation of the invigorated administration of Cuba."

As pirates were tracked down by British and American patrols, they turned their back on the sea, and became robbers on land, where they attacked Cuban plantations. The brigands became the Spanish army's problem, and a number were caught and executed. Charles Gibbs himself was caught and handed over to the American authorities. Tried in New York and hanged in 1831, he was one of the last pirates to use the Caribbean as a base.

above: *A contemporary map of the New Orleans area exaggerates the river's width.*

below: *New Orleans and the harbor looking south toward Barataria Bay, and* **inset**, *the northern coast of Cuba, whose ports became pirate havens.*

David Porter

THE US NAVY'S PIRATE HUNTER

The United States President sent Porter to Key West off the southern tip of Florida to establish an anti-piracy base. A skilled strategist with an uncanny ability to outguess his opponents, he proved to be the ideal man for the job. Within two years his "Mosquito Fleet" had swept the waters of the Caribbean.

below: *Small boats of Porter's anti-piracy Mosquito Fleet attack a vessel commanded by the Cuban pirate Diabolito in 1823. Most of the pirate crew escaped ashore, where the US naval force was unable to pursue them.*

The late wave of piracy in the Caribbean during the 1815–20 period severely disrupted shipping on the Atlantic seaboard, the Gulf of Mexico, and the Caribbean. In 1820 alone, 27 American ships were attacked and plundered, and insurance companies raised their premiums to levels that even surpassed those charged during the War of 1812. As the losses of American ships increased, ship owners and the American public demanded action be taken. Six US warships already cruised the Caribbean, but they were insufficient to stem the tide. In 1821, President Monroe authorized the establishment of an anti-pirate squadron, commanded by Commodore David Porter.

David Porter first went to sea as a midshipman in 1798, serving onboard the *USS Constellation*. A year later he participated in the frigate action against the 40-gun French frigate *L'Insurgente*, and Porter distinguished himself. He served as a lieutenant in the US Navy's attack on the Barbary pirates in 1801, and was captured when the *USS Philadelphia* ran aground off Tripoli. After spending a year in a Barbary prison he was repatriated and promoted to command the brig *USS Enterprise*. During the War of 1812 Porter commanded the *USS Essex*, but after a successful cruise against British shipping he was captured by frigate *HMS Phoebe*. He was paroled and given free passage back to the United States, on the condition that he would not again fight the British.

Porter was regarded as a naval hero, and served in Washington as a member of the Board of Naval Commissioners until he

was called on to fight pirates once again. He was promoted to the honorary rank of commodore and sent to Key West off the southern tip of Florida. Porter was 42, and commanded the largest peace-time collection of American ships that had yet been assembled by the young country.

Commanding the Mosquito Fleet

This US Naval force was known as "The Mosquito Fleet," due to its use of small and shallow-drafted vessels. It included 16 vessels—naval brigs, rapidly-converted Baltimore schooners, an early paddle steamer, and even a decoy merchant ship, armed with hidden guns. The Mosquito Fleet chose Key West as its base because of its central location in pirate waters. The island was then known as Thompson's Island, and soon the fledgling township boasted the busiest naval base in the United States. The phrase "Mosquito Fleet" had extra meaning for the American sailors, since in summer months the insects carried yellow fever and malaria, and the wards of the island's naval hospital were filled with fever patients.

Porter's orders were to suppress piracy and the slave trade, protect the commerce and citizens of the United States, and transport American specie when required. "The Mosquito Fleet" had a daunting range of tasks, but by early 1823 he was ready and his ships scoured the Caribbean, the Bahamas, and the Gulf of Mexico. They hit hard at pirate bases, escorted American ships, and captured pirate ships. One of the problems was the elusiveness of pirates, who disguised themselves as fishermen and local traders, but turned to piracy when the opportunity arose.

Porter's fleet scoured the known pirate havens of Puerto Rico, Mexico, Cuba, and the Florida Keys. They sought out and destroyed pirate vessels wherever they were encountered. Cuba was a particularly difficult target, since the Spanish resented the American presence and almost seemed to condone the piratical activities of their seamen. Porter walked a political tightrope, but as his successes grew

Spanish merchants encouraged the Cuban authorities to support his activities.

One of Porter's greatest successes was the defeat of the notorious Cuban pirate Diabolito (Little Devil) and his band in April 1823. The US naval force surprised the pirates off the northern coast of Cuba and forced them to abandon their ship and take to the land to hide. The Spanish authorities then complained to Porter that many former pirates found it safer to become Cuban brigands (bandits) on land. Porter's fleet ended the careers of other pirates, such as Charles Gibbs and Jean Laffitte. With hundreds of pirates captured, safe maritime trade was restored and, by 1825, piracy virtually ceased to exist in American and Caribbean waters.

above:

Commodore David Porter was an able naval thinker who managed to clear the Caribbean Sea and the Gulf of Mexico of pirates during a two-year naval campaign.

Canton
Whampoa
Pearl River

MOUTH OF
THE PEARL

SOUTH
CHINA SEA

LANTAO ISLAND

Kowloon
HONG KONG ISLAND

Macao

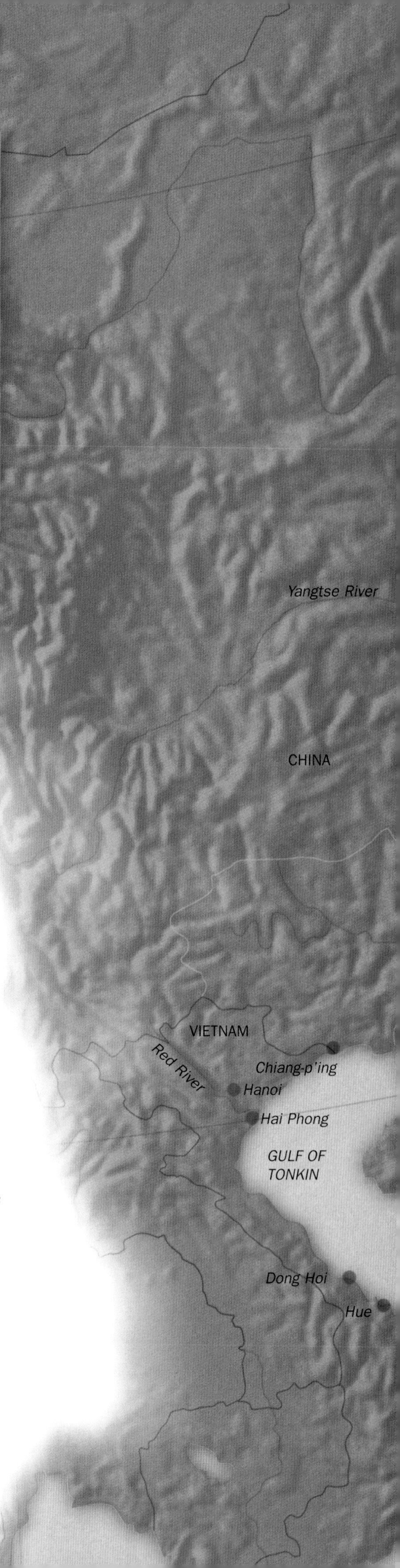

Yangtse River

CHINA

VIETNAM
Red River
Chiang-p'ing
Hanoi
Hai Phong

GULF OF
TONKIN

Dong Hoi
Hue

CHAPTER TEN

Piracy in the Far East

Piracy in the South China Sea was conducted in a way that was unique in world history. Piracy and politics were frequently combined to produce virtual pirate empires powerful enough to influence the rise and fall of Imperial dynasties. Further to the south, in the waters of southeast Asia, piracy was conducted in a tribal nature, where cultures fought each other, as well as preying on the vessels of passing Oriental and Occidental merchants. While the Chinese emperor often appeared powerless to stop the practice of piracy along his shores, he adopted unusual tactics to curb maritime lawlessness. Piracy in the Far East was eventually suppressed by the European powers, whose steamships and modern armament were able to decimate the older fleets of pirate junks.

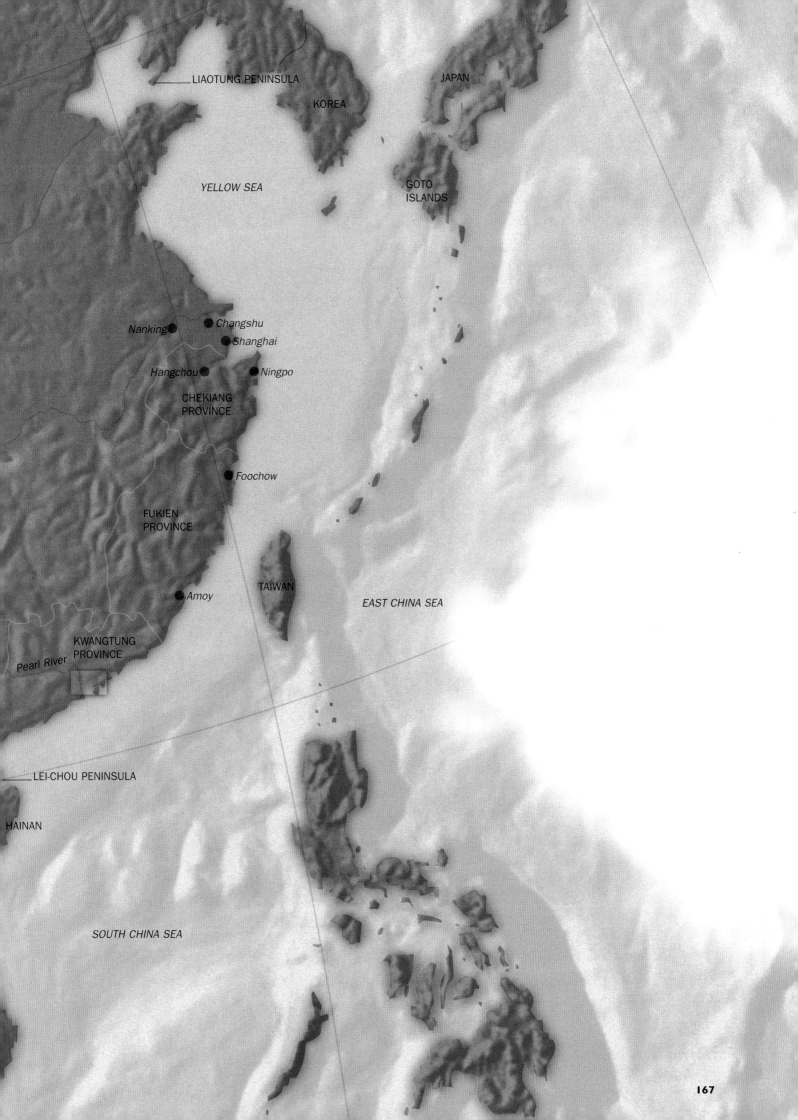

LIAOTUNG PENINSULA

JAPAN

KOREA

YELLOW SEA

GOTO
ISLANDS

Nanking *Changshu*

Shanghai

Hangchou *Ningpo*

CHEKIANG
PROVINCE

Foochow

FUKIEN
PROVINCE

TAIWAN

EAST CHINA SEA

Amoy

KWANGTUNG
PROVINCE

Pearl River

LEI-CHOU PENINSULA

HAINAN

SOUTH CHINA SEA

167

PIRACY IN THE FAR EAST

Pirates have been recorded in the waters of the South China Sea since before the establishment of the Sui Dynasty in AD 589. As China was fragmented into petty states, Chinese waters were plunged into lawlessness. The end of the Han Dynasty in AD 220 had created a political void, and local rulers took full advantage of their freedom. Minor warlords dominated stretches of the Chinese coast, trading where they could and raiding their neighbors' shipping.

While central control was reestablished and then lost during the centuries between the rise of the Sui Dynasty and the foundation of the stabilizing Ming Dynasty in 1368, Imperial power was frequently unable to control the coastal waters of the vast Chinese Empire.

Although maritime trade flourished during the 13th and 14th centuries, and Chinese merchants established contact as far afield as the basin of the Indian Ocean, it was only in the 15th century that the Ming rulers regained control of Chinese

below: *The capture of the British sailor John Turner by Ching Yih's pirate band in 1806. Turner survived to tell the story of his experiences as a prisoner of the Chinese pirates.*

waters from the pirates who infested it. This control was often based on the less than expedient policy of paying local rulers to suppress piracy; setting a thief to catch a thief. This policy was repeated until the 20th century.

In the 16th century European sea travelers reached the Far East and opened up trade routes between China, Japan, the Philippines, and Europe. They reported pirate activity in Chinese waters and also further south, in the confined waters of the Indonesian archipelago. While the threat from Japanese pirates diminished in the 16th century, rival Chinese pirate empires sprang up along the coast bordering the South China Sea, and tribal piracy prevailed in southeast Asia.

The same European traders saw the rise of the first pirate empire of the 17th century, created by the merchant-turned-warlord Cheng Chih Lung, and later wielded as a political tool by his son, Kuo Hsing Yeh. For the first time piracy and politics were firmly united in China, a practice that continued with the establishment of later pirate empires.

The demise, resurgence, and ultimate end

Piracy was conducted on such a massive scale that the controllers of the pirate empires were sucked into China's swirling politics. Kuo Hsing Yeh in particular conducted piracy on a strategic level, an achievement that was never repeated elsewhere. By the start of the 18th century, the reestablishment of a powerful Ch'ing Dynasty would temporarily end widespread piracy in Chinese waters.

During the 18th century piracy extended into Vietnam, and the political upheavals in the country produced a conducive atmosphere for sea robbers. Pirate fleets

220	605–10	1206	15th century	1592–98	16th century	1610	1641
Chinese warlords take advantage of the end of the Han Dynasty; piracy is rife around much of the coast.	The Grand Canal is constructed to connect the Yellow River, China, with the Yangtze.	The Mongols begin their conquest of Asia, led by Genghis Khan.	Rulers of the Ming Dynasty regain control of Chinese waters from the pirates.	Korea is devastated by Japanese invasion.	New trade routes between Far East and Europe attract pirates to Chinese and Indonesian waters.	Galileo is the first to observe the stars through a telescope.	Chinese emperor ends Chih Lung's piratical empire by appointing him Admiral.

into a force powerful enough to resist attack from all-comers, including the forces of the emperor of China. As ever, Imperial intrigue and the absorption of piracy into the legitimate commercial umbrella of the empire brought piracy to an end through political rather than military means.

The growing power of the European colonial powers in the Far East eventually brought widespread piracy to an end. After humbling the Chinese in the Opium Wars of the mid-19th century, Europeans assumed the responsibility for maintaining the region's sea routes. In a series of punitive attacks in the South China Sea and the Indonesian archipelago, piracy was largely eradicated in China and the Far East, allowing European commerce to thrive. A millennium of piracy was ended by European technology; the days of the great and powerful pirate empires of the East were finally brought to a close.

left: *For centuries the South China Sea and the Indonesian archipelago were plagued by large bands of organized and highly efficient pirates.*

below: *"A Boatload of Piratical Rascals." Watercolor by Edward Cree. Cree was a Royal Navy surgeon who participated in the destruction of Shap-'ng-Tsai's pirate force in 1849, and the sketch portrays prisoners from his fleet.*

combined with local rulers to attack rivals and terrorize their shipping, a situation mirrored in the political and tribal petty rivalry of the Indonesian archipelago.

By the end of the century widespread piracy reemerged in the South China Sea, first under the secure banner of the Tay Son Dynasty in Vietnam, and later in the form of the piratical dynasty of Ching Yih, who led the largest pirate confederation in history. While Tay Son provided a safe haven for pirates who operated as their allies, Ching Yih organized pirates

1778	1791	1807	1821	1823	1845	1849	c.1850
Captain James Cook discovers Hawaii and passes through the Bering Strait.	The Constitution Act divides Canada into French- and English-speaking territories.	Ching Yih's pirate confederation includes over 600 pirate junks and 150,000 men.	Michael Faraday invents the electric generator and electric motor.	President Monroe delivers the Monroe Doctrine.	Famine in Ireland due to potato blight causes emigration to the United States.	Shap-'ng-Tsai's pirate fleet massacred by British navy in delta of the Tong King (Honghai) river.	Europeans eliminate pirates from China and the Far East.

The Junk

Since the days of Marco Polo, the junk has been the standard form of sailing craft in the Far East. While ideally suited as a maritime trader, a junk could also be fitted out as a formidable warship or pirate ship.

opposite page top: *The sail plan of an oceangoing junk is simple but highly effective. Although this model dates from the 19th century, the basic design had remained unchanged for centuries.*

The Chinese junk was the universal maritime vessel of the Far East, and by the arrival of Europeans to the region in the late 16th century it had developed into a clearly defined ship type. The name "junk" was first applied by the Portuguese, who named it *junco*, a word based on the Indonesian name for the vessels, the *djong*.

The origin of the junk is shrouded in legend. One chronicler recorded that Emperor Fu Hsi, the child of a sea nymph, taught the Chinese how to build the craft. For centuries it had been the mainstay of Chinese and southeast Asian maritime traffic and, under the Ming Dynasty,

Chinese merchant fleets traveled as far afield as Africa and Japan. By the 17th century an introverted Chinese policy led to the confinement of shipping to local waters.

Marco Polo was impressed by the junk, which he saw as superior to anything in his native Venice. He recorded that: "they have a single deck, and under this the space is divided into small compartments, more or less according to the size of the vessel, some furnished as a small living quarters for a merchant. They are fitted with only one rudder. They have four masts with as many sails, and some have a further two which can be raised and lowered when necessary. In addition to the cabins already spoken of, some vessels of the larger sort have their hulls fitted with thirteen partitions which are made of thick planks joined together. The purpose of these is to protect the vessel if she springs a leak by running against a rock."

The junks used by the pirates of the South China Seas in the 17th, 18th, and 19th centuries were similar to the vessel described by Marco Polo, although usually fitted with only two or three masts. Modern Chinese junks are similar, but adapted for marine engines. This makes the junk the longest-serving vessel type in human history.

Piracy as a family business

After Marco Polo European travelers reported seeing fleets of hundreds of heavily armed warships and thousands of trading ships; all junks. Other variations on the basic design were encountered by Europeans elsewhere in Asia; the *twaqo* of Malaysia and the *rua chalom* of Siam and Burma, plus the junks found in Japanese waters. These were mostly small local

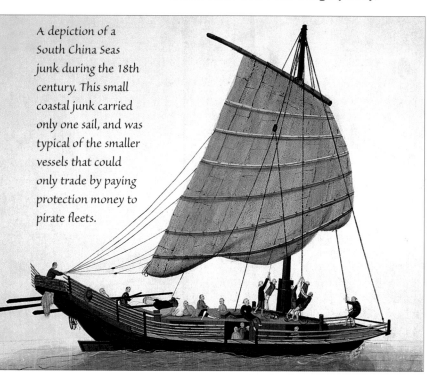

A depiction of a South China Seas junk during the 18th century. This small coastal junk carried only one sail, and was typical of the smaller vessels that could only trade by paying protection money to pirate fleets.

craft, but it was the Chinese junk that amazed the European traders of the 17th century. They were also alarmed at the way it was adapted for use as a pirate vessel.

Most pirate junks were converted from trading junks captured by pirates. These were armed with both large guns and a type of swivel gun known as a *lantaka*, but like most pirates, the hope was that they could capture a prize without resorting to gunfire. Some of the largest pirate junks were over 100 feet (30.5m) long, with a beam of 20 feet (6.1m), although most vessels were smaller. Larger junks carried three masts, while others carried two, these smaller vessels had an average length of around 45 feet (13.7m).

At least in 1807 and probably earlier, Chinese pirate junks were run almost as family ventures. The captain and some of the crew would have their families onboard, and while the captain lived in a stern cabin, the crew were housed in the main hold area. These seagoing pirate junks had substantial cargo space, part of which was taken up with a gunpowder magazine and weapons store.

Although Europeans in the 19th century described junks as "primitive looking craft," their sail plan was responsive and well suited to the waters of the South China Sea. Junks were usually seaworthy and could be fast, if handled correctly.

Pirate crews varied in number from a few dozen on small craft to almost 200 men for larger junks. The large, well-armed crew of a pirate junk was more than a match for the sparsely manned trading junks they attacked, and they often also outnumbered the crews of Imperial warships.

below: *Pirate junks being destroyed by the East India Company paddle-powered warship Nemesis near Hong Kong in 1841.*

Kuo Hsing Yeh

THE PIRATE WHO FOUGHT TO SAVE AN EMPIRE

In the mid-17th century, Kuo Hsing Yeh's pirate fleets controlled the entire South China Sea. He allied himself with the Ming emperor in a failed attempt to drive out the Manchu invaders. After his death, the pirate warlord became a Chinese folk hero, revered for his resistance against foreign invasion.

above right: *A Chinese junk pennant and,* **right**, *model of a trading junk, the main target for the Chinese pirates.*

K uo Hsing Yeh, sometimes recorded as "Koxinga," was born in 1624, probably in Nagasaki, Japan. His mother was Japanese and his father, Cheng Chih Lung, a successful Chinese merchant from Fukien province in southeast China. By the late 1620s his father owned a substantial fleet of war and trading junks, based in the bustling port of Hsiamen (Amoy Island), Fukien. His fleet traded with Europeans, who were becoming increasingly common in Chinese waters.

A power vacuum allowed Cheng Chih Lung to expand his powerbase and, by the early 1630s, his ships controlled most of the coast of Fukien province and the neighboring island of Taiwan. He was the

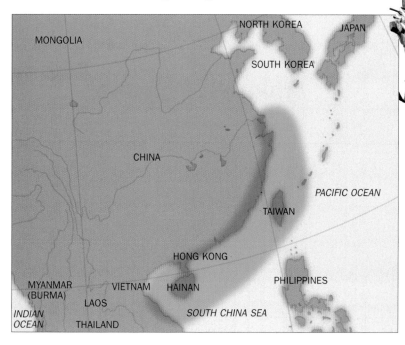

virtual overlord of the area, maintaining a tightly guarded monopoly of maritime trade.

His war junks guarded trade, but also operated in a less paternal manner. Acting as pirates, Cheng Chih Lung's junks raided shipping from the mouth of the Yangtse river to the island of Hainan. Other maritime traders had to pay protection money to his captains or face the loss of their ships and cargo.

By 1641 Cheng Chih Lung's position was so strong that the Chinese Ming emperor in Nanking bowed to the inevitable and appointed him "Admiral in charge of pirate suppression," which came with a salary! The emperor hoped to be able to use the pirate as an ally, if he needed one. When invading Manchu forces captured Nanking in 1644, Cheng Chih Lung invited the emperor to set up court in Foochow, in Fukien province. He used the emperor as a political pawn, and two years later reached a deal with the Manchu Dynasty. He submitted the province to their authority and almost certainly had the Ming emperor killed. The warlord then traveled to the Manchu court in Beijing, where he was rewarded for his defection by imprisonment and execution.

Conducting piracy, seeking revenge

Kuo Hsing Yeh took over his father's home-made empire, and since Fukien province was occupied by Manchu forces, the 22-year-old pirate escaped into exile on Taiwan, taking much of his father's fleet with him. While the Manchus dominated the mainland, the pirates retained naval supremacy in the Formosa Strait, and were relatively safe from attack.

After they had killed his father, Kuo Hsing Yeh saw the Manchu Dynasty as his enemy, and he acted as a rallying point for the remaining supporters of the Ming Dynasty. His junks attacked Manchu shipping and effectively blockaded the mouth of the Yangtse river, cutting Nanking off from all European and Chinese maritime commerce.

In 1649 or 1650 he launched an amphibious invasion of Hsiamen and captured the port. Using this as a base,

the rebels cleared Fukien province of Manchu troops within a year. For the time being, his power base was secure. He resumed his father's activities, his pirate fleets dominated the region, and his trading junks sailed as far afield as Japan. The less powerful Manchu navy abandoned the South China Sea and for a decade Kuo Hsing Yeh maintained complete control of its coastal waters, from the Yangtse river to the Mekong delta.

Like his father before him, his downfall came through meddling in politics. In the late 1650s he agreed to join a Ming offensive to drive the Manchu Dynasty out of Nanking. In 1659 he sent a fleet up the Yangtse river as part of a combined land and sea assault on the Manchu city. Instead, his ships were trapped and destroyed. With Ming power destroyed, the Manchus swept south, forcing Kuo Hsing Yeh to abandon Fukien province for Taiwan a second time.

He resented the growth of the European presence in his own province of Taiwan and drove the Dutch from the island in 1661. This maintained his business monopoly, and his trading and pirate fleets continued to dominate the region until his death in 1683. Today, Kuo Hsing Yeh is idolized as a national hero in Taiwan, and amazingly is regarded as both a valiant defender of Ming culture and civilization, and also a ruthless pirate warlord.

below: *An illustration from a broadsheet of 1836 shows a Chinese pirate chasing a Chinaman in order to chop off his head. Terror tactics kept the population of coastal areas firmly under the control of the pirate warlords.*

Ching Yih

THE LARGEST PIRATE CONFEDERATION

During the early 1800s, the South China Sea was controlled by a large confederation of pirates that attacked vessels and extorted protection money. Ching Yih was head of the confederation and he defied all attempts by the Chinese navy to defeat him.

Ching Yih (also written as "Cheng I") was born the son of a Chinese pirate in 1765, probably in Vietnam. His father and fellow pirates were engaged in a Vietnamese civil war, but the son had other plans. In 1801 Ching Yih was the commander of a fleet of pirate junks. He left Vietnam and sailed to Kwangtung province, where he gained control of the pirate fleets who dominated the Chinese coastline.

Within four years he combined the fleets into a large pirate confederation that he organized along rigid lines. This was divided into six fleets, each identified by a particular color (black, white, red, blue, yellow, or green). Each fleet was allocated its own area of operations, which ensured that they would not fight each other, and each fleet was given its own coastal base. Each fleet had the latitude to operate as it saw fit, but Ching Yih maintained a loose control over the whole pirate confederation, while he directly controlled the red fleet, based near Canton. At the start the confederation comprised 200 pirate junks, but his force steadily grew.

In 1804 he blockaded the Portuguese-held city of Macao, ostensibly because the Europeans refused to pay him protection money. A Portuguese relief force drove him off after several weeks, but nonetheless, he had demonstrated his power as a maritime warlord.

The British Royal Navy assumed responsibility for patrolling the coast off Hong Kong and Macao, but its strength was insufficient to reduce the pirate threat appreciably. By 1807 Ching Yih directly commanded over 600 pirate junks and around 30,000 crew, while the organization as a whole contained over 150,000 men, making it the largest pirate confederation in history.

Spouse and lover

During the first decade of the 19th century, the Chinese emperor tried to bring an end to piracy in the region. Naval attacks on the pirates were largely unsuccessful, and a subsequent Imperial amnesty produced disappointing results. One reason for the failure of the Chinese initiative was the apparent invulnerability of the pirates. If a base was threatened, other colored fleets would be summoned and the threat repelled.

Protection money was extorted from ship owners all around the basin of the South China Sea, and the pirate confederation completely dominated the region, attacking or extorting money from the vessels they

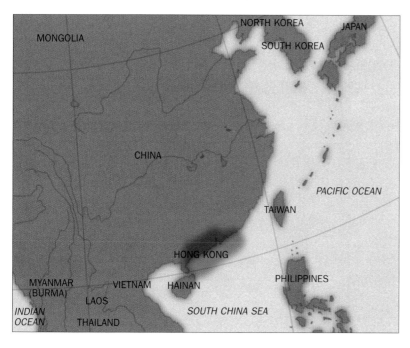

above: Cutaway model of an armed junk, c.1800. This is typical of the seagoing junks that were built to carry cargo, but became ideal pirate ships after their capture. Ports were cut in the sides for broadside guns, and swivel guns were mounted on the rails.

encountered. The exceptions were usually European trade ships, since Ching Yih realized that while he was able to repel any Chinese punitive expedition sent against him, the Royal Navy could not be so easily deterred.

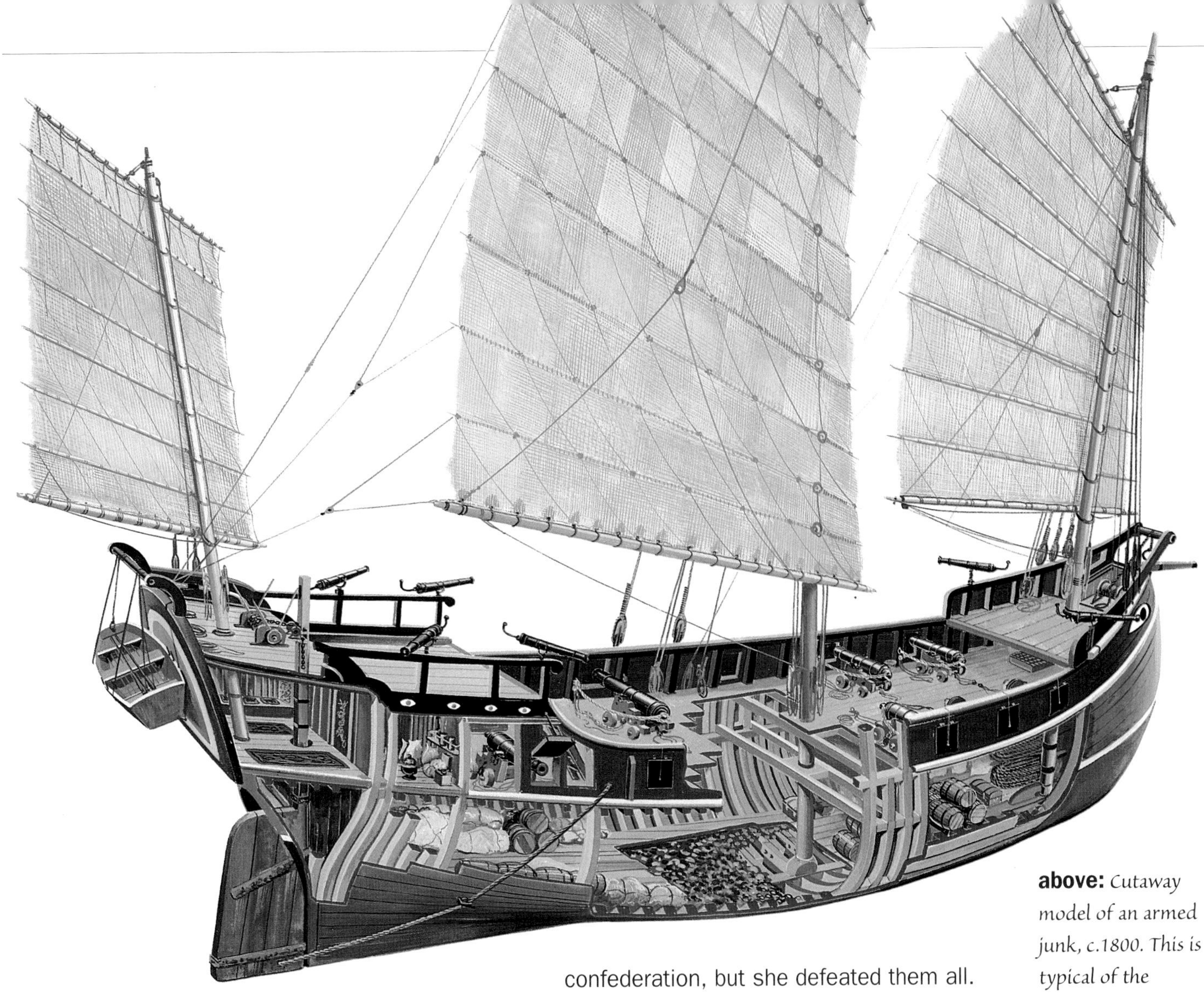

The pirate warlord died at the height of his power in late 1807, probably washed overboard in a storm. When his wife Cheng Yih Sao took over control of the red fleet, Ching Yih's bisexual male lover Chang Pao became the new mate of the late pirate's wife. Cheng Yih Sao (also written as "Cheng I Sao") developed into a fearsome pirate leader, and her fleet dominated the approaches to Canton and the European enclaves. Within three years she was elected as head of the confederation.

Unlike her husband, Cheng Yih Sao was not intimidated by Europeans and she attacked their ships. Several Chinese expeditions were sent to crush the confederation, but she defeated them all. While the emperor failed by military means, he did succeed through political maneuvers. Pardons were offered to the pirates, and, by 1810, the confederation was in disarray, since many saw the benefits of being legal, which opened up lucrative Imperial markets for former pirate ship owners. Colored pirate fleets began fighting one another, which further diminised their influence.

Cheng Yih Sao bowed to the inevitable and accepted a pardon, although she maintained her position at the head of a major smuggling operation well into the 1840s. Chang Pao surrendered the red fleet *en masse*, received a commission into the Imperial navy, and turned pirate-hunter. For the next decade the ex-pirate scoured the waters of the South China Sea, until he destroyed all traces of the massive pirate empire that had been created by his former lovers.

below: A pirate sword, decorated with tufts of human hair, that was captured during a Royal Navy anti-piracy expedition.

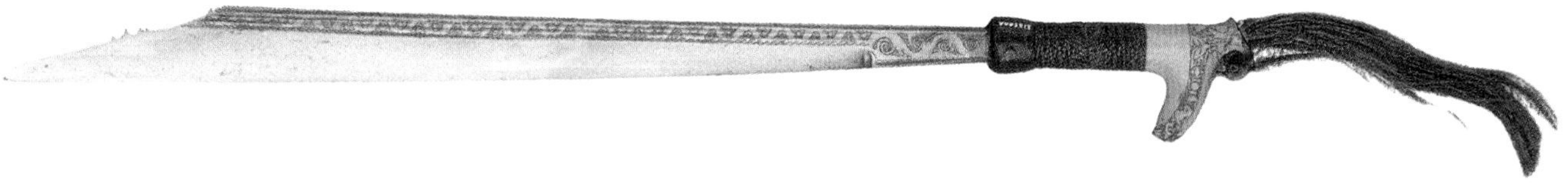

Shap-'ng-Tsai

LAST OF THE GREAT CHINESE PIRATES

A pirate who thrived on the illegal trade in opium, Shap-'ng-Tsai maintained a fleet that dominated the waters around the British colony of Hong Kong. By 1849, the British had had enough, and sent a powerful force to crush the sea raiders. The stage was set for a clash between pirates and steam-powered naval gunboats.

below: *Following the destruction of Shap-'ng-Tsai's pirate fleet, Vietnamese villagers massacred the survivors of the pirate band as they swam toward the shore.*

Friction created the opium trade led to the eruption of warfare between the Chinese and the British in 1839. The First Opium War (1839–42) resulted in the decisive defeat of the Chinese, and the emperor was forced to sign a humiliating treaty with the Europeans. China ceded Hong Kong to Britain, and five ports were opened up to European trade, including Canton in Kwangtung province. The opium trade was big business, and in 1843 alone over 40,000 chests of opium were shipped from China to Britain. The war devastated the Chinese Imperial navy along the South China Sea coast, and the British Royal Navy only concerned itself with protecting European interests. As a result, many Chinese turned to piracy, and a new pirate infestation threatened the region.

Like Ching Yih before him, Shap-'ng-Tsai was a pirate who operated in Kwangtung province. Based at Tin Pak, 175 miles (282km) west of the British treaty port of Hong Kong, he rose to prominence as the leader of a pirate band soon after the war.

By the end of the 1840s Shap-'ng-Tsai's pirate fleet had grown to include over 70 vessels, and his group extorted protection money from Chinese traders from Hong Kong to Haiphong in Vietnam. His men also attacked British and American vessels off the treaty ports, capturing one American and three British opium-carrying clipper ships. Shipping entering and leaving the British treaty ports of Kwangtung province was disrupted, as were trade links to the ports occupied by other colonial trading powers.

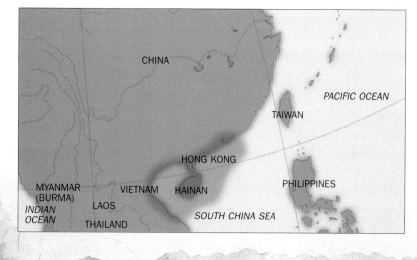

CHINA

PACIFIC OCEAN

TAIWAN

HONG KONG

MYANMAR (BURMA) VIETNAM HAINAN PHILIPPINES

INDIAN OCEAN LAOS

THAILAND SOUTH CHINA SEA

The Royal Navy's commander of the Far East squadron based at Hong Kong agreed with East India Company officials to take steps to bring these pirate attacks to a close. A punitive expedition was organized and, in September 1849, they struck. A naval squadron of steam warships led by Commander Dalrymple Hay entered the pirate base at Tin Pak, only to find that the pirates had flown, forewarned by spies in Hong Kong.

Caught by surprise

The British captured over one hundred junks in the harbor, prizes that the pirates had intended to hold for ransom. In a bizarre twist, the British kept the junks and sold them to their former owners under the laws of international salvage. To the ship owners, the result was the same as if the pirates had held onto the vessels. A second pirate base at Bias Bay, east of Hong Kong, was also destroyed, although many of the pirates escaped inland.

The Royal Navy pursued Shap-'ng-Tsai and his pirate fleet into the Gulf of Tong King (Tonkin). By October they had discovered the new pirate lair in the delta of the Tong King (Hongha) river, among the channels and delta islands north of the port of Haiphong in Vietnam. Commander Hay blockaded the mouth of the river to prevent escape, then steamed into action. His force consisted of two steam warships and the East India Company paddle-steamer *Phlegethon*, accompanied by a squadron of Imperial Chinese junks.

The pirates were caught unprepared and were at anchor when the British and Chinese warships arrived. After crossing the sandbar at the entrance to the river, the warships bombarded the pirate junks, which were unable to swing around and effectively return fire because of the river's fast current. Over 1,800 pirates were killed and 58 pirate vessels were sunk or captured. Shap-'ng-Tsai escaped up-river, accompanied by a handful of pirates and six small junks. He soon took advantage of an offer of an Imperial pardon and a commission into the Chinese navy, a typical Chinese method of combating piracy.

From 1849 onward, the British maintained a permanent naval presence in the South China Sea, based at Hong Kong. Although there were continued incidents of piracy throughout the remainder of the 19th century, the superior technology of their warships ensured that pirates were no longer a serious threat.

The Indonesian Archipelago

A RAG-TAG COLLECTION OF PIRATE COMMUNITIES

For centuries the waters around Indonesia provided a safe haven for small-time pirates. Often operating on tribal lines, these cutthroats forced shipping sailing from the Far East to Europe to run the gauntlet of coastal pirate bases.

opposite right: *A Dyak warrior in 1897. Their head-hunting habits mean that the the Sea Dyaks were feared pirates.*

below: *The sad tale of a young man who suffered at the hands of Malay pirates in the Strait of Malacca.*

The islands of southeast Asia created an ideal pirate haven. Bands of local tribal pirates preyed on the shipping of colonial European powers and the craft of other local peoples. During the 18th and 19th centuries, apart from enclaves controlled by Europeans, most of the region was split into a patchwork of small tribal areas. The centralized power of Javanese and Malayan rulers in the archipelago was broken by the arrival of the Dutch, and the political fragmentation of the region continued until the late 19th century.

Frequently changing alliances between these groups and almost incessant warfare meant that no single power dominated the archipelago and its sea lanes. Many of these minor kingdoms and tribal groupings used piracy as a means of support, and it frequently formed part of their official policy.

The increased presence of Europeans, mainly through the establishment of Dutch trading posts, altered the unstable nature of this regional patchwork. With their lack of respect for local alliances, the colonial Europeans continually interfered through first their support of, and then abandonment of local favorites. The consequence was that, by the 19th century, Europeans were distrusted and their ships singled out for pirate attack.

Ships sailing between Europe and China were the most vulnerable, since they had to pass through the narrow Strait of Malacca between Malaya and Sumatra—a hotbed of pirate activity. From there they had to sail through the South China Sea, running a further gauntlet of the numerous pirate havens bordering the shores of Borneo, Malaya, and the Philippines.

Of all the pirate groups in the Indonesian archipelago, the most feared were the Ilanun pirates of the Philippines and the Balanini pirates of Sulu, northeast of Borneo. The Ilanun pirates not only plagued the waters of the Philippines but also raided far out into the South China Sea. Early observers, including the buccaneer William Dampier, described the Ilanun people as being peaceable, so their reliance on piracy must have developed during the 18th century.

Vessels of the Indonesian pirates

Ilanun raids were often designed to gather slaves, which were then traded in the markets of Sumatra and Java. These large-

---

TO A GENEROUS PUBLIC.

I am a poor young man who have had the misfortune of having my Tongue cut out of my mouth on my passage home from the Coast of China, to Liverpool, in 1845, by the Malay Pirates, on the Coast of Malacca. There were Fourteen of our Crew taken prisoners and kept on shore four months; some of whom had their eyes put out, some their legs cut off, for myself I had my Tongue cut out.

We were taken about 120 miles to sea; we were then given a raft and let go, and were three days and three nights on the raft, and ten out of fourteen were lost. We were picked up by the ship James, bound to Boston, in America, and after our arrival we were sent home to Liverpool, in the ship Sarah James.

Two of my companions had trades before they went to sea, but unfortunately for me having no Father or Mother living, I went to sea quite young. I am now obliged to appeal to a Generous Public for support, and any small donation you please to give will be thankfully received by

Your obedient servant,

WILLIAM EDWARDS.

P.S.—I sailed from Liverpool on the 28th day of May, 1844, on board the Jane Ann, belonging to Mr. Spade, William Jones, Captain. Signed by Mr. Rushton, Magistrate, Liverpool, Mr. Smith, and Mr. Williams, after I landed in Liverpool on the 10th December, 1845.

scale raids were augmented by attacks on Spanish shipping around Manila, and the occasional foray against passing Dutch and British shipping. Like many Indonesian pirates, they used prahus, shallow-drafted canoes rowed by slaves.

The Balanini pirates were based on the island of Jolo and, like the Ilanun pirates, they were well placed to engage in slave raiding and attacks on Spanish vessels around the Philippines. Their preferred craft was the corocoro, a fast-sailing vessel fitted with outriggers that could be powered by sail or oar. Corocoros could displace as much as 100 tons (91 tonnes) and carry as many as 60 pirates, although most were smaller.

Other pirate groups included the Bugis of Sulawesi (the Celebes), who combined trading with piracy, depending on economic conditions. They were described as "the most mercenary, bloodthirsty, inhuman race." To the west, the Atjeh (Achin) and Riau pirates of Sumatra specialized in harassing ships in the Malacca and Sunda straits. The Sea Dyak pirates of Borneo used a variant of the prahu called the bangkong. By the 1830s, the Dyaks were the most feared pirates of the region.

In 1819 Stamford Raffles founded the British colony of Singapore, which was ideally placed to dominate the waters of the Strait of Malacca. In 1836 a combined Royal Navy and East India Company squadron was based in the port, charged with sweeping the strait of pirates. Following the success of this operation, the British launched punitive expeditions against the Sea Dyaks and the Malay pirates and destroyed their power bases.

By the 1860s the Ilanun and Balanini pirates had been destroyed by Spanish and British naval expeditions, and although piracy was never completely suppressed, the Indonesian archipelago was considered safe for shipping. Descendants of the Indonesian pirates would revert to piracy during the late 20th century, but they would be armed with assault rifles, not spears.

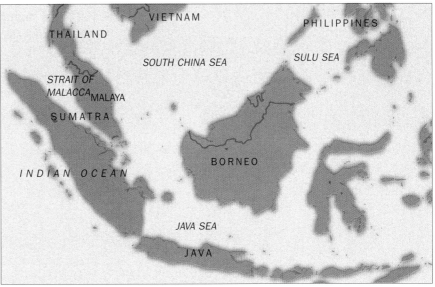

CHAPTER ELEVEN

Modern Piracy

Piracy never completely ended when the Caribbean was cleared in the 1820s, and the Far East by the 1860s. Isolated incidents continued, although these were rare in waters outside the Far East. As had been the case for centuries, one of the main causes for piracy was the collapse of a political, military, or economic system somewhere in the world, with the result that an opportunity for lawlessness was provided.

This was the case with piracy in the waters of the Persian Gulf in the early 19th century, the Balkans during the late 19th century, and the Far East of the early 20th century. The rivers and coastal waters of China were a particularly dangerous area, and piracy thrived in traditionally infested areas such as the Yangtse river or the province of Kwangtung. The British took a tough line and sent repeated expeditions to wipe out pirate groups as late as the 1920s. Similar punitive expeditions attacked suspected pirate lairs in Siam, India, and the Indonesian islands.

A similar lawlessness had made the west coast of Africa a haven for pirates. When the slave trade was made illegal, outlaw traders combined coastal raiding with small-scale piracy until they were crushed by European military attacks during the 19th century. More widespread piracy or privateering was a naval tool of the past, although during the American Civil War (1861–5) the Confederacy made extensive use of commerce raiders.

The World Wars saw the launch of unrestricted U-boat warfare, and although these were conducted for national rather than personal goals, the British and American press branded the German submariners "pirates." This epithet came from the submarine's underhanded form of warfare, but it shows how widely the term "pirate" could be misused. Naturally, submariners enjoyed the romanticism attached to the name, some putting pirate symbols on their boats and even flying pirate flags. As late as 1982, when *HMS Conqueror* returned from the Falklands War after sinking the Argentine cruiser *Almirante Belgrano*, its commander flew a skull and crossbones when he sailed into his home port.

Sailing through a U.N. loophole

Following the boom in maritime shipping that came after the end of the Second World War, piracy appeared to have been outstripped by progress. This changed in the early 1980s when a fresh wave of piratical attacks swept the waters of the Indonesian archipelago. Other incidents of piracy have occurred in the Caribbean (where they are almost certainly related to drug trafficking), off the coast of Africa, and in the rivers and ports of Brazil. The rise of this phenomenon was aided by circumstances we have already discussed, and that have encouraged piracy since the days of the Ancient Egyptians.

The response of the international maritime community has been hindered by international law. The United Nations defined piracy as being "any illegal act of violence or detention, or act of depredation committed for private ends by the crew or the passengers of a private ship directed on the high sea." The problem for the victims is in proving that the attack was made for private gain, and that it was committed on the high seas.

Many attacks in the Far East occur in coastal waters, and there have been frequent claims from "pirates" that they are really part of regional independence movements and, therefore, not pirates at all. Some victims have found that in appealing to local authorities, they are talking to the mystery men behind the pirate activity. Still other attacks are conducted by representatives of the local governments, such as the Philippines Coast Guard, who illegally seized a Japanese merchant ship in 1995 and were

subsequently convicted of robbery in Manila.

Others are often local fishermen, who operate fast outrigger craft that are well suited for pirate attacks. Instead of carrying fishing nets, they carry a crew of pirates armed with automatic weapons. These small craft are ideally suited for hit-and-run attacks on passing shipping in the confined coastal waters of Southeast Asia and the Philippines. They are also difficult to catch. So long as the regions' governments are unwilling to crush piracy in their waters, the situation will continue.

left: *Philippines, 1991—automatic weapons are often paid for by corrupt governments and used to terrorize local seafarers.*

below: *Filipino pirates capture a small boat (top) and make the victims cower in the bows (bottom), their fate as yet undecided....*

Today's Pirate Hotspots

THE TRADITION CONTINUES

The South China Sea has long been a haunt of pirates, but modern pirates use new methods. During the 1990s victims reported attacks by what appeared to be gunboats carrying uniformed Chinese crews. While the Chinese Border Patrol have been held responsible for many of these incidents, other groups may be impersonating government officials to escape detection.

Chinese authorities also admitted that local naval patrols may have been over-zealous in their pursuit of pirates and smugglers. This enthusiasm extended to attacking non-Chinese ships in international waters. Filipino gangs have also been identified as the perpetrators of numerous attacks; regional, religious, and political tensions have given them the excuse to operate openly in Philippine waters. While most of these attacks are mounted against coastal fishermen operating in the Sulu, Mindanao, and Celebes seas, others are more daring. Government officials and coastguard crews have been linked to pirates, and court cases have proven many either condone or participate in the attacks.

In the waters of Indonesia and Malaysia, pirate attacks have been reported from the mid-1980s, where vessels carrying Vietnamese "boat people" have been attacked, often by coastal fishermen. In the 1990s, non-violent attacks on ships passing through the narrow Philip Strait or the long Strait of Malacca began to concern the Singapore authorities. These were hit-and-run crimes by robbers using fast boats, where the perpetrators made off with money and valuables.

A crackdown on crimes in the waters surrounding Singapore saw a marked decline in these attacks. The government initiative was backed by maritime surveillance, increased patrolling, and a fearsome judicial system that combined brutal corporal punishment with lengthy custodial sentences.

Elsewhere in the region, the revolution in Jakarta in 1998 highlighted the problems facing the government. Guerrilla movements have eroded government authority, and a fresh wave of small-scale pirate attacks have been reported in Indonesian waters. As ever, political instability is creating the perfect environment for opportunistic piracy.

In the Americas, drug-related attacks have become increasingly common since 1980, and, as Colombia and Venezuela are gripped in a war with the drug barons, they are still on the rise. Similarly, Brazil is suffering from a wave of lawlessness that has led to widespread attacks on ships in her ports, principally in Rio de Janeiro. Since the mid-1990s the Brazilian authorities have been put under intense pressure to clean up their home waters, and since 1995 Brazilian ports have been

below: *Positioned just off the northeastern tip of Borneo, Twai-Twai on the Philippine island of Bongao is a meeting place for modern Filipino and Dayak pirates.*

deemed to be the most dangerous in the world. Similar riverine attacks have been reported on the Amazon.

Attacked by African officials

Piracy was a serious problem in African waters during the 1970s and early 80s. The end of colonial rule sparked an eruption of coup d'états, guerrilla fighting, civil war, and tribal conflict. The Nigerian Civil War (1967–70) and similar power struggles along the West African coast plunged the region into a period of anarchy and lawlessness. By the late 1970s even peaceful countries such as Sierra Leone had been engulfed in the violence, and incidents of shipping attacks grew.

Some West African attacks were made by naval gunboats supposedly engaged in policing, and spread to involve international shipping. In 1981 Nigeria was declared the world's most dangerous coast. As military rule was established over most of the region, the incidences of piracy diminished.

In the 1980s and 90s the Indian Ocean and the Red Sea became dangerous waters for passing shipping, as Somalia and Ethiopia became embroiled in civil war. Ships using the Suez Canal were attacked as they sailed through these hostile waters, as were ships using the ports of Mogadishu and Djibouti. Liberation movements attacked vessels to fund their activities, while even government officials seized ships, claiming they were infringing territorial waters. These incidents are less widespread than they were in the mid-1990s, but the region remains a volatile one.

Piracy continues to thrive in unstable regions of the world, and to the victims of these crimes, be they local fishermen, passing yachtsmen, or the crew of large merchant ships, it has no romanticism.

Pirate Appearance

Fiction and Hollywood have given us an impression of what pirates looked like and what they wore—necessarily colorful. In fact pirates were just like other seamen, and their dress was largely dictated by fashions of their time ... and practicality.

below: *Pirates dressed for life at sea, often in whatever was to hand—and they enjoyed their rum; many died from alcohol abuse.*

The modern image of a pirate from the "Golden Age of Piracy" is based on the archetypal Hollywood model. Bicorn hats adorned with a skull and crossbones plus a splendidly decorated long-tailed captain's coat are the standard attire for any pirate leader. The crew tend toward head scarves, plain white shirts, and seamen's baggy trousers, adding ear-rings and tattoos for extra effect. Although the portrayal of the crewmen is almost accurate, much of the image is carried to extremes, and the figure of Captain Hook with his wig, ruffed sleeves, and trimmed beard would have been laughed out of the Caribbean.

During the Golden Age, as throughout history, pirates were seamen, and turned to piracy out of desperation or a desire for personal gain. They did not adopt a special uniform, and retained the clothing they wore when they remained within the law. There are numerous instances where pirate crews were passed off as privateer crews or as hands onboard a legitimate slave ship or merchant vessel. This meant that a pirate's appearance was the same as that of other early 18th-century seamen. All seamen adopted forms of clothing that set them apart from "landsmen," worn for practical reasons rather than a desire to be conspicuous. Even naval ratings during the early 18th century wore no special uniform,

although naval captains frequently adopted one for their own barge crew or shore party. In the early 18th century, landsmen wore knee breeches, sleeved or sleeveless vests, and long overcoats, worn over a basic white linen shirt. European settlers in the Americas wore the styles found throughout contemporary Europe.

A practical wardrobe

Seamen wore an adapted version of this dress. Short woolen coats known as fearnoughts, usually made from a heavy blue or gray material, were frequently worn in port. At sea, canvas jackets were worn, or fearnoughts waterproofed with tar or wax, with a linen or cotton shirt beneath. Shirts were usually white (or off-white), although checkered blue and white shirts have been depicted in contemporary illustrations. Sailors often just wore a shirt or went bare-chested, unless the weather was particularly bad.

Linen neck cloths were frequently worn to absorb sweat. Canvas pants—"sailor's petticoats"—were standard dress for seamen, although woolen breeches like the ones worn on land were also used. Aboard ship, seamen usually went barefoot; shoes were saved for visits ashore.

There was a marked difference between this seagoing attire and clothes saved for "a run ashore." Some form of head covering was a vital part of a sailor's dress in the tropics. Typical forms included head

scarves, tricorn or "slouch" hats, and woolen "Monmouth" or montero caps.

Unlike other sailors, pirates had the opportunity to amass stolen clothing, and there are instances where less practical forms of stolen clothing were used by pirates at sea, including silk shirts and hat feathers! These finer clothes may have been worn when going into action, as was probably the case in the contemporary navy.

Pirate captains were elected from the crew, and in theory would wear the same clothing as the rest of the crew. They also frequently had to pass themselves off as officers of a privateer or merchant ship, which meant wearing breeches, a vest, and a long blue "sea coat" (Edward England was described wearing "a short coat, but without shoes or stockings").

Probably the best dressed pirate of the Golden Age was Bartholomew Roberts. When he was killed in 1722, his dress consisted of "a rich crimson damask waistcoat [vest] and breeches, a red feather in his hat, a gold chain round his neck, with a diamond cross hanging to it." Roberts probably looked more like the archetypal Hollywood swashbuckler than any other pirate leader; simpler, more practical clothing was the rule. Blackbeard wore a plain "sea coat" when he was killed, and even the well-born Stede Bonnet was captured wearing a plain gentleman's coat. At sea, practicality triumphed over elegance.

above: *Peter Pan and the Lost Boys take on the flamboyantly-dressed Captain Hook and his evil crew.*

above: *As Hollywood's head swashbuckler, Errol Flynn was invariably a practically-dressed rogue who left the more fanciful costumes to names below the title.*

The Pirate Code

Although pirates operated beyond the law, they frequently established their own codes of conduct. These codes were designed to avoid disputes over the division of plunder, and even made provision for looking after pirates wounded in battle. For its time, these charters were remarkable documents.

The image of pirates is one of a lawless band, but they often imposed codes of conduct upon themselves. This was more to prevent disputes than for any social motives. Most pirate crews drafted these tenets and lived by them. Of particular importance was the election of the captain, who could be removed if the crew disapproved of his actions, as happened to both Charles Vane and Edward England. Charters included rules against gambling, womanizing, fighting, and drinking; all pastimes that have traditionally been associated with pirates. Although many pirate charters are alluded to, the following example drawn up by the crew of Bartholomew Roberts is one of the few to survive:

right: *A captive is tortured by "sweating"—forced to run around the mast at spearpoint until he passes out from exhaustion.*

1. Every man shall have an equal vote in affairs of moment. He shall have an equal title to the fresh provisions or strong liquors at any time seized, and shall use them at pleasure unless a scarcity makes it necessary for the common good that a retrenchment may be voted.
2. Every man shall be called fairly in turn by the list on board of prizes, because over and above their proper share, they are allowed a shift of clothes. But if they defraud the company to the value of even one dollar in plate, jewels or money, they shall be marooned. If any man rob another he shall have his nose and ears slit, and be put ashore where he shall be sure to encounter hardships.
3. None shall game for money, either with dice or cards.
4. The lights and candles shall be put out at eight at night, and if any of the crew desire to drink after that hour they shall sit upon the open deck without lights.
5. Each man shall keep his piece, cutlass and pistols at all times clean and ready for action.
6. No boy or woman to be allowed amongst them. If any man shall be found seducing one of the latter sex and carrying her to sea in disguise, he shall suffer death.

7. He that shall desert the ship or his quarters in time of battle shall be punished by death or marooning.

8. None shall strike another aboard the ship, but every man's quarrel shall be ended on shore by sword or pistol in this manner: at the word of command from the Quartermaster, each man being previously placed back to back, shall turn and fire immediately. If any man do not, the Quartermaster shall knock the piece out of his hand. If both miss their aim, they shall take to their cutlasses, and he that draws first blood shall be declared the victor.

9. No man shall talk of breaking up their way of living till each has a share of £1,000. Every man who shall become a cripple or lose a limb in the service shall have eight hundred pieces of eight from the common stock, and for lesser hurts proportionately.

10. The Captain and the Quartermaster shall each receive two shares of a prize, the Master Gunner and Boatswain, one and one half shares, all other officers one and one quarter, and private gentlemen of fortune one share each.

11. The musicians shall have rest on the Sabbath Day only, by right, on all other days, by favor only.

This pirate code emphasized the division of plunder, where elected officers received a higher share, commensurate with their duties. This is a fraction of the share found in naval service, where over half was allocated to the officers. Privateers were a half-measure between the two forms of division, but a high percentage was retained for the financial backers, which soaked up much of the profit. This was part of the reason behind William Kidd's adoption of piracy, since his privateering contract offered little financial reward.

One notable aspect of Roberts's pirate code is the provision of financial aid for injured crewmen. While injured naval ratings were cast ashore to beg or starve, pirates looked after their own. Pirate codes were revolutionary social charters for their time.

above: *A 19th-century depiction of an 18th-century event, where a prisoner is tied to the mast and used as target practice for pistols and broken bottles.*

below: *Many pirates divided their booty according to set codes, which had been agreed upon beforehand. "How the treasure was divided." Oil painting by Howard Pyle.*

The Legacy of Piracy

WHAT IS THE APPEAL OF PIRACY?

below:

Mythmaker—the frontispiece from Exquemelin's "Adventures of the Buccaneers in the Indies." Many authors would follow.

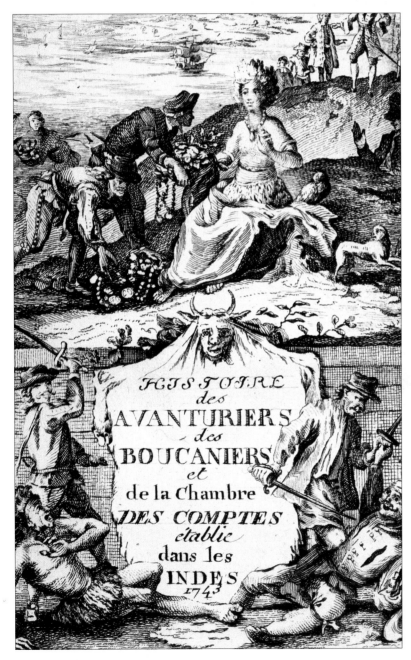

Ever since Charles Johnson published his pirate history in 1724, piracy has gripped the popular imagination. Today it is so intertwined with our culture that the romanticism associated with it cannot be removed. The childhood daydreams of treasure maps, buried plunder, and sailing the seas have become ingrained in our subconscious.

While calling someone a "pirate" can be used in the same context as the appellation "shark," it carries a deeper meaning, and is altogether more favorable. It still retains a roguish quality, similar to the romance of "gangsters," as opposed to the realities of the mob. At the wild street celebrations of Mardi Gras in New Orleans and Fantasy Fest in Key West, the author has noticed that pirates are the most popular costume theme. What is the appeal of this distinctly criminal element?

Pirates are a recognizable and emotive image that represents a freedom of action that is denied to most law-abiding modern citizens. The adult city-dweller often dreams of a "getaway" vacation to the sun, where a tropical climate, sun-kissed beaches, and a week of lazy opulence are seen as the ultimate form of escapism. This same tropical setting formed much of the backdrop to the Golden Age of Piracy, and the vacation destinations of the Caribbean and Indian Ocean were once the haunt of pirates. In the same way as vacationers in Key West might envy the locals who live in the sun all the year around, they might also envy the pirates of the past. The feeling is often transitory, and they return to the familiarity of a more mundane existence without regret.

In *Treasure Island*, Robert Louis Stevenson made Long John Silver describe the pirate lifestyle: "Here it is about gentlemen of fortune. They live rough, and they risk swinging, but they eat and drink like fighting cocks, and when a cruise is done, why it's hundreds of pounds instead of hundreds of farthings in their pockets. Now the most goes for rum and a good fling, and to sea again in their shirts." Not only does Silver have a tropical cruise, he also makes a profit, and has a major party whenever the cruise reaches a port of call! Piracy represents a romanticized form of escapism, freed from the constraints of modern society.

Piracy—a modern-day reason for a party!

While the romanticism of piracy as portrayed by novels, plays, and films has been a major influence in this appeal, there must be more to it than that. Piracy would have to retain an intrinsic appeal for people to remain interested in these fictional interpretations of piracy, so the fascination must have deeper roots. Interest in piracy is similar to a love of the Wild West, another victim of fictional portrayal. Like the pirate, the life of a Western gunfighter was distinctly unromantic, but the brutal realities of the past have been given a glamorous coating, so that fact and fiction are difficult to disentangle.

The city of Tampa in Florida hosts an annual Gasparilla Invasion, based around the local pirate, José Gaspar. "Pirates" capture the city's mayor before settling down to a weekend of revelry. Tampa treats the event as a major attraction; the city named their football team the "Tampa Bay Buccaneers" and raised a statue to the pirate. The drawback is that Gaspar never existed! Research indicates that around 1900, an elderly local fisherman called John Gomez claimed to have once been a pirate, serving under Gaspar. Lack of evidence for Gaspar was not allowed to interfere with the tale, providing an excuse for a major pirate festival where today thousands let their hair down.

The truth is that pirates left us with no legacy except an aura that they never deserved. Fiction and imagination added to this, so that today, the pirate image is an enduring romantic creation far removed from the historical realities from which it was spawned. Perhaps it is unnecessary to challenge this image; better to present the difference between myth and reality for those who want to peer behind the romantic legacy of piracy.

index